Accounting Theory

Research, regulation and accounting practice

Accounting Theory

Research, regulation and accounting practice

PEARSON
Education
Australia

Michael Gaffikin

Pearson Education Australia
Unit 4, Level 3
14 Aquatic Drive
Frenchs Forest NSW 2086

www.pearsoned.com.au

Senior Acquisitions Editor: Karen Hutchings
Project Editor: Sandra Goodall
Editorial Coordinator: Angela Peters
Copy Editor: Kathryn Lamberton
Proofreader: Julie Ganner
Cover and internal design by Natalie Bowra
Cover illustration fromArt Box Images
Typeset by Midland Typesetters, Australia

Printed in Malaysia (CTP - VVP)

1 2 3 4 5 12 11 10 09 08

National Library of Australia
Cataloguing-in-Publication Data

Gaffikin, M.J.R. (Michael John Renny).
Accounting theory: research, regulation and accounting practice/author, Michael Gaffikin.
Frenchs Forest, N.S.W.: Pearson Educaiton, 2008.

Includes index.
978 1 7410 3070 9 (pbk).

Accounting.

657.01

An imprint of Pearson Education Australia
(a division of Pearson Australia Group Pty Ltd)

Brief contents

Contents in full

contents in full

Preface

I t is contended early in this book that many accounting students dislike theory, but it is also asserted that for practice to be effective it must be *reasoned* practice. Theory provides this reasoning. However, in the past most accounting theory books have fallen well short of presenting a coherent explanation of the basis for theory and its relation to accounting practice. Some have simply described current research trends; some have described existing practices as if their mere existence was reason enough for their continued use; while others have deferred to restating current regulations with the implication that they were the theory of accounting!

As the title implies, this book links theory to research and practice and indicates where regulation is necessary to substitute for independently derived theory. There are several themes in the book. First, the conventional elements of theory and theorising are explicated. Theory is inextricably linked to research and, although well known, too often there is confusion over the meaning and permissible uses of these elements. Fundamental to all theory and research is how we view the world and our relationship to it. So it is important to acknowledge the (philosophical) ontological position we assume; all else follows from this. There are numerous factors—our ontological predilections—affecting our vision, so it is essential that we do not restrict this vision to the narrow perspective of only that with which we are familiar. It is vital in approaching matters of theory and research that we adopt a wide breadth of vision, seek out the unfamiliar and maintain a true spirit of inquiry. This will involve challenge to and critique of extant knowledge as well as interdisciplinary exploration. It will be through these processes that some of the issues facing accounting can be examined and questions resolved.

There are many issues facing accounting today, not all of which can be resolved in purely economic terms. These will be familiar to most people involved in accounting. For example, there are the effects of increasing globalisation, the speed of information transfer made possible by information technological innovations, the increasing demands for ethical business behaviour, and the problems that loom large for society

preface

from climate change (as well as other environmental concerns). Therefore, this book examines not only conventional economic perspectives of theory (and research) but addresses these other concerns affecting accounting knowledge. There has been a growing awareness in the recent accounting literature that not only is accounting affected by the demands placed on it, both economically and by society, but accounting, in turn, affects society through its processes and enabling of the technologies of economic control. That is, by its very nature and appearance, accounting imparts power to those with the knowledge and skill to so employ it. This takes place from the fundamental level of the treasurer (financial officer) of a social club to large corporations, governments and international financial institutions.

Accounting's claim to professional status necessitates its members working to serve the public interest. Prospective accountants need to be made aware of this and left to accommodate it in the development of their own personal principles and ideals. In order to do this they need to be made fully aware of the issues involved—so that they can draw on notions developed in the many and varied disciplines that make up the stock of human intellectual endeavour.

I subscribe to the view that all knowledge is subject to the interlinked elements of language, history and culture. Knowledge is only seen to be knowledge when it is communicated. The dominant media of communication is language, a system of signs and symbols accepted within and by a society and culturally agreed upon. This system evolves through time, not in any linear fashion but as and when the need arises, which suggests meanings are never absolutely fixed. Consequently, we need to be aware of the importance of language when developing theories, research or regulation. For example, international financial reporting standards devised in one language may not mean precisely the same in another language—it is not possible to totally map one language against another, and regulators are aware of this. This is even more apparent when acronyms are used—devised in one language (usually English), they have to be applied in another language which may even use a different character set.

A further theme developed in this book is the growing importance of regulation. In some respects regulation can be viewed as a substitute for theory. This being the case, it is important to have an understanding of the bases for regulation—why and how they are developed. Where regulation is devised it has to be done on a reasoned basis. Therefore, developing effective regulation will at times involve similar processes to theory development. There are different theories of regulation and these are briefly discussed before examining accounting regulations and their rationale.

To be a truly intellectual activity a discipline must embrace a broad appreciation of human thought and knowledge. Accounting influences decisions made in a great many areas. This is often recognised with some derision—after all, we are merely the 'bean counters'. If we are to rid ourselves of this yoke, accountants must take a broader perspective of their profession to advance it beyond simply reflecting economic considerations, although these are undoubtedly important. Accountants are not equipped to decide on broader social policy decisions but they can certainly work with those who have more specific expertise. If knowledge is power then accountants must use their power judiciously. A profession is defined in terms of its public service. Accountants must not hide behind the misguided mantle of merely being there as neutral representors of an economic reality. Such economic 'reality' has been created by many societal and political forces, and in order to properly serve the public interest accountants must be aware of that. This book draws attention to some of the many different dimensions accounting theorists must recognise if they are to provide a responsible accounting practice. ■

Ackowledgements

As with any book there are many people who indirectly contribute to its ultimate publication. I would like to publicly thank these people as without their contribution I would not have been able to fulfil a long-held desire to write a book on accounting theory.

My wife Angela provided continual spiritual support and proved to be an excellent sounding board for some radical ideas, two very necessary pillars for a writer. I am very grateful to Karen Hutchings, acquisitions editor for Pearson Education Australia, who maintained the faith that, despite being long overdue with the manuscript, I would someday complete the project—thank you Karen. Some colleagues read and commented on earlier drafts of chapters and often 'put me right' (changing the views of someone so stubborn was sometimes difficult). For this I am especially grateful to Jane Andrew and John Trowell of the University of Wollongong, and Geeta Singh of the University of Ballarat. Honours students at the University of Tasmania also proved to be willing and uncomplaining participants in the 'trialling' of ideas for the book—thank you to Sue Conway, Jill Hall, Trish O'Keefe and Xenia Stathopoulos.

There have been many others who have influenced my thinking over the years but, of course, I alone am to blame for the conclusions I have drawn. Project editor for Pearson Education, Sandra Goodall, and copy editor, Kathryn Lamberton, took my typescript and are responsible for converting it to the fine end product—thank you. ■

About the author

Michael Gaffikin

Michael Gaffikin has a Bachelor of Commerce and an MBA with first class honours from universities in New Zealand and a PhD from the University of Sydney. He also has a Diploma in Teaching and is a Fellow of CPA Australia. Michael is currently Emeritus Professor of Accounting and Finance at the University of Wollongong where he was previously Head of the Department of Accounting and Finance and later Associate Dean (Research) of the Faculty of Commerce. Prior to joining academe he worked as a financial accountant in industry.

Although having taught many different subjects in accounting and finance Michael's primary teaching interests have always been accounting theory, history of accounting thought and research methods. He has successfully supervised over 40 doctoral students who now work in various parts of Australia and in many places throughout the world. He has an international reputation as a teacher and researcher having published several books and articles in many leading international journals. He serves on the editorial boards of a large number of international accounting journals and has presented papers and seminars at international conferences and universities in all continents throughout the world (except Antarctica!). Michael continues to be an active researcher working in many areas associated with the theoretical development of the discipline such as ethics, language, accounting for sustainability, professionalism and the history of accounting thought.

Michael has worked closely with accounting professional bodies, having been Chair of CPA Australia's Education and Membership Committee and its Universities Committee (NSW) as well as serving on several branch, state and national committees. He has also served on many other professional body and academic body committees such as the (then) AAANZ and the advisory committee for designing professional body accreditation regulations. Michael has won awards for service to the profession. ■

Acronyms

AAA	American Accounting Association		EMH	efficient market hypothesis
AARF	Australian Accounting Research Foundation		EU	European Union
			FAF	Financial Accounting Foundation
AASB	Australian Accounting Standards Board		FAS	Financial Accounting Standard
ACCC	Australian Competition and Consumer Commission		FASB	Financial Accounting Standards Board
			FIFO	first-in, first-out
AcSB	Accounting Standards Board		FRC	Financial Reporting Council
AICPA	American Institute of Certified Public Accountants		GAAP	generally accepted accounting principles
AISG	Accountants International Study Group		GRI	Global Reporting Initiative
			GTE	government trading enterprise
APB	Accounting Principles Board		IASB	International Accounting Standards Board
APESB	Accounting Professional and Ethical Standards Board Limited		IASC	International Accounting Standards Committee
ARD	Accounting Research Division			
ARS	Accounting Research Studies		IASCF	International Accounting Standards Committee Foundation
ASIC	Australian Securities and Investments Commission		IBRD	International Bank for Reconstruction and Development (also called the World Bank)
ASOBAT	*A statement of basic accounting theory*			
ASRB	Accounting Standards Review Board			
BCCI	Bank of Credit and Commerce International		ICAA	Institute of Chartered Accountants of Australia
CAPM	capital asset pricing model		ICAEW	Institute of Chartered Accountants of England and Wales
CCA	current cost accounting			
CDA	critical discourse analysis		IFAC	International Federation of Accountants
CIMA	Chartered Institute of Management Accountants		IFRIC	International Financial Reporting Interpretations Committee
CLERP	Corporate Law Economic Reform Program		IFRS	International Financial Reporting Standards
CoCoA	continuously contemporary accounting		IGC	Implementation Guidance Committee
CPA	Certified Practising Accountants (in the US, Certified Public Accountant)		IMF	International Monetary Fund
			IOSCO	International Organisation of Securities Commissions
CSR	corporate social responsibility			
DSOP	draft statement of principles		LIFO	last-in, first-out

MCA	Minerals Council of Australia	SATTA	A *statement on accounting theory and theory acceptance*
MNC	multinational corporation		
NIA	National Institute of Accountants	SD	sustainable development
NPV	net present value	SEC	Securities and Exchange Commission
NRV	net realisable value		
NYSE	New York Stock Exchange	SER	social and environmental reporting
PAT	positive accounting theory	SFAC	Statement of Financial Accounting Concepts
PCAOB	Public Company Accounting Oversights Board		
		SIC	Standing Interpretations Committee
RC	replacement cost	SOX	Sarbanes-Oxley Act
RCA	replacement cost accounting	TNC	transnational corporation
RVA	replacement value accounting	UIG	Urgent Issues Group
SAC	Statement of Accounting Concepts	WTO	World Trade Organization

The Need for Theory in Accounting

1

Understanding Theory

CHAPTER 1

Understanding Theory

This chapter explains the need for theory and some of the essential considerations involved in the process of developing theories. It very briefly looks at how, in Western societies, these considerations emerged and how they have changed over time. Many of them were developed in the discipline of philosophy and subsequently used in all other disciplines. The significance of these elements of philosophy for accounting theory is also explained. ■

Many students and practitioners of accounting eschew theory. That is, they try to avoid what they conceive as abstract discussion of what they believe to be a very practical activity. However, this practical activity did not just appear from thin air. The techniques and tools accountants employ in engaging in their 'practical activity' were devised in a systematic and orderly manner such that this activity results in an output which is useful to those who require the services of accountants. A famous Classical Greek scholar, Aristotle, claimed that practice emerges from theory. This probably means that all rational actions are based on good reasons, and implies that all actions are carefully considered and undertaken to achieve some end result. Actions are taken in the present for some anticipated or expected consequence. Actions vary in complexity from simple, everyday functions, such as drinking to quench a thirst, to highly complex activities, such as neural surgery or space travel. In taking such actions we would like to be confident that they will in fact lead to the desired aims being achieved, but we can never be certain that they will. Therefore, we need to be able to understand the factors that will impact on our decisions: we need to have a soundly reasoned basis for our decisions, and this is where theories come in.

Generally speaking, theories provide the reasoned basis for actions—for practice. So, very broadly, the process of theorising is designed to obtain an understanding and then provide an explanation of phenomena to serve as the basis for practice. An acceptable theory of accounting would thus serve as the basis for the best accounting practice. Some people even claim that theories facilitate prediction. We will return to these different perceptions of theory later in the chapter.

No precise definition exists for **theory**. The word is derived from the Classical Greek word meaning 'viewing, speculation and contemplation'. It could be defined as 'a set of propositions which provides principles of analysis or explanation of a subject matter' (Mautner 2000, p. 562). Alternatively, it could be more formally defined as:

> any set of hypotheses or propositions, linked by logical or mathematical arguments, which is advanced to explain an area of empirical reality or type of phenomenon (Jary and Jary 1991, p. 658).

Or:

> any abstract general account of an area of reality, usually including the use of formulation of general concepts (Jary and Jary 1991, p. 658).

There is no one view of a theory that would permit a single definition acceptable to all. However, from the above it can be seen to involve things such as reasoning, propositions, concepts, logical analysis, hypotheses, explanations, phenomena, reality and abstraction. No *one* view exists because all of these elements (and many others) are frequently looked at very differently by different people as they attempt to devise a theory. In fact, as will be discussed in later chapters, there are very many different *types of theories* that have been proposed over the years. This is as true in accounting as it is in all other disciplines. A theory depends on how the would-be theorist views the world and the phenomena under consideration, the assumptions they make about the behaviour of people and the phenomena, and their aims in developing the theory.

In developing theory, a theorist will undertake research. The procedure is rather circular as theoretical assumptions will be made during the research process undertaken to support or create theory. Therefore, the terms used often mean the same thing or something very closely related. This will be demonstrated as we develop the discussion. Theoretical assumptions will be made from research and (successful) research reinforces theory: existing theory and the construction of (new) theories.

In fact, research will be undertaken also to improve practice. This is done to better explain elements of practice or to understand phenomena such that predictions can be made as to their behaviour. For example, to put a man on the moon it was necessary to understand the very many factors involved in space travel as well as to predict where the moon would be by the time the spaceship arrived and so on. Research is undertaken in a climate of change in order to predict when extraordinary, unusual or potentially devastating events, such as cyclones, are likely to occur. Similarly, in business it is important to understand the behaviour of economic actors in the choice of a particular accounting treatment, such as the valuation of inventories, as this gives rise to theory in accounting.

A prerequisite for a full understanding of accounting theory is an awareness of the processes involved in developing a theory and the implications of these for practice. Evidence for the need for such a theoretical understanding exists in the many business failures and the legal and other actions taken against accountants for incorrect or negligent practices. This century has already witnessed some of the largest ever business failures. Such failures are not new and not purely the result of poor or inadequate accounting. However, the fact that they exist and seem to be getting bigger is reason to examine what possible role accounting played in these corporate demises and whether improvements in accounting practices could have assisted in preventing them. In addition, where accountants have been accused of negligent or inappropriate behaviour, what accounting practices could have been developed to prevent such undesirable actions?

If this aim is to be met, it is necessary to determine and understand the elements of theories and theory construction. The discipline of philosophy is where most of these elements have arisen and been discussed and debated. Consequently, it is to a brief introduction to philosophy and philosophical terms that we need to turn our attention.

Philosophical foundations

In looking at theories we are looking at the basis for making claims to knowledge: that is, on what basis can we make the claim that what we state is knowledge is *reliable* knowledge? How do we know what we claim to know? In such a discussion there are at least four fundamental terms which we need to understand.

Ontology

Ontology is the theory of being; it is designed to determine the nature of the fundamental kinds of things that exist. Theorists all have an **ontological commitment**, which is the assumptions about what there is and what sorts of things are assumed to exist.

It is usually assumed that we all see the world in the same way; that is, we all think of the world as existing as a solid reality and we regard anyone who does not see it this way as being somehow 'not normal'. However, there are different views of how we perceive the world and these sometimes emerge when we engage in deep discussion or argument. The direction of our argument will depend on the ontological position we adopt—the assumptions we make as to what exists and what does not or cannot exist. The conventional view of the world is one that sees the world as full of solid things which make up reality; things exist. This view is described as a **realist ontology**. Such an ontology is based on the belief that objects in the world have an existence independent of us. That is, it is possible to distinguish the known (the object) from the knower (the human).

But there can be alternative ontological assumptions. For example, a popular deep philosophical question (a Buddhist cone) concerns the sound of a tree falling in a forest when there is no one there to hear it. Does it make a sound? How can we know this if there is no one to experience it in some way (hear, see, smell or feel [!] it)? This question can be generalised to consider the world without the existence of human beings. Maybe such a world would have no 'meaning'—certainly no 'meaning' as we understand the expression. So, it is possible to claim that the world exists only insofar as we create it. We describe the world in language and we ascribe meanings to the words (signs) that make up that language. Thus, the world is **socially constructed**: we 'make' the world and can only understand it in terms of how we describe it (in language). We are concerned with how we know of the existence of things, and if there is no one there, we can never know of them so their existence is irrelevant. This is a **non-realist ontology**. An extreme example of a non-realist world is that of the solipsist, the person who claims that only he or she exists and everything else is a fabrication of his or her mind.

In evaluating a theory it is important to be aware of its underlying ontological commitment. Do things we cannot 'see' exist—for example, sub-atomic particles, quarks, genes? What about abstract entities like properties and numbers?

Epistemology

The process by which we obtain knowledge is called epistemology. Epistemology is usually referred to as the theory of knowledge and consists of the 'rules' of how and whether knowledge is acquired. An epistemology is any theory of what constitutes valid knowledge.[1] The word has it its origins in the Classical Greek 'episteme' meaning knowledge and 'logos' meaning theory. It is that branch of philosophy that studies the nature and limits of knowledge; it is concerned with the structure, origin and criteria of knowledge. It is also concerned with the relation between the knower (the human— that is, the researcher) and the object known (the object of the inquiry—that is, the researched), possible kinds of knowledge and the degree of certainty for each kind of knowledge, and the nature of truth. Epistemology and ontology are generally held to be the foundation of all knowledge.

Methodology and methods

Methodology is a much abused word as it is often confused with methods. It is the framework of the means for gaining knowledge. Methodology investigates and evaluates methods of inquiry and thus sets the limits of knowledge. All too often it is used to indicate the techniques used to gather data and information—the methods. Methodology is about methods but it is not the same thing. A famous economist once said:

> Methodology, in the sense in which literate people use the word, is a branch pf philosophy or of logic ... Semiliterates adopt the word when they are concerned neither with philosophy nor with logic, but simply with methods (Machlup 1963, p. 204).

Each of these terms is subsumed by the higher level one. That is, the methods employed will be determined by the methodology, which in turn will be dependent on the epistemology adopted, which is dependent on the ontology (the ontological commitment). In other words, how one views existence (the world) will determine how one perceives knowledge is created, which will then indicate the framework for

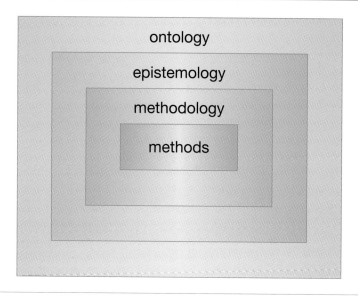

Figure 1.1 Foundations of knowledge

ontology

epistemology

methodology

methods

how this knowledge will be obtained, which will dictate the techniques and tools that will be used in determining the knowledge. Figure 1.1 describes this schematically.

It is very important to understand the relationship between ontology, epistemology, methodology and methods. The ontological position adopted by a theorist will determine what she or he sees as valid claims to knowledge. A realist ontology will lead to a realist epistemology. Therefore, if a theorist has a realist ontological commitment, as discussed above, she or he believes that things exist independently of anyone wishing to know of the thing. Consequently, that person will believe that, if we wish to have knowledge of the thing, then we can employ a methodology that leads to the methods of physically examining the thing. This examination of the thing will enable us to understand it and subsequently explain it. This will lead some to claim that we then know the 'truth' of the thing. On the other hand, if we adopt a social constructionist ontology, the thing only exists insofar as it has a social context. Our understanding will be determined by the (social) context in which we are interested in the thing. Thus, any 'truth' will be dependent on the (social) context in which the thing is being considered. Hopefully, these differences will become more evident as we examine the processes of theorising.

The development of Western knowledge

In order to understand how we gain our understanding of ourselves and our environment and therefore how we create theories to assist us in this understanding, we need to examine the *origins* of these terms and concepts. These days it is often claimed that we live in a knowledge society. What we regard as 'knowledge' is very much bound up with how we live or want to live, how we organise our existence.

Consider, for example, a so-called primitive tribe. It exists as a closed society in which knowledge is bound up with superstition and ritual. The essential defining character of its members' knowledge would be existence or survival. Therefore, an important element of their knowledge would concern day-to-day matters such as food, shelter, and defence against external threats. Knowledge of these matters would have been determined from past experiences—actual and recounted—combined with explanations for certain phenomena. For example, this could have involved a system of supra-human beings who controlled aspects of their daily lives such as the weather or the seasons. That is, aspects of everyday existence were personified or deified and often sacrifices were made to appease, placate or mollify the often less pleasant actions of these 'gods'. Nevertheless, in the absence of extraordinary events this knowledge was quite satisfactory for the society.

The demands of a contemporary developed society are far more complex. Generally we believe we are far better than the primitive tribe because we are more sophisticated, despite the fact that our fundamental needs are similar. We use such expressions as 'primitive', 'developed' and 'sophisticated' in a judgemental way. Our lives are considered to be easier than the near-subsistence lives of the members of the tribe, and this is because we 'know' more. However, we have many more alternatives to choose from so our lives may not be easier. In fact, some would argue that it is debatable as to just who is 'better off' in terms of existence—the tribe or us. The point here is that knowledge is very much bound up with existence. If we do not want to be part of a team that sends humans into space, generally speaking, then we do not feel the need to acquire the knowledge that would enable us to do so. We are content to use highly sophisticated electronic devices without fully understanding how they are constructed. However, in order for us to have such devices, *some* people need to have the knowledge to be able to create them; for example, engineers and technologists. They are our modern-day 'witchdoctors'—they have the specialist knowledge to help us 'survive' in our contemporary, sophisticated societies. Underlying such technical knowledge (and, indeed, all knowledge) will be some conceptual or theoretical knowledge. On the whole, the more complicated the knowledge, the more complex the underlying theory.

If we are to seek the origins of our Western knowledge then we must first look to the Ancient Greeks for it is there that we find the basis of our current thinking. At least three of the Classical Greek scholars stand out in terms of their contribution to Western thinking—Socrates, Plato and Aristotle. Along with their contemporaries, they questioned our existence and the basis for knowledge. Not only did they suggest solutions to these deep questions, many of which are still relevant, but they also provided us with the tools for constructing knowledge. Amongst other things, they laid the foundations for such concepts as rationality, objective knowledge, definitions, deductive logic, induction, ethics and many other notions, all of which are important for our development of theories.

If we adopt a realist ontological commitment to the study of some phenomenon then we have to accept that it exists separate from us—there is a distinction between the knower (the researcher or the person interested in the phenomenon) and the known (the object of knowledge). Plato claimed this was a very necessary first step to gaining knowledge of the phenomenon. If we accept the phenomenon's separate existence we can then define it and we do so according to our perceptions of its characteristics. This was possible, Aristotle suggested, if we examined and observed it. Many still hold the view that we can know something only if we observe it. Therefore, for example, if we want to know the effect of a certain accounting technique we should observe how it is employed in practice. Aristotle also gave us the system of reasoning known as deductive logic. The basis of deductive logic is the **syllogism**. A syllogism is a form of argument in which a conclusion follows from several premises. For example:

Premises:

All animals with fur and four legs are cats
Tom has fur and four legs, (therefore)

Conclusion:

Tom is a cat.

This is a *valid* syllogism because it follows the pattern for a valid argument. This is so despite the fact that its 'truth value' may be a little questionable—for example, Tom may be a rabbit! In other words, first and foremost, a syllogism is a matter of the *form* of the argument rather than any truth value. Therefore, a deductive argument is assessed on its validity rather than its truth value. For the argument to be true the premises must be true. To be an *effective* deductive argument, the premises must be framed carefully. In the above example we know that cats are not the only animals with fur and four legs. And, sometimes, as a result of an accident, cats do not even have four legs but still exist. Consequently, a syllogism is a powerful tool of analysis but its use must be carefully considered if it is to be successfully employed in constructing knowledge or theories.

A more precise syllogism is:

All asset accounts have debit balances in the ledger
Plant and equipment is an asset, (therefore)
The plant and equipment account has a debit balance in the ledger.

Scholars like Socrates, Plato and Aristotle were arguing in opposition to other Greek philosophers called the sophists. The sophists held (amongst other things) that all knowledge was relative. That is, what we know is dependent on our place and time, such that there is *never* any permanent knowledge. Thus, an earlier scholar, Heraclitis (c. 500 BC), claimed that we can never really know anything with certainty and he used the metaphor of a river: we can never step into the same river twice because the water is constantly flowing (that was before our rivers became too polluted) so it is never exactly the same river. Hence the world is constantly changing so our knowledge of it is also ever changing. Plato's arguments were so strongly opposed to those of the sophists that the term developed pejorative connotations. Someone may have said to you that your argument was pure sophistry—you were arguing for the sake of it without any concern for the **truth**. Similarly, **relativism** has mostly been out of favour in Western intellectual circles.

The period in Western history from about 300 to 1400 AD is often referred to as the Dark Ages.[2] It is so called partly because the spirit of inquiry that the Greeks held dear was lost. Society was based on a feudal system with a strict hierarchy, at the top of which were the divinely established kings. That is, the king (very rarely queens) obtained his authority from God so all knowledge had to be reconciled to God's will. This will was determined by (Christian) religious (clerical) scholars. These scholars were referred to as **scholastics** and their primary duty was to interpret the word of God as written down in sacred texts, mainly the Bible. This interpretation was referred to as **hermeneutics** (from the Greek word meaning 'to clarify or reveal')—the interpretation of the written word. It was believed that the Greeks had determined all there was to know about the physical world so this knowledge had to be reconciled with the 'word of God'.

Modernity

The period in history known as the **Renaissance** (15th and 16th centuries) is so called because it acknowledged the rebirth of confidence in the human capacity to learn, understand and explain the world. It marks the beginning of individuals increasingly examining and attempting to explain the world without resorting to the sort of metaphysical explanation that was essential for the scholastics. Attention was directed to human achievements and ideas. It started in the Florentine state at the start of the

15th century and spread across Europe over the next two centuries. It marked the rediscovery of thought and work, but most importantly the inquiring spirit of the Classical (Greek) scholars.

The Renaissance ushered in the era of **modernity**: the replacement of traditional (non-industrialised) society by modern social forms. The characteristics of modernity have been and continue to be debated rigorously. However, most commentators are agreed on the impact it has had and continues to have on our societies: for example, its emphasis on **scientific reasoning** and its globalising nature. Much of this is manifested in what is referred to as the Age of Reason, or more specifically the 'Enlightenment project', a movement centred around Parisian intellectual life in the 18th century, which continues to influence intellectual thought today.

A paramount tenet of the Enlightenment was that the source of human misery was the ignorance and superstition on which traditional societies were based. This could be destroyed only through knowledge, science and reason, which would be the basis of modern societies. As Hollinger (1994) states:

> [It] is based on the assumption that ignorance is the basic source of all human misery and that the elimination of ignorance, and its replacement with scientific knowledge, would pave the way for endless human progress (p. 7).

Moreover, in modern societies there was an emphasis on secularisation, capitalism and modern economic individualism. Attempts to understand the process of modernisation gave rise to the social sciences (partly as a response to the growing influence of Newtonian physics). The aim was to *understand, predict and control human behaviour* in the same way that physical objects were studied—the scientific study of human nature.

Despite being regarded as a French movement, the development of the Enlightenment was influenced by two English philosophers. The first was Thomas Hobbes (1588–1679), founder of **rational choice theory** and **social contract theory**, both of which were incorporated as essential elements into modern neo-classical economic theory which, in turn, has so influenced present-day accounting thought. The label 'psychological egoism' (pursuit of self-interest) is used to describe Hobbes's ideas. They involve a belief in the notion that human behaviour responds to a choice between pain and pleasure, and that 'obviously' people will choose the latter. In Enlightenment terms this was 'rational behaviour' or, as it later came to be known, **rational self-interest**. Thus, human behaviour was predictable and controllable.

The other British philosopher was John Locke (1632–1704), generally regarded as the father of **empiricism**. Empiricism means that *we can only know things through our sensory experience of them*. That is, we can only know those things that we see, hear, touch, smell or taste. Empiricism has been the dominant influence on Western thought throughout the last 300 years.

Another British writer, Adam Smith (c. 1723–1790), incorporated Hobbes's ideas into his work, *The wealth of nations*, in which rational self-interest becomes a **moral virtue** and hence we are guided by an 'invisible hand', the unintended consequence of intentional action. This, too, forms a cornerstone of contemporary economic thought and has become the justification for a belief in free markets.

The ideals of the Enlightenment have shaped thought in many spheres of life in the last three centuries, and continue to do so. The notion of universal knowledge made possible through the use of a single (scientific) method brought us the encyclopaedia, a major Enlightenment project. These ideals were also behind political revolutions— in the US (the American War of Independence) and in France (the French Revolution)—and are credited with the thought that enabled the Industrial Revolution. They are believed to have contributed significantly to considerable progressive elements in human 'development'. However, there also have been some less desirable and sinister implications of the Enlightenment principles such as the use of the guillotine during the French Revolution.

The apparent spectacular successes of rational scientific inquiry, as evidenced in technological advances, have reinforced the Enlightenment's domination of Western thinking. 'Objectivity, knowledge, truth, and method become intertwined by definition. Whatever falls outside this orbit becomes subjective and value laden' (Hollinger 1994, p. 61). It became, essentially, a dogma of methods.

The object of understanding of most scholarship up to the 19th century was the natural (physical) world. But then a French philosopher by the name of Auguste Comte (1798–1857) believed that social phenomena could be understood and explained on the same 'scientific' basis—through observation and experience—and it is to him that we owe two important terms: **sociology** and **positivism**. That century saw the application of this methodology to developing methods of understanding social phenomena from which emerged the social sciences (such as economics).

The tenets of positivism determined the (scientific) status of knowledge claims, including:

- Scientific statements had to be empirically grounded.
- Scientific observations had to be repeatable.
- A single (scientific) method was necessary to ensure the universality of statements and observations.

■ Science would advance through theories which, if empirically verified, would become scientific laws.

■ Scientific laws in time would be integrated into a single system of knowledge and truth.

Positivism also involved notions of reduction, causality and simplicity. **Reduction** means making generalisations on the basis of perceived common characteristics, such as reducing all social sciences to (a few) statements of human behaviour. For example, after observing that most people act to their own advantage, a reductionist statement would be that *all* humans are greedy and self-interested. **Causality** is the assumption that a linear relation exists between one event and another, such that the first event is said to have caused the second. It forms the basis of discussions of cause and effect. For example, the owner of a beauty salon noted that custom was down and also that the operators were a bit depressed and irritable. She concluded that the behaviour of the operators had caused the fall-off in customers. However, it may well be the other way round—the operators were depressed because there were fewer customers! A belief in causality is that it is possible to determine an event, or an action, that leads to something else happening. The determination of causal laws is a primary objective of positivism. **Simplicity** is the belief first expressed by William of Ockham (c. 1285–1347) (hence Ockham's razor) that, where there is a choice between expressing something in a complicated way or in a simple way, the simple way is to be preferred. All three of these notions are ontologically and epistemologically closely related.

These principles formed the basis for judging knowledge claims. Early in the 20th century they were modified, by a group of philosophers known as the Vienna Circle, to include deductive mathematical and philosophical statements which could be used to structure the knowledge into theories. This was referred to as **logical positivism** and it came to totally dominate Western thought in the 20th century. Only knowledge that fitted logical positivist principles was worthy of being called scientific knowledge; all else was non-scientific and meaningless.

A central doctrine of logical positivism is the principle of **verification**—that only knowledge verified by sensory experience is valid knowledge. Verification necessitates testing, so for the logical positivists meaning and **testability** are the same thing. Consequently, a proposition, or a statement, is factually meaningful only if it is verifiable; all other statements are meaningless. Thus, only experiential knowledge is admitted; that is, it is an **empiricist epistemology**. Consequently, logical positivism is concerned with facts (which are verifiable) and not values (which are not verifiable). The language in which a theory is described comprises propositions which are only meaningful if they are tautologous. Logic and mathematics are tautologous: they obtain their meaning internally and do not have any real-world referents. That is, logical statements are expressed as syllogisms and mathematical terms derive meaning from their internal proofs. Therefore, in describing the theory, the principle of empiricism is not violated. As it is an empirical epistemology, all propositions must be **verifiable** (or tautologous). The theory is based on a realist ontology and the position that all knowledge is **objectively determined**. Consequently, under this interpretation, ethical, aesthetical and theological statements are meaningless.

Most members of the Vienna Circle agreed with Comte that the methods of science could be applied in the social sciences, so not only did logical positivism dominate the pure sciences but it also became the standard for social science theorising, including economics and accounting, in which it was held that to be considered meaningful knowledge had to be:

- empirical
- objective (value neutral)
- scientific
- inductively derived
- verifiable (or confirmable).

These ideas have strongly influenced accounting research and theorising, as will become evident as we turn to discuss them later in this chapter and in Chapters 2 and 3. Unfortunately, they have been accepted into our disciplines almost without question. However, by the end of the 20th century, in most disciplines, they were generally rejected as the way to develop relevant, useful theories, although their influence is still very much apparent in accounting.

Requiring knowledge claims to be empirical means that only those things that we can sense (with our five senses—for most of us) have meaning. This claim has attracted considerable debate over the years and some philosophers have strongly opposed it. Although empiricism seems appealing because it is a basis for rejecting superstition, obscure and false claims, and irrationality, there are certain things which we seem to know without any direct empirical referent. This knowledge is said to be what we know *a priori*. Pure or naïve empiricism—simplistic statements or conclusions on the belief of observation—has been rejected in most disciplines. However, this does not mean that empirical knowledge has been rejected. A distinction can be made between an empiricist inquiry in which *only* empirical knowledge is admitted (such as pure or naïve empiricism) and an empirical inquiry which involves referring to empirical elements without making ontological or epistemological assumptions: looking at 'the facts' without claiming that only those things which we can experience should be considered. As we shall see later, a great deal of accounting research adopts an empiricist commitment.

As explained earlier, in order to claim to admit only objective knowledge, a person adopts a realist ontology. That is, objectivity assumes that the object under consideration exists independently of any opinion of it. Accounting has long had this as a fundamental principle. This means that people have believed that accounting can be practised in a value-neutral manner. In other words, it is believed that accounting exists as a purely independent and technical activity which does not involve any personal opinions of those practising it. Value neutrality, or objectivity, is enshrined in fundamental accounting statements such as those that form an essential part of the *Conceptual framework* and the *Framework for the preparation and presentation of financial statements* (discussed in Chapter 5).

In Western societies science has long been held to represent the most rigorous way to determine knowledge. The social sciences are those disciplines that concern social activity but wish to employ scientific methods to study them. This, as explained above, is part of the Enlightenment legacy. Many accounting researchers believe that only by employing scientific method can we establish a sound theoretical foundation for accounting.

The process of **induction** was introduced by Aristotle, who believed that in order to know about something one needed to observe and examine instances of it. Induction involves inference from a finite number of particular cases to a general conclusion. For example, we can observe a thousand white swans and conclude that all swans are white. Likewise, we can observe a thousand instances of companies announcing a (positive) profit followed by an increase in the share price and conclude that a (positive) profit announcement leads to a rise in share prices. If we are going to engage in induction, then we are also going to have to draw on the tools of statistics. For example, in our observations of the many instances of a particular phenomenon we would want to be able to have a level of confidence in any conclusion we derive—a confidence level. Therefore, **statistical inference** plays an important role in inductive research. Often this use of statistics becomes very sophisticated and complicated. Whereas induction involves an empirical inquiry, it does not necessarily mean an empiricist inquiry.

An important role for auditors has been to check the veracity of the financial statements issued by a company; this is independent verification. In a similar way, for logical positivists knowledge must be verifiable or confirmable, meaning that another researcher should get the same result as the original investigator. This is known as the **verification principle** and is obviously an empiricist principle because it holds that to be meaningful knowledge it must be possible to determine the truth-value of that knowledge (statement) by means of sensory experience. Realising that it would often be difficult to get verification as it is not always possible to observe *all* cases, the position was later weakened to confirmation, a high level of (statistical) confidence in the conclusions. Philosopher Karl Popper later argued that it was not even really possible to get confirmation so he 'reversed' the principle to state that a statement is meaningful if it can be **falsified**. That is, a proposition is meaningful only if it can be falsified through testing. Those propositions that are not able to be falsified are non-scientific. The central doctrines of religion or ethics are not verifiable, confirmable or falsifiable, and so are regarded as scientifically meaningless—they are neither true nor false. One implication of this tenet is that **testing** assumes a crucial role. So, if, for example, we wish to suggest that a (positive) profit announcement will lead to a rise in the share price, we would need to undertake rigorous testing that would convince everyone that our proposition was true.

Scientific revolutions

In 1962 a philosopher of science, Thomas Kuhn, published a book which had a significant impact on thinking in almost all disciplines, including accounting. His book, *The structure of scientific revolutions*, challenged the view that knowledge is cumulative. Kuhn demonstrated that throughout history all advances in scientific thought had emerged during a revolutionary process. That is, each new major theory represented a break from the existing accepted views and was thus a revolution in thought. The new theory (he used the term **paradigm**) dominated thinking until it was 'overthrown' in another revolution with the emergence of a newer paradigm. It is not possible to compare paradigms because they represent totally different systems of thought—they are **incommensurable** (fundamentally so different as to be unable to be measured against each other). As a philosopher of science, Kuhn used examples from the history of science to demonstrate his position.

In an article published in 1976, Wells argued that similar revolutions had occurred in accounting. One of the major problems that accounting had not been able to solve had been financial reporting in times of fluctuating—usually rising—prices. The use of historical cost for reporting did not reflect the current 'economic reality' of the items being reported. Various theorists had suggested new systems of accounting to overcome this problem but each was very different from the others' systems. Wells argued that it was not possible to make a simple comparison of the suggested alternatives because the underlying assumptions employed in each theory were dramatically different from those in the other theories. They were incommensurable so that a commitment to any one theory was like a matter of faith—a belief that a particular theory was the most appropriate basis for meaningful financial reporting. Kuhn argued that one paradigm would attract most of the working scientists and it would become the new dominant theory. Proponents of other paradigms, he argued, would gradually die (even literally) out. In accounting, proponents of *all* the then suggested theories did 'die out' as none of the theories emerged as dominant. This is one of the major criticisms of accounting as a discipline—we never seem to resolve some of the 'big questions' and just move on to another, more fashionable theory. This suggests that we do not understand the process of developing sound theory. However, the purpose of this book is to create an understanding of just that—how we evaluate theories!

Kuhn was not the only one to question the received wisdom of how theories in science develop. Lakatos (1974) suggested that it was through research programs rather than a single paradigm—that is, a group of very similar theories centred around a common core of knowledge. A research program would dominate thinking until superseded by a more successful one. Feyerabend (1975) was far more radical. From his investigations of the history of science, he argued that there was no *one* way in which scientific theories developed, which implied that 'anything goes', so even magic and witchcraft could be regarded as sciences and be judged on the same basis as other more conventionally regarded sciences.

The important point to appreciate in respect of these new world views of how theories are created in science is that they called into question some of the Enlightenment principles mentioned above. For example:

■ A single (scientific) method was necessary to ensure the universality of statements and observations.
■ Science would advance through theories which, if empirically verified, would become scientific laws.
■ Scientific laws in time would be integrated into a single system of knowledge and truth.

As indicated above, in Western thinking, science was held to be the ultimate in intellectual rigour, and the scientific method was the basis for establishing true and meaningful knowledge. However, what Kuhn and others demonstrated was that there is no *one* method of science that can be applied to establishing *all* knowledge claims. Moreover, the so-called laws of science change. What was held to be an inviolate scientific law in Newtonian mechanics was demonstrated to be not so under the system of Einstein, or under quantum mechanics or particle theory.

If we are to establish acceptable theories in accounting we need to be aware of the work of Kuhn and others and not simply accept the outdated belief that a method of science exists for establishing all knowledge claims. We also need to question whether any method of scientific inquiry is appropriate for establishing theory in accounting, as it is a socially constructed system for economic measurement and reporting rather than a discipline that deals with physical objects.

The purpose of this brief historical examination of the concepts used in theory and theory construction has been to show the context in which some widely held views originated. In addition, it is important to be aware of the tools for theoretical development and the assumptions underlying their use. With such an understanding it is possible to make a more rigorous and informed assessment of theories in accounting, which is the aim of any course in accounting theory.

The discipline of accounting

To say that accounting is what accountants do is to acknowledge that accounting changes over time. What accountants did 150 years ago is different from what they did 50 years ago, which is different from what they do now. There are common elements but a large part of their activities are different. The common elements include the technical system, bookkeeping. Any theory of accounting is going to have to incorporate the changing nature of accounting or we will continually need different theories. The Enlightenment ideal of a single system of knowledge and truth would suggest the former, but is it possible? Once again, it is useful to look back and see how the discipline of accounting originated in order to better appreciate what it is today. We can examine the ancestry of accounting as a discipline in a manner similar to how we look at our forebears—via the family tree. This is what a well-known philosopher, Nietsche (pronounced 'nee-cha'), referred to as **genealogy**.

The need for order in modernity led to the creation of disciplines. There are two meanings of the word 'discipline'. One is the action necessary to ensure that individuals conform to accepted social behaviour. Thus, a student at school is disciplined if they break the school rules. This, of course, is also true in many other social institutions, for example, the road rules and the rules of sport. In this sense, discipline is designed to seek control and order—normal, acceptable behaviour—and punish deviations from that behaviour.

The other general meaning of 'discipline' relates to the setting of the boundaries of a subject—the discipline of economics, the discipline of finance, the discipline of accounting. A further examination of the word reveals that, in essence, the meanings are similar. In determining the discipline of economics there is an attempt to determine what is acceptable and normal behaviour for those engaged in the study of economics. Activities which do not conform to acceptable behaviour are considered to fall outside the discipline's boundaries. In disciplines where there are strong professional bodies, activities that are not considered acceptable are punished. For example, a law society, a medical association or an accounting body can discipline its members. In so doing they contribute to defining the boundaries of their discipline; they are exercising power over individuals to conform.

If we look at the 'family tree' of accounting, we can discover those groups or entities that have exercised power over individuals involved in accounting activity and who thereby have defined the discipline of accounting. Over time there has been pressure brought to bear by various groups on what accountants do. Generally speaking, accountants have acquiesced; they have accepted these pressures and this has changed the discipline. However, whereas some of the entities asserting power over accountants are obvious, some are much less so. But if we are to know just what accounting is then it is important that we are aware of all these influences. This, then, is why it is useful to look back at the ancestry of the discipline.

At this stage, we will look only briefly at some examples, but as we move further into our analysis of accounting theory we will be aware of this sort of pressure—the power exerted by entities that leads to changes in the practice of accounting. (Those interested in detailed historical accounts can refer to the many works on accounting history.)

However we view the discipline there are seemingly distinct arms of accounting. The Industrial Revolution gave rise to many manufacturing organisations. One of the major concerns of the owners of these new entities was to carefully monitor costs of production. They turned to those who they believed were the experts to assist them in determining the costs and design systems for controlling these entities. Initially, these people were the engineers, but as time progressed more and more it became the role of people called bookkeepers or accountants. Thus, the accountants served the needs of the new class of entrepreneurs; they were what today we would term 'management accountants'. Industrialisation and the growth of transport systems demanded greater amounts of capital and led to the development of the joint stock company and a separation of ownership (the investors) from control (the managers). In order to protect the owners the law required the managers (the company) to be accountable to those who had provided the capital—the shareholder owners. This accountability included the furnishing of financial statements which were to present a true and fair record of the affairs and position of the company. The reports were required to be independently audited. This was the job of financial accountants and auditors. Thus, 'what accountants do' was again dictated by the needs of other groups.

Given that accounting is usually seen as a service discipline the above is probably obvious. However, the fact that it is seen as a service discipline suggests that it will never be accountants that define accounting but those whom accountants serve. As business and society have become more complex so too has the task of knowing who is defining accounting. It is also obvious that it will be those with the greatest 'political power'.

The period of the late 1920s and the 1930s was one of tremendous economic disruption in almost all Western societies. It was a period of economic depression and subsequent experiments to overcome such depression. In the US there had been many spectacular corporate failures and accounting was held to have been a key element in those failures. A direct result was a call by the Stock Exchange to the accounting profession to develop accepted accounting principles and the creation of a powerful corporate regulatory body, the Securities and Exchange Commission (SEC), which today exerts enormous pressure in determining what is acceptable accounting practice.

In Australia, from the 1980s there has been a period of 'business unease' with accounting. It seems that pressure from the finance industry has resulted in corporate law reform which has impacted directly on accounting. The apparent aim has been to make Australian business more 'international' in outlook and form, resulting in dramatic changes in the regulation of accounting practice (which will be discussed in greater detail later in the book). Here, then, is yet another illustration of accounting practice being determined from outside and subject to those groups with the political power.

What these illustrations are designed to show is that there has been no linear development of accounting. Rather, it has responded to various power influences at various times. Thus it is not a science like some of the physical sciences which are defined by the phenomena of interest; for example, geology is the science of earthly things and examines the earth in general. Accounting is concerned with a socially constructed world. In developing a theory for (or of) accounting we will need to take this into consideration. As it is concerned with human activity, accounting will never be a completely objective, value-free body of knowledge, as some would argue are the physical sciences.

If it is to continue as a separate, independent discipline, accounting is going to have to change and its exponents will have to *recognise* this change. It has done this for many years, but there has been a recent disturbing trend of many of those practising accounting not wishing to be referred to as accountants. Developments in information technology have changed the tasks of accountants. Many accountants are now involved with the provision of financial advice rather than mechanical recording and reporting procedures. This, however, is not new, as accountants have done this almost since the beginning of their existence, but the form of this advice has changed. That is, whereas it once involved cost reporting and analysis and financial statements, it now involves modern information technology media.

The involvement, at the beginning of this new century, of accountants in some of the largest corporate collapses in history is evidence of a need to recognise the changed nature of the discipline and the need for a reliable theoretical understanding of it.

NOTES

1   Unfortunately, there is some circularity of reasoning necessary here: if epistemology is a theory of knowledge then it must also refer to itself. This is a common 'problem' when 'defining' terms, but understanding would be difficult without such attempts to describe meaning.

2   Sometimes the period to 1100 is referred to as the Dark Ages and the period 1100 to 1400 as the Middle Ages.

REFERENCES AND FURTHER READING

Feyerabend, PK 1975, *Against method: outline of an anarchistic theory of knowledge*, New Left Books, London.

Hollinger, Robert 1994, *Postmodernism and the social sciences: a thematic approach*, Sage Publications, Thousand Oaks, CA, US.

Jary, David & Jary, Julia 1991, *Collins dictionary of sociology*, Harper Collins, UK.

Kuhn, TS 1962, *The structure of scientific revolutions*, University of Chicago Press, Chicago, US.

Lakatos, I 1974, 'Falsification and the methodology of scientific programmes', in Lakatos, I and Musgrave, A, *Criticism and the growth of knowledge*, Cambridge University Press, Cambridge, UK.

Machlup, Fritz 1963, 'Introductory remarks', *The American Economic Review*, vol. 53, no. 2, p. 204.

Mautner, Thomas, ed. 2000, *The Penguin dictionary of philosophy*, Penguin Books, London.

Popper, Karl 1968, *The logic of scientific discovery*, Hutchinson, London.

Wells, MC 1976, 'A revolution in accounting thought?', *The Accounting Review*, vol. 51, pp. 472–482.

CHAPTER 2

Towards a Science of Accounting

This chapter describes the development, largely in the first 70 years of the 20th century, of what has been regarded as accounting theory. It demonstrates that a major motivation for the development of this theory was the generally accepted belief in the need for greater conceptual rigour in accounting theory and research. A big part of this theorising was designed to solve a major accounting problem—that is, accounting in periods of changing prices, notably inflation. The process of scientific theory construction and the elements necessary for it are explained, as are the endeavours of some accounting scholars who attempted to use their theories in their work. ∎

As indicated in Chapter 1, the general aim of theory is to provide a reasoned basis for practice. Attempts at constructing accounting theory were made with a view to improving accounting practice. Prior to the 20th century there were few attempts at providing an accounting 'theory', the main aim being simply to provide instruction in accounting. However, in the 20th century, the accounting profession sought to determine a more theoretical foundation for accounting from which appropriate practice could be derived. This search took many forms, from mere descriptions of extant practice to the use of highly sophisticated data collection and analysis, including complex tests for statistical significance, as well as, at times, fiery philosophical debate.

To be successful a theory must win acceptance—it must be acceptable to the vast majority of those involved in the practice of the discipline. Throughout the 20th century there were many attempts to develop an acceptable theory, and they appeared in many different forms. This chapter is devoted to examining some of them to determine why and how they arose and to make some assessment as to their success.

As also previously mentioned, in order to comprehend how we gain an understanding of ourselves and our environment, and therefore how we create theories to assist us in this understanding, we need to examine the origins of the terms and ideas used in these theories. Consequently, we need to employ some of the tools of the historian. But this is not to imply that we merely establish a chronology—a list of dates on which events occurred—or any linear cause and effect. What we want to do is to uncover the context in which the ideas arose in order to better appreciate them. In the 20th century there were several major social upheavals which had a considerable impact on all aspects of human societies, including how accounting was practised. Knowledge of the circumstances surrounding these social disruptions and changing practices better helps us to understand our present. It does not mean that we recreate the past or implement past solutions to present problems, but merely that our understanding of such past occurrences *may* assist in our better appreciating the present. For example, we can ask ourselves: what was the impact on accounting practice of both world wars, economic depression, increasing complexity in business ownership and control, rapidly changing information technology, economic internationalisation then globalisation, the development of new financial instruments, and so on?

Early attempts

Accounting, as we know it, is based on the system of recording known as double-entry bookkeeping. Although accounting did exist before double entry, it is now difficult to imagine accounting without it. It is so important that, to some extent, its appearance may be viewed as the origins of modern accounting. No evidence exists that can accurately date the emergence of double entry but the oldest surviving written record of it is in an appendix to a book, *Summa de arithmetica, geometria, proportioni et proportionalita* (The collected knowledge of arithmetic, geometry, proportion and proportionality), by Fra Luca Pacioli, published in 1494, and so for many years he was regarded as the inventor of double-entry bookkeeping and the 'father of accounting'. Others have argued that it existed long before it was included in Pacioli's book and had been in use outside Europe many years before it was adopted there—perhaps in China, Korea or India, or maybe in the Arab-dominated mediaeval world. This is not the place to enter into a debate on the origins of double-entry bookkeeping. The important point is that it has been a dominant feature of the European business environment since that time.

If we are interested in the genealogy of (modern) accounting, then the adoption of double entry is of real significance. So why did double entry appear and very quickly come to dominate accounting? An accounting writer, AC Littleton (1933), has suggested reasons for its appearance. He refers to the seven antecedents of accounting or, in other words, the conditions that arose that made it inevitable that double entry would emerge and be quickly adopted. He divided his antecedents into two groups. There were those that he classified as media, namely, writing, arithmetic, and money; and those he referred to as institutional, namely, commerce, capital, private property, and credit. All have become so much a part of our everyday life now that we take them for granted, but there was a time when they did not exist as we now know them. All were either emerging or becoming more important in the 15th-century Italian states— in the Early Renaissance, the beginnings of modernity. Previts and Merino (1998) in a table in the Preface to their book, *A history of accountancy in the United States*, indicate that most of Littleton's antecedents existed in some form well before this time (p. xvi). However, what is important is that they coalesced around this time to provide an impetus for the development and growth of trade and commerce, which forms the basis of the 'modern economy'.

The growth of the modern economy

The meanings of the terms 'modern', 'modernity' and 'modernism' are constantly debated. However, for our purposes here, we will define the first two only. In everyday use, 'modern' usually means up to date with recent developments, whether it be in fashion, music or technology. If it is used in reference to art, it popularly means 'non-representational'—abstract art or art since the middle of the 19th century. The term 'modernity', particularly in relation to the history of ideas, is used to indicate the break from traditional societies brought about by the Renaissance or, more particularly, the Enlightenment, as traditional feudal societies were perceived as hindering economic development. Modernity is used to describe the period of radical changes in economies, which led to industrialisation, specialisation and the greater and more creative use of capital, resulting in the development of a system that promoted the effective use of capital—capitalism.

Facilitating the growth and expansion of economic modernity was the device known as double-entry bookkeeping. This was largely due to the fact that it was an ordered system of maintaining financial records and was able to provide decision makers with information vital to the maintenance of businesses. Later, as it developed into accounting, it also enabled the establishment of systems of (cost) control. The Enlightenment ideals were an essential foundation for modernity and many aspects of social activity went hand in hand with it. For example, the growth of (modern) science produced new technologies that could be exploited economically, hence the growth of trade and commerce and the expansion of capital needed to develop the new technologies.

The Enlightenment influenced very many aspects of society. Some of the influences were very positive but some were not so desirable. In some parts of the world the new ideals led to political revolution (for example, in France and the United States), while the United Kingdom, a 'nation of shopkeepers', was bringing about an industrial revolution that gradually spread to other parts of the world.

The legacy of the Enlightenment has been constantly debated through the centuries by scholars with very diverse interests. What is certain is that modernity through its progress has greatly influenced all aspects of life and continues to do so today.

The birth of modern accounting?

While the above is a rather simplified description, it draws attention to some of the implications of the spread of modernity. Whether double-entry bookkeeping resulted from the growth in industrialisation and the development of the business organisation, or whether bookkeeping made possible the growth of industrial development and business organisations has been debated widely. What is clear is that the ordered system of double-entry bookkeeping was extended by new and additional developments to accommodate the expanded forms of business and economic activity and organisational structures. It could be claimed that at this stage bookkeeping became 'modern' accounting. That is, previously bookkeeping fulfilled a stewardship function in that it made possible the recording of the results of economic activity to indicate to the providers of the capital the success or failure of various ventures.

However, with the growth of factories and industry, financial information was used to assist in everyday decision making: What was the cost of material? What were the cost and productivity of labour? How were price and cost related (break-even analysis)? Gradually these activities became part of what is regarded as accounting—information of a financial nature became the domain of bookkeepers and later accountants.

It should be noted that manufacturing and industrialisation had existed earlier. It is claimed that:

> . . . a market-based economy led to the development of techniques for gathering cost information for manufacturers in, for instance, fourteenth-century Italian, English, Flemish and German commerce (Chatfield and Vangermeersch 1996, p. 180).

Nevertheless, it was the greatly increased manufacturing activity of the Industrial Revolution starting in the latter part of the 1700s that created increased demand for different and new forms of financial reports and information.[1]

The joint stock company

The Industrial Revolution contributed to major changes in the form of business organisation and ownership. The magnitude of some of the new economic activities required additional financial resources. It became increasingly difficult for individuals or small groups of individuals to provide these resources so larger groups of people contributed the necessary capital, which led to the development of the modern corporation—the joint stock company. The company enabled the accumulation of the larger amounts of capital needed to meet the greater costs associated with industrialisation. It also resulted in the increasing separation of management from ownership as management became more specialised. A new accountability relationship developed between the management and the owners. New laws were created to facilitate the development of the company and protect all those who dealt with these new organisations—especially the shareholders, as providers of the capital. This accountability was satisfied by the provision of information on the management of the company to the shareholders. A large part of this was in the form of an annual report containing financial statements. This was reinforced by the additional legal requirement of an independent assessment of the veracity of the financial statements: the birth of modern financial auditing.

This is a simplified description of the history of accounting. However, the intention is to draw attention to the fact that accounting has grown in response to social and institutional developments. Thus, accounting is very much a social construction. It has responded to a demand created by dominant economic and social forces. Modernity brought about new processes of economic activity and accounting grew to facilitate these developments. Therefore, accounting has been very much a part of the dominant economic ideology, the belief in certain economic ideas that were seen as best suited to economic progress and development. As the economic activity expanded, it needed novel concepts of cost determination and control, capital accumulation and accountability, periodic profit determination, and many other aspects of accounting which are now taken for granted. In so doing, it served to protect the interests of capital providers, a notion which went unquestioned until the latter part of the 20th century. For example, employees were seen as a 'factor of production' and as such there was a belief that cost of labour needed to be controlled like all other costs. As a result, many systems for the monitoring and control of labour were devised by innovative entrepreneurs and their accountants who sometimes seemed to have been unaware that workers were their fellow humans.

Professionalisation of accounting

Another consequence of the additional demand for accounting and accountants was the formation of professional accounting bodies to protect and monitor the activities of those offering accounting services. Professionalisation is a process of socialisation. That is, if the activities of those offering accounting services can be controlled, this may be a great social advantage, protecting societies from the behaviour of unscrupulous individuals and also ensuring some consistency in what services accountants provide. However, professional bodies can also control and direct the activities of their members. In so doing, the question arises as to whose interests the professional bodies see themselves as serving—their members, the business community or society at large?

Early theorising of accounting

One of the problems the historian faces is that history is always the subject of interpretation by those presenting it. Therefore, the claim that accounting theory is a 20th-century phenomenon is likely to be questioned. However, for the present purposes, the claim will be made. Prior to this, much of the accounting literature was designed to serve as instruction in (bookkeeping and) accounting. By the end of the 19th century dissatisfaction with the existing texts led some to attempt to provide a more intellectually rigorous treatment of the subject.[2] In 1908 Charles Ezra Sprague published *The philosophy of accounts* which, over the next 15 years, went through five editions in an attempt to add theoretical rigour and consistency to the teaching of accounting and to replace the previous practice of students having to learn by rote a series of rules of a logical and rational system. It was he who also introduced the algebraic notation of the accounting equation (A = L + P). Some of the ideas in his book were determined by earlier writers, but Sprague was one of the first authors to present a rationalisation of accounting and an articulation of its various elements. For example, proprietorship increased through profits. He thus restated what had been alluded to by several authors before him—capital represented the owner's interest in the entity. This stressing of the ownership elements was referred to as the **proprietary theory**: the owner (proprietor) was the centre of accounting interest. This became the dominant view presented in most texts published in the first four decades of the 20th century; for example, both Sprague (1908) and Hatfield (1909) supported the theory.

At about the same time as proprietorship theory was being formalised and accepted, an alternative view emerged. This was known as the **entity theory**.[3] Its emergence as an important consideration for accounting at this time is directly related to the changing nature of the modern corporation. As corporations grew in size and significance the separation of ownership and control became more pronounced. Some believed that, as the corporation existed as a separate legal entity, accounting for the company should reflect the interests of the company and not what the proprietorship theorists held: the shareholders (the owners). In entity theory, the shareholders became just one group of equity providers so profit measurement was not to be viewed as the determination of potential dividends for shareholders. Profit was what was available to management to distribute to owners *and* to other parties, for example, through interest payments and taxes. Therefore, management had a right to retain profits for the future development of the company because it had accrued to the company not the owners.

Taken at face value, there appears to be little difference in terms of bookkeeping between the two theories. However, each represents a very different set of assumptions. Assumptions form an important part of theorising, as we saw in Chapter 1, so the differences will be reflected in the elements that comprise the accounting theory. For example, proprietary theory holds that profits are increases in the capital of the shareholders, while entity theory holds that profits are attributable to the company itself. Consequently, the important elements of determination may change such that the former will view the balance sheet as the most significant statement and so all measurements should be at historical costs. Entity theory, on the other hand, is designed to reflect economic rather than legal considerations and profit therefore becomes a major element in the company's survival such that the profit and loss statement becomes the more significant document with resources measured in terms of their future economic benefits (that is, to maintain the future continuation of the company). With entity theory, profit becomes a measure of managerial efficiency and an indication of future earnings.

The best known exponent of entity theory was William Paton and its expression is found in his book of 1922, *Accounting theory*. Paton was to exert an immense influence on accounting in the United States, but his strong advocacy of entity theory did not win full acceptance by the accounting community for very many years. However, elements of it did find their way into accounting thought and practice. His realisation of the changing nature of the corporation was perceptive, as the corporation has come to dominate the economic affairs of most societies and they (corporations) have long since departed from what was probably the original intention of merely accumulating capital to permit expanded economic activity.

Corporations, crises and accounting

In the 20th century there were several major social disruptions which impacted on accounting. The development of accounting thought and theory for most of the century was dominated by developments in the US. Although there were some developments in some European countries, the ideas behind which significantly impacted US accounting thinking, most of the overt developments in accounting found expression in the US.

Consolidated financial statements

As alluded to earlier, there were significant developments in the corporate form of business organisation towards the end of the 19th century. The dominant economic ideology was laissez-faire capitalism—minimum government regulation of economic activity. Businesses developed and grew stronger, and bigger. One method of growth was by stronger businesses subsuming weaker ones. As legal entities, companies started buying the shares of other companies, leading to some corporations owning a proportion of the issued capital sufficient to enable them to 'control' that company: the former became the holding company, the latter its subsidiary. Consistent with an entity theory type of philosophy, the holding company then issued consolidated financial reports which reflected the financial position of the economic unit rather than the strictly defined legal entity (entities). Because corporate financial reporting was regulated through the Companies Acts in the UK and the Commonwealth countries, such as Australia, consolidated financial statements were not commonly encountered until after their recommendation in the legislation of the 1930s. However, in the US they were common before the First World War (1914–1918) and were expected to be prepared by investors and investment advisors in the 1920s. Thus, the changing nature of the company was shaping developments in accounting, which supports the view that accounting responds to social pressures.

The business optimism of the 1920s is well known, as is its abrupt end in the 'Crash' of 1929 which started in the US but soon spread around the (Western) world. This crisis proved to be one of the most important influences on accounting thought. There was first the issue of professionalism: who could be an accountant or offer accounting services? Then, how were the activities of these 'accountants' to be regulated? Thirdly, there were questions concerning the lack of a conceptual or theoretical basis for accounting practice that would lead to consistent and uniform practices. Accounting practices in the 1920s were many and varied, some deliberately designed to mislead, some highly questionable as a result of the ignorance of those carrying them out, but all lacking a 'principled' basis. In the remainder of the 20th century the accounting profession sought those principles that would be generally accepted by the practising community—GAAP (generally accepted accounting principles).

The professional bodies' search for principles

One immediate consequence of the economic crash and the ensuing public outcry was the establishment of the Securities and Exchange Commission (SEC), a governmental regulatory body whose responsibilities included ensuring appropriate and full disclosure of accounting information by listed companies to their shareholders. Regulation was viewed as a challenge to the professional status of accountants, so to avoid total government regulation of accounting the profession responded by seeking those GAAP that would ensure accounting information would be reliable. This 'search' lasted for the rest of the century, taking slightly different forms but with essentially the same basic idea, namely, the establishment of a theoretical foundation for accounting.

There are three broadly defined periods in which the profession in the US attempted to determine this theoretical base, each marked by a different organisational structure:

1 1938–1958: Committee on Accounting Procedure (CAP)
2 1959–1973: Accounting Principles Board (APB)
3 1973 onwards: Financial Accounting Standards Board (FASB).

It was the express intention of CAP to develop a theory of accounting to help solve the problems in accounting. However, the task proved too big and CAP was reduced to issuing, over its life, 51 *Accounting Research Bulletins* (ARBs). Although well intentioned, these pronouncements were criticised as representing a 'bushfire' approach, that is, a problem emerged and an ARB was issued to 'put out the fire'. CAP was a volunteer organisation comprising members voluntarily giving their time. It never succeeded in achieving a firm authoritative status. Consequently, it could not 'enforce' its pronouncements and even its own members disagreed significantly over proposed solutions to problems (Zeff 1984).

In 1959 a new approach to determining an acceptable accounting theory was created. The APB was established with a semi-autonomous, full-time research division, the Accounting Research Division (ARD), charged with providing Accounting Research Studies (ARS). Called *Opinions*, and issued by the APB, they were to be the basis of the accounting standards. The APB had 18 to 21 members who, as with CAP, were all part-timers and all accountants. The APB did not last as long as its predecessor and, after considerable controversy and debate, it was replaced by the Financial Accounting Standards Board (FASB), a body that continues to exist today. Members of the FASB are full time and not all are accountants, as other 'interested parties' (stakeholders) are represented.

Others' search for principles

The professional bodies' response to the demand for principles on which to base accounting practice was mainly through its committees described above. Some felt that it would not be possible for practitioner bodies to develop a sound theoretical foundation as there was always the potential for a conflict of interests if a proposal affected the reported financial position of a major client. Therefore, attention was turned towards the largely academic body, the American Accounting Association (AAA), which it was felt was more disinterested and therefore capable of establishing accounting principles. The AAA issued a series of statements, the first of which was published in 1936 under the heading of 'A tentative statement of accounting principles affecting corporate reports'. It was reissued in revised form in 1944 and 1948. Practitioners believed the statement departed too much from practice—accounting principles should be no more than reflections of existing practice. The professional body responded by commissioning another report from Sanders, Hatfield and Moore, which was published in 1938 under the title, *Statement of accounting principles*. The report consciously sought to catalogue best practice and the statement was merely a listing of what practitioners believed to be best practice with no 'theoretical' speculation or conceptualisation.

In 1940 the AAA published a sponsored monograph by WA Paton and AC Littleton entitled *An introduction to corporate accounting standards*. This was to be one of the most influential works in the accounting literature (AAA 1977, p. 9), and it went through various reprints and is still used in some university courses today. It was significant in that it represented the work of two of the most influential accounting professors in the US and took a conscious 'theoretical' approach. It introduced notions such as the matching concept and, unlike other works of the same period, represented a serious attempt to establish an entity theory perspective.

The reason for the brief historical background to the search for accounting principles above is that the search was for a theoretical foundation for accounting, a rational basis for accounting practice. In each of the attempts described (and others) there were features the authors believed were necessary for the construction of a theory of accounting. Various terms were used to indicate these elements. In fact, so many terms were introduced into the literature that there was at times confusion as to what they indicated. It is important to appreciate these terms in order to appreciate the process of theorising, the construction of theories.

So much energy was expended in the search for generally accepted accounting principles that it seems that most people believe a principle to be an important and fundamental element in a theory. The word 'principle' has various shades of meaning. In one sense it means a rule, law or belief which determines actions. For example, you live by your principles. It also means a fundamental truth or proposition on which many other truths or propositions depend. The American Institute of Certified Public Accountants (AICPA), in sponsoring the search for generally accepted accounting principles by the ARD, used the term in both senses by describing a principle as:

> A general law or rule adopted or professed as a guide to action; a settled ground or basis of conduct or practice . . . (Moonitz 1961, p. 1).

They also claimed that postulates would form the basis of principles:

> . . . initially, accounting postulates are derived from experience and reason; after postulates so derived have proved useful, they become accepted as principles of accounting (quoted in Moonitz 1961, p. 1).

Accounting research studies

Consequently, the ARD first undertook to establish the basic postulates of accounting, published as ARS1: *The basic postulates of accounting* (Moonitz 1961) on which broad principles for business enterprises, published in ARS3: *A tentative set of broad accounting principles for business enterprises* (Sprouse and Moonitz 1962) could be built. In seeking the principles, the authors claimed that GAAP to date had been directed to accounting for large corporations; they intended to establish principles to apply to accounting for *all* entities.

Both ARS1 and ARS3 were consciously developed on modernist theory construction lines. Many other terms were employed, such as axioms, concepts, assumptions, definitions, propositions, hypotheses, premises, primitives. There is very little difference in the meaning of postulates and axioms, as both are regarded as self-evident truths which cannot be proved; similarly with definitions and primitives. There are fine shades of difference in the meanings but for everyday purposes these are not important. However, the terms are used by different writers in different situations, which tends to confuse the uninitiated. Propositions, hypotheses and premises are also similar in meaning but are generally used in different contexts. They are all conjectural statements. Premises are statements used in (deductive) logic and must be true or false[4]; propositions are used in theory construction and are statements about the relationship between two or more concepts; and hypotheses, which are empirically testable theoretical propositions, are employed in research used to establish theories. Unlike the earlier described terms, propositions, hypotheses and premises can be true or false and research is often designed to prove their truth or falsity. Concepts are not true or false but are single or compound terms.

A conceptual framework

Unfortunately, all these terms and expressions are found in the accounting literature so it is important to be aware of their meaning if there is to be an understanding of accounting theory. This is evident in the Accounting Research Studies 1 and 3—one refers to postulates, the other to broad accounting principles. In fact, the profession, as described above, was searching for generally accepted accounting principles which would form the basis of a theoretical foundation of accounting. With the demise of the APB and its ARD the profession turned to establishing a conceptual framework for financial reporting. This was to be the theoretical basis on which to build an accounting theory.

Figure 2.1 presents a simplified visual scheme of the process of theory construction. The starting point for the process of theorising is based on assumptions. These are beliefs about the area to be subject to research or theorising. They include what some writers refer to as objectives. That is, an objective will emerge from an assumption that there is some 'problem' worth theorising or researching. Advocates of modernist theorising could not provide an answer to the question of how assumptions emerged.

In order to overcome the problem of not being able to describe the initial stages of theorising, philosophers of science distinguished between a **context of discovery** and a **context of justification**. It was to the latter that they directed attention because they believed that it was not possible to reconstruct (and describe) the former, which was 'psychologism'. That is, they believed it was not possible to recreate and explain how theorists came up with their original ideas—it was a creative activity and part of their psychology (mind) in the same way an artist conceived of a work of art. Therefore,

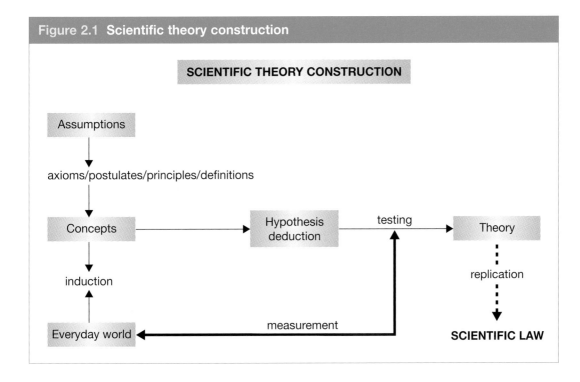

Figure 2.1 Scientific theory construction

descriptions of modernist scientific method have concentrated on how theories are 'proved' and demonstrated to solve problems—how they can be justified.

Assumptions will be based on past knowledge, or knowledge and understanding gained to date. Some will clearly be derived from observations of the everyday world and these are said to be derived **a posteriori**—knowledge derived from experience. Others will be derived **a priori**—knowledge independent of experience. These are ideas we have without being able to precisely state why we have them in terms of direct experiences. Although the terms are Latin, the distinction between the two types of knowledge is derived from Aristotle. They have been the subject of considerable debate in Western philosophy. They have also been employed in accounting, with *a priori* coming to mean an inferior type of knowledge.[5] The field of ethics relies on *a priori* knowledge in that we assess it in terms of prior beliefs and prejudices, the derivation of which we cannot necessarily specify other than through general statements such as 'it is a result of my upbringing'. On the other hand, we can observe the effect on share prices of a change in accounting method, so our knowledge is directly related to experience and is said to be derived *a posteriori*.

False dichotomies

The claim that some accounting theories are *a priori* and others are *a posteriori* is, as will become clear later, one of great misconceptions in accounting. Another great accounting misconception is the claim that some theories are deductive and some inductive.[6] It is clear from Figure 2.1 that modernist theory construction employs both inductive and deductive (recall the syllogism described in the previous chapter) reasoning. The only difference is in the emphasis placed on deduction or induction. However, they are *tools* of theorising not different *types* of theorising. Hypotheses will be derived from a process of deduction using concepts derived from *a priori* knowledge (such as postulates and principles) and *a posteriori* knowledge (a process of induction through observations of the everyday world). Some theories will make greater use of induction (claiming to describe reality) while others will combine observations (induction) with previously held theories and beliefs. However, even the so-called descriptive theories will be based on a set of prior beliefs and assumptions about the phenomena being theorised or researched.[7] The emphasis will then turn to the context of justification; that is, how systematic the testing is (see, for example, Nelson 1973, especially pp. 14–16). Consequently, there will certainly be a difference in emphasis, but all will employ the same basic tools of theorising—induction and deduction—as well as *a priori* and *a posteriori* knowledge.[8]

A simpler description of this theorising process is referred to as **hypothetico-deductivism** (sometimes referred to as the 'covering law model' or 'deductive-nomological method') which philosophers such as Karl Popper believe to be the essence of scientific method. In this form, a hypothesis is proposed and certain statements are made as premises (antecedent conditions) from which a conclusion (theory?) is deduced which will then need to undergo a process of rigorous empirical testing to determine whether the hypothesis is 'true' or not. For example, we could start with the hypothesis that lead is heavier than water, from which we could deduce certain conclusions, such as that lead would sink in water. We could then test the proposition by experimentation—placing lead in water. If it sank we would have confirmed the original hypothesis. While this is a simple example, a series of such confirmed hypotheses can be interrelated to make up a complex system of theories. The emphasis is on empirical testing to confirm the proposition. As explained in the previous chapter, testing was initially thought to be able to *verify* theories. However, because of the problem of induction, Popper (1968) proposed that testing should be used to try to falsify a proposition and until—after extensive testing—a proposition was demonstrated to be false it should be accepted as 'true' or confirmed. His ideas are referred to as falsificationism, or critical rationalism.

Measurement

Many people believe that accounting is a measurement–communications process. Sterling (1970) believes that 'accounting ought to measure something and then communicate that measurement' (p. 454). Christensen and Demski (2003) state that 'surely accounting is a formal financial measurement system. It . . . reports measures of accounting stocks on the balance sheet and accounting flows on the income statement' (p. 4).

If measurement is the application of numbers to properties or attributes of things or events, then it is an important aspect of accounting. Financial reports are money number representations of economic events and resources or commitments of an entity. However, there has been debate in accounting as to what properties of these events, resources and commitments are being measured. To Sterling they would be measuring values, while Christensen and Demski, as accountants, claim that they are measuring informative events. Thus, the latter claim that the goals are different—the first view is of valuation as an end in itself, whereas the other perspective views valuation as necessary only to convey some information (content). The distinction is difficult to discern as those who see accounting as measuring values are, as Sterling asserts above, only doing so to communicate that information to users.

There are various aspects to measurement. There is a hierarchy of measurement types—measurement scales. On the simplest level, if numbers are simply replacing names, as in the numbers allocated to a football team, there is very little we can do with the numbers. The number may represent the position of the footballer—that is the information being conveyed by the measure. Adding the numbers would not produce any meaningful information. This measurement is referred to as the **nominal scale**. If we ranked objects in order—first, second, third and so on—similarly no meaningful information would be produced if the numbers were added. This is referred to as the **ordinal scale**. In neither of these two scales is there any indication of magnitude between measures. Someone could come first in a race but the third-place getter could be quite a distance back. So, while the ordinal scale provides more information than the nominal scale, both are very restricted in the information they convey and would not seem to be of much use in accounting. Accounts could be represented by numbers rather than by verbal descriptions and they could be ranked in some order of importance, but neither type of measure would be useful in conveying financial information to users.

A third scale, the **interval scale**, comprises numbers with a fixed interval between each measure. This is much more relevant to accounting as numbers in monetary units indicate considerably more information. Two dollars is twice one dollar and the reason is that there is a rational zero and then numbers in equal increments (one dollar is 100 cents). Most accounting measures would be on this scale. A fourth scale is the **ratio scale** in which, as its name implies, the relationship between two or more measures is the objective. For example, in accounting, financial analysis involves determining the relationship between different measures—the measure of current assets is twice that of current liabilities.

The significance of being aware of measurement scales lies in the permissible mathematical operations (addition, division, multiplication, etc.)—how the numbers can be used and related to each other.

A further distinction in measurement is *how* the measures are obtained. If they are directly derived from the object or event, they are said to be **fundamental measures**. If they are the result of two or more fundamental measures they are said to be **derived measures**. A fundamental measure is supposed to bear a direct relationship to the properties being measured. For example, the statement 'I have $200 in my wallet' means that I have notes (and coins) that add up to 200 monetary units (that is, dollars), which can be directly observed. Although in some instances there would be general agreement as to this measure, there are very significant ontological implications of measures—that is, to what extent they represent a 'reality' or the 'truth'. Largely as a result of the inability to get agreement as to the most appropriate measures, there is another type of measurement increasingly being used in accounting: measurement by **fiat**. This is where a measure is arbitrarily determined and mandated. As the world moves towards global accounting standards—International Financial Reporting Standards (IFRS)—there is a strong tendency for the regulators to dictate how to measure various items. Measurement by fiat is measurement by decree.

Measurement in theory construction

Measurement is important in modernist theory construction (see Figure 2.1) as it relates to how and what information is used to construct the theory and to determine the success or not of the theory. Observations are inductively derived so if they are to be useful they will probably have to be converted to a common basis as the input to the theory. This will usually involve conversion to numbers. For example, many theories rely on descriptions of stock market reactions to an accounting event and so will be reflected in share prices at a point in time or over a period of time. Once the hypotheses have been determined it will be necessary to test them. This will also necessitate comparison of data (numbers) with observations, which will provide the feedback to the theory—if the observations conform to the predictions in the hypotheses, then the theory will be accepted; if not, the theory process will continue. Consequently, it is vital to know whether the numbers used are dependable, reliable and accurate. Here too there are epistemological and ontological questions, but these will need to be raised in detail later as a modernist position holds that the numbers can accurately reflect reality.

It seems that the American Accounting Association (AAA), the primarily academic accounting professional body, published a statement of accounting theory in every decade. In 1966 it published *A statement of basic accounting theory* (popularly known by its acronym, ASOBAT) and in 1977 it published *A statement on accounting theory and theory acceptance* (SATTA). (Earlier it had issued tentative and other statements on accounting principles and standards.) Both statements were the work of committees of very senior members of the profession. Their contents indicate a major shift in thinking about theories taking place after the first and before the second was published. In ASOBAT there was an optimism about the possibility of a single accounting theory; in SATTA there was a distinct pessimism about this possibility as little common acceptance had been found of the various attempts that had been made to create an accounting theory. Whereas ASOBAT consciously set out to determine parameters for an accounting theory (Preface, p. v), the SATTA Committee viewed its task as surveying the accounting theory literature (p. 49).

A feature of later modernity, or late capitalism, is the increasing process of **commodification**. This is the process in which goods and services are increasingly produced for 'the market'. In Western societies almost every aspect of social life is discussed in terms of its commodification. This has also spread to non-Western societies so it can be considered a hallmark of globalisation. The change in emphasis from ASOBAT to SATTA was evidence that accounting was not immune to the processes of commodification in that accounting was increasingly seen as a 'commodity' to be exchanged in markets. That is, accounting produced information and the information was seen as a 'good', subject to the conventionally viewed economic pressures of supply and demand. The implications of this were that new concepts emerged such that there was an emphasis on *users* of accounting information and *usefulness* to these users. Previously, accounting had been viewed as an 'institutional structure'; now it was a process of information generation that was subject to the vagaries of market supply and demand. Therefore, whereas ASOBAT, like ARS1 and ARS3, was seeking structural elements which could serve as the foundations for an accounting theory, this newer view saw them as irrelevant. This is illustrated in the belief of Milton Friedman (the well-known economist) that the realism of the underlying assumptions of a theory is irrelevant so long as its predictions are accurate.[9]

Therefore, despite the statement in ASOBAT that 'No one really knows what individuals or any organization wants [in respect of accounting information], or what they should want' (p. 69), there was a change in accounting theory formulation to an emphasis of satisfying users' wants. This was a major message implicit in SATTA.

The contribution of accounting theorists

Throughout the 20th century there were several individual accounting writers who made major contributions to accounting thought. SATTA includes a useful summary of the work of many of these writers.[10]

One very important feature of 20th-century accounting thought was its close association with the discipline of economics. In fact, so strong was this relationship that it led many to view accounting merely as applied economics and others to believe accounting to be based on the current dominant economic theory. If this was true, then there was little point in attempting to develop an accounting theory as accounting would become a technological extension (the measurement aspect) of economic theory!

The influence of economics came early, as the teaching of accounting in universities (first in the US and then in other countries) was invariably carried out from departments of economics.[11] Consequently, the doctoral dissertations of early accounting professors were written by members of economics departments as economics theses (for example, Paton's *Accounting theory*, 1922). Some were written by people who referred to themselves as economists. For instance, JB Canning was professor of economics and head of the Division of Accountancy at Stanford University, and wrote a book entitled *The economics of accountancy* (1929) in which he attempted to restate accounting in economic terms: for example, assets to be measured as future economic benefits rather than as the result of other valuation processes. Evidence of this strong influence of economics is also seen in the work of other accounting writers and it is interesting to note the differing economic theories. DR Scott's book, *The cultural significance of accounts* (1931), shows the influence of Thorsten Veblen's institutional economics, while Chambers' work, *Accounting, evaluation and economic behavior* (1966), appears to have been influenced by von Mises (an Austrian economist) and Hayek. There are many other examples. The work of late 20th-century accounting writing is heavily dependent on neo-classical economic theory, which will be discussed in the next chapter.

To many, this influence of economic theory on accounting will not be at all surprising. However, what is often forgotten is that economic theory does not remain constant. Accounting will therefore reflect the current economic hegemony—the current dominant economic ideology. As such, accounting is ontologically reliant on economic ideology. It is evident, after examining the perceived major accounting problems in the 20th century, that accounting thought changed to reflect an economics basis for attempted solutions. Thus, there was a change in emphasis away from the balance sheet as a statement of valuations at a point in time (stock concept) to the income statement to reflect the return on investment/capital (flow concept). This became so strong in the later part of the century that accounting was believed by many researchers to reflect the interests of one group of stakeholders—the investors in publicly listed corporations. This belief stills holds dominance in this century despite many economic crises and accounting catastrophes.

In the middle of the 1950s there was a marked change in the type of accounting theory literature. Two articles, one by Raymond Chambers (1955) and the other by Richard Mattessich (1956), made calls for greater intellectual rigour in accounting through the use of the works and ideas of philosophers of science, and in making such calls they were clearly aligning themselves with the modernist movement. One outcome of this was a decade of considerable methodological debate and the publication of several major theoretical books (see below). These works represent a major part of the intellectual heritage of accounting. In other disciplines the works of 'past masters' are respected and studied. For example, in physics the work of Newton, Maxwell and many others has not been forgotten even though many of their theories have been replaced by those of Einstein and 20th-century quantum mechanics. Similarly, the works of Marx, Weber and Durkheim are studied in sociology despite many of their notions being replaced by newer theories. People in sociology study these classical theorists because they provided theories with many innovative ideas, which laid the foundation for subsequent sociological theorists.

A major issue in accounting in the 1960s was asset measurement in times of rapidly changing price levels: how was it possible to present users with reliable financial statements when there was such rapid inflation that the figures in the traditional accounts were quickly outdated and meaningless? Theorists suggested various solutions, some of which were relatively conservative, while others required a radical overhaul of accounting as it was then practised. Some even tried to justify the status quo.

Two economists were among the first to publish a major theoretical work in the 1960s— Edwards and Bell (1961). As economists they argued that the use of historical cost measures by accountants resulted in totally meaningless information for those concerned with the survival of the firm (company). Accountants should try to produce information of what it would cost the firm to continue operating at the same level. Thus they advocated measuring resources at their current market prices—it was replacement cost accounting. Although revenues would remain much the same as under historical cost, expenses would reflect the replacement cost at the time they were incurred. Deducting these expenses from the revenues would result in a measure of *current* operating profit. A complication was that the system also required recognising that if assets were measured at replacement cost during periods of rising prices there would be what they called a 'holding gain' or 'holding loss'. For example, the increased (replacement cost) measure of an asset over its (recorded) historical cost would indicate a holding gain. These holding gains (and any holding losses) should be separated from current operating profits and disclosed as such.

This was, according to Professor Raymond Chambers of the University of Sydney, too artificial. In his works he argued that those making decisions about possible courses of future action most needed to know what resources they had at their command that would enable them to undertake future activities. The replacement price of an asset indicated the amount needed to replace an asset but gave no indication of how that cost could be met. Therefore, he argued, the most relevant measure of all items was the *current market selling price*, and his system came to be known as 'continuously contemporary accounting' (**CoCoA**). Critics argued that this was contrary to the going-concern postulate as it implied the sale of assets. However, they missed his point—he never advocated the sale of assets (which would likely result in 'low' prices, as in a forced sale situation) but what measure of resources the company had at its command if it sold its asset(s) in the normal everyday course of business. This was the current cash equivalent at the command of managers. A shift to CoCoA would have required a radical change in the actions of accountants; this seemed too much for the professional community and his ideas were never fully accepted. However, some companies did produce published financial statements with CoCoA measures. Moreover, it is interesting to note that regulators now require some assets to be reflected in the accounts at 'mark-to-market'—which, of course, is essentially the current market selling price advocated by Chambers.

CoCoA was not the only contribution Chambers made to accounting thought: he is probably the largest single contributor to the accounting literature. As indicated above, Chambers sought to add greater intellectual rigour to accounting thought and his work covered many aspects of accounting theory and related fields. He also believed that he should not remain in the 'academic ivory tower', so took an active role in the affairs of the professional bodies and was at one stage the national president of (what is now known as) CPA Australia. In his work he drew from a diverse range of disciplines and he was committed to making accounting a discipline that was equal to any science. For this he can be classified as one of the greatest accounting scholars, albeit a modernist thinker.

Like Chambers, Richard Mattessich was committed to establishing an intellectually rigorous discipline of accounting. However, they differed in how to achieve this and at times they clashed intellectually. Whereas Chambers was intent on creating a new theory of accounting (CoCoA), Mattessich was more concerned with establishing a sound intellectual base for accounting practice as he saw it. He too was a modernist thinker with a strong commitment to establishing the scientific credentials of accounting and, like Chambers, he drew from a diverse range of disciplines for support. In his early career Mattessich was situated at the University of California, Berkeley, where he worked with many other major contributors to accounting thought such as Moonitz (the author of ARS1 and ARS3 discussed above) and Carl Devine.

Another author to publish a major work in the 1960s was Yuji Ijiri, whose prime objective was to establish a sound theoretical base for historical accounting. The central theme of Ijiri's work is measurement. His book is entitled *The foundations of accounting measurement: a mathematical, economic and behavioral inquiry* (1967), which gives an indication of its content.

An age of intellectual rigour

There were many other major contributors to the accounting theory literature during this period but it is not appropriate to discuss them all here.[12] However, it is important to note that there was a substantial response to the call by Chambers and Mattessich for greater intellectual rigour. This was seen to lie within the methods of science and much of the argument was drawn from the conventional descriptions of scientific method in the philosophy of science. It is also important to note that these efforts were consistent with the general thrust of the profession since the 1930s: namely, a search for the theoretical foundations of accounting. All shared a modernist vision— that is, they sought to establish a science of accounting, believing that science represented the highest standard in determining intellectual rigour—but they were unaware that the debate on science and its 'method' was undergoing dramatic revision, initially in response to the ideas produced by Kuhn (1962) and later by many others. However, around 1970 these efforts took a new turn, which is the subject of the next chapter.

NOTES

1 There are several works on the history and development of cost and management accounting; see, for example, Wells, MC 1977, 'Some influences on the development of cost accounting', *Accounting Historians Journal*, pp. 47–61. One of the most influential sources is Paul Garner's *Evolution of cost accounting to 1925*, Garland, New York, 1990, although it makes the modernist assumption of steady progress and development—that is, evolution.

2 For example, George Soule published his *Soule's new science and practice of accounts* in 1881.

3 Once again, the history of entity theory has been traced back to much earlier than the turn of the century.

4 For the conclusion of a syllogism to be true, rather than valid, the premises must be true.

5 See Nelson, Carl L 1973, 'A priori research in accounting', in N Dopuch & L Revsine, eds, *Accounting research 1960–1970: a critical evaluation*, Centre for International Education and Research in Accounting, Champaign-Urbana, Illinois, US.

6 This was probably introduced into accounting by one of the earliest textbooks on accounting theory (Hendriksen, ES 1965, *Accounting theory*, Richard D Irwin, Illinois), but has persisted in theory texts and other accounting literature ever since.

7 Similarly with so-called positive and normative theorising: for example, Hakansson (1973) makes the statement 'In examining the literature of the social sciences, one is struck by the intertwinement of the positive, or descriptive, and the normative, or prescriptive' (p. 139).

8 This was first made clear by the great philosopher, Immanuel Kant (1781), in the 18th century and has been a part of the Western philosophical tradition ever since: see Kant, Immanuel 2003, trans. JMD Meiklejohn, *Critique of pure reason*, Dover Publications, New York.

9 This is a very well-known feature of Friedman's methodological position and further information on it can be obtained from a very wide range of references on neo-classical economics and the work of Friedman.

10 However, it classifies them as inductivists or deductivists, thus perpetuating the mistaken classification of textbook writers such as Hendriksen as mentioned above.

11 This was not always the case—remember that Sprague wanted a reliable statistical base for accounting practice. However, long before the 20th century, both disciplines were concerned with similar phenomena (for example, the notion of capital), each arriving at a distinctly different conclusion.

12 A more comprehensive discussion can be found in Gaffikin (2003).

REFERENCES AND FURTHER READING

American Accounting Association (AAA) 1966, *A statement of basic accounting theory*, AAA, Evanston, Illinois, US.

American Accounting Association (AAA) 1977, *A statement on accounting theory and theory acceptance*, AAA, Sarasota, Florida, US.

Canning, JB 1929, *The economics of accountancy*, Ronald Press, New York.

Chambers, RJ 1955, 'Blueprint for a theory of accounting', *Accounting Research*, vol. 6, pp. 17–25.

Chambers, RJ 1966, *Accounting, evaluation and economic behavior*, Prentice Hall, Englewood Cliffs, New Jersey, US.

Chatfield, Michael & Vangermeersch, Richard, eds 1996, *The history of accounting: an international encyclopedia*, Garland Publishing Inc, New York.

Christensen, John A & Demski, Joel S 2003, *Accounting theory: an information content perspective*, McGraw-Hill, New York.

Dopuch, N & Revsine, L, eds 1973, *Accounting research 1960–1970: a critical evaluation*, Center for International Education and Research in Accounting, Champaign-Urbana, Illinois, US.

Edwards, EO & Bell, PW 1961, *The theory and measurement of business income*, University of California Press, Berkeley.

Gaffikin, MJR 2003, 'The a priori wars: the modernisation of accounting thought', *Accounting Forum*, vol. 27, pp. 292–311.

Hakansson, Nils H 1973, 'Empirical research in accounting, 1960–70: an appraisal', in Dopuch & Revsine, op. cit., pp. 137–173.

Hatfield, HR 1909, *Modern accounting*, D Appleton and Company, New York.

Ijiri, Yuji 1967, *The foundations of accounting measurement: a mathematical, economic and behavioral inquiry*, Prentice Hall, New York.

Kuhn, TS 1962, *The structure of scientific revolutions*, University of Chicago Press, Chicago, US.

Littleton, AC 1933, *Accounting evolution to 1900*, University of Illinois Press, Urbana, US.

Mattessich, RV 1956, 'The constellation of accountancy and economics', *The Accounting Review*, vol. 31, no. 4, pp. 551–564.

Mattessich, RV 1964, *Accounting and analytical methods: measurement and projection of income and wealth in the micro- and macro-economy*, Irwin, Homewood, Illinois, US.

Merino, Barbara D 1993, 'An analysis of the development of accounting knowledge: a pragmatic approach', *Accounting, Organizations and Society*, vol. 18, pp. 163–186.

Moonitz, M 1961, *The basic postulates of accounting* (ARS1), AICPA, New York.

Nelson, Carl L 1973, 'A priori research in accounting', in Dopuch & Revsine, op. cit., pp. 3–19.

Paton, William 1922, *Accounting theory*, Ronald Press, New York.

Popper, Karl 1968, *The logic of scientific discovery*, Hutchinson, London.

Previts, Gary John & Merino, Barbara Dubis 1998, *A history of accountancy in the United States*, Ohio State University Press, Columbus, US.

Scott, DR 1931, *The cultural significance of accounts*, Scholars Book Club, Kansas, US, reprinted 1976.

Sprague, CE 1972 (1908), *The philosophy of accounts*, Scholars Books, Kansas, US.

Sprouse, R & Moonitz, M 1962, *A tentative set of broad accounting principles for business enterprises* (ARS3), AICPA, New York.

Sterling, Robert R 1970, 'On theory construction and verification', *The Accounting Review*, vol. 45, pp. 444–457.

Zeff, Stephen 1984, 'Some junctures in the evolution of the process of establishing accounting principles in the USA: 1917–1972', *The Accounting Review*, pp. 459–462.

CHAPTER 3

Accounting Research and Theory

The theorising described in Chapter 2 was rejected as not providing sufficiently general theories, and attempts to theorise accounting took a new direction, informed now by theories in economics and finance (and other disciplines such as psychology), and aided by the use of computers. Large data collection and analysis emphasised a purportedly more systematic empirical approach to developing theory. ∎

Around 1970 there was a dramatic change in the approach to accounting research. Several reasons have been suggested for this change in methodological direction by those reviewing the development of accounting thought. For many, a major distinction was a change in direction away from attempts to prescribe a theory of accounting to developing theory from a description of extant practices. To advocates of the latter, previous attempts to develop a theory of accounting were futile as there could never be agreement over the many inputs into the theory such as the postulates, principles and, most specifically, the assumptions. Although very inaccurate descriptions, the two approaches were labelled **normative** (the prescriptive theories that dominated prior to 1970) and **positive** (the descriptive research that has dominated mainstream accounting research since 1970).

With its emphasis on description, the most defining characteristic of mainstream research since 1970 is its commitment to empiricism. In their book on accounting theory, Henderson et al. (1992) refer to this research as neo-empirical research: a most apt nomenclature. As mentioned, the dominating characteristic was empiricism. It is 'neo' (new) because, although earlier research had relied on empiricism in that it sought to establish 'theory' from best practice, the emphasis after 1970 was on a more *systematic* use of empirical evidence. This was largely made possible because of the availability of large financial databases to which sophisticated statistical techniques could be applied to test hypotheses. This, in turn, was greatly facilitated by the increasing availability and use of computers.

All neo-empirical accounting research has the underlying assumption of the efficiency of markets—the **efficient markets hypothesis** (EMH). It is referred to as an 'hypothesis' because, despite more than 40 years of research designed to test the hypothesis, all attempts to date have failed to confirm it. Therefore, consistent with the process of theory construction described in Chapter 2, which states (simply) that a theory is a *confirmed* hypothesis, it remains a hypothesis.

The EMH emerged in the 1960s from the work of researchers at the University of Chicago trained in economics and finance and engaged in the area known as portfolio theory, and employing the **capital assets pricing model (CAPM)**. It was then taken up by accountants also working and studying at the University of Chicago and, as stated, it has been the cornerstone of a considerable amount of research over the last 40 years. The EMH is an assumption about the relationship between information and security prices. The research area is usually referred to as 'capital markets research' but the EMH has had implications for other research areas as well. Two Australians working at the University of Chicago, Ray Ball and Phillip Brown, are regarded as the first to have engaged in capital markets research in accounting, and their work (Ball and Brown 1968) has been widely cited. Another seminal work is that by Bill Beaver (1968).

There are various forms of market efficiency, but they discriminate only on the degree of efficiency, in a similar way to how economists describe a market: perfect, imperfect, etc. Nevertheless, in the literature reference is made to three types of EMH: the strong form (markets very efficient); semi-strong; and weak (markets not very efficient). A strongly efficient market would be one in which security prices *fully* reflect all available information, and do so immediately the information becomes available: all new information has been immediately absorbed by the market. A leading figure in the development of the EMH in finance, Eugene Fama (1970), states that a market is efficient if 'security prices fully reflect all available information' (p. 384). It should be noted that available information includes *all* information that investors use to make investment decisions, and accounting is only a part of such information.

Capital markets research

Prior to the 1960s the emphasis in finance was on fundamental analysis—that is, attempting to determine a valuation (an intrinsic value) of securities based on past and present financial information (mainly financial statements) and industry and other macroeconomic data. The aim of the analysis was to uncover mispriced securities (in order to take advantage of the mispricing): to trade in these securities in the knowledge that the prices were not 'correct'. Employing the new theories in economics and finance, Ball and Brown's (1968) study attempted to determine the information content (for the securities market) of accounting numbers (in this case, income measurements). Through empirical examination of stock-market prices Ball and Brown (and later many others) believed they could determine the effect on stock prices of (new) accounting information. Stock prices were taken as objective external indicators of the usefulness of the information in accounting reports.

Underlying the developments in finance and financial economics, and subsequently accounting, was the notion of portfolio selection; that is, which investments should be made and included in a 'portfolio of investments'? In 1959 Harry Markowitz had published a book under the title, *Portfolio selection: efficient diversification of investments*. Starting from this work, in the mid-1960s two financial economists, Sharpe and Lintner (working at the University of Chicago), developed the CAPM which was designed to determine an appropriate return on a single asset, given a level of risk.

The notion of **risk** is an essential element in determining investment. All investment is made at some level of risk. On the assumption that investors are risk averse (they try to avoid risk as much as possible), portfolio theory seeks to determine the appropriate mix of investments that should be held in order to minimise risk. An investor will undertake a risky investment so long as there is a **return** sufficient to induce the investment to be made—there is a trade-off between risk and return. Both risk and return are crucial elements in the valuation of securities. The expected return from an investment will determine the price an investor is willing to pay, but this must be offset by some measure of the risk associated with the investment. At the simplest level, the value of an investment represents the present value of the expected future dividends from that investment. That is, the *expected* future dividends will be discounted at a rate of return adjusted for the risk associated with the investment.

Portfolio theory, as indicated, is designed to determine a portfolio of assets. On the other hand, CAPM is designed to provide a measure for a single asset. It does this by comparing the expected return from an asset in relation to a measure of risk—β (beta). The beta of a security indicates the riskiness of holding the asset as part of a thoroughly diversified portfolio; it is the risk associated with a specific asset compared with the average overall market risk.

An assumption of market efficiency is essential to both portfolio theory and CAPM. Accounting research in the 1970s tended to support market efficiency; in the 1980s market efficiency was assumed by researchers; since the 1990s research has found evidence inconsistent with market efficiency (Fields et al. 2002, p. I-280). An underlying assumption of market efficiency is the economic rationality of investors. With evidence suggesting that markets are not rational, much recent research has turned its attention to the behaviour of investors (who do not necessarily act economically rationally). In 2004 *The Wall Street Journal* reported that even the 'father of EMH', Eugene Fama, at a conference to honour him held at the University of Chicago, conceded that markets may not be efficient and there may be 'poorly informed investors' who do not act rationally.[1]

Nevertheless, there are still many accounting researchers who want to believe in market efficiency and undertake research that continues to test for efficiency or assumes it exists. As indicated in Chapter 1, Kuhn (1962) showed that researchers will continue to believe in a paradigm as a matter of faith despite mounting evidence against it.[2]

Capital markets research and accounting

Much of the capital markets research in accounting has been in the form of event studies, which were first used in finance. An **event study** investigates the association between an information announcement and the behaviour of share prices. As Kothari (2002) states:

> In an events study, one infers whether an event, such as an earnings announcement, conveys new information to market participants as reflected in changes in the level or variability of security prices or trading volume over a short time period around the event (p. I-116).

There are also **association studies**, which Kothari says are:

> . . . tests for a positive correlation between an accounting performance measure (e.g. earnings of cash flow from operations) and stock returns . . . (p. I-116).

Most studies have been one or the other but Ball and Brown's (1968) study is both. It provides evidence that there is information content in accounting earnings announcements and correlates the signs of the abnormal stock returns in the period of an earnings announcement.

There has been a considerable amount of capital markets research in accounting over the last 40 years. The studies can be classified according to the researchers' motivation, as Kothari (2002, p. I-121) has done.[3] Although there is considerable overlap among the areas, he has listed them as:

1   Methodological capital markets research
2   Evaluation of alternative accounting performance measures
3   Valuation and fundamental analysis research
4   Tests of market efficiency
5   Value relevance of disclosures.

As its name implies, the first, methodological capital markets research, is concerned with examining the significance of and the relationship between various variables when trying to determine the relation between security returns and financial statement information. For example, questions related to items such as the information content of additional information or alternative measures, the effects of governance structures in respect of the amount and timing of company information releases, and other matters are of interest to researchers.

In evaluating alternative accounting measures, the second on Kothari's list, researchers are concerned with perceived deficiencies in some existing performance measures. The term 'quality of earnings' has often been used in relation to this type of capital markets research, most being association studies.

As noted above, much of the research in finance prior to the 1970s was termed fundamental analysis. However, there has been a considerable body of capital markets research in accounting and finance that attempts to incorporate a more systematic empirical analysis of the information in investigating the problems of valuation. This is the third of Kothari's classifications. Underlying it is the fundamental value assumption that the value of equity is equal to the present value of future expected dividends. Fundamental analysis research is undertaken to try and identify mispriced securities (as earlier). It does this by comparing an 'intrinsic value' of a security to the 'market value'. Because of the fundamental assumption, it follows that this type of research is heavily dependent on forecasting. For example, what will be the future flows of cash, revenues and expenses? The research includes financial modelling and a good example is that by Feltham and Ohlson, which is discussed at length by Beaver (2002) who argues that it is an excellent example of an attempt to provide an accounting theory. As such it has led to considerable empirical research as researchers have attempted to provide empirical support for the model.

As indicated previously, market efficiency is a necessary assumption in almost all accounting (and other) capital markets research. Research first supported efficiency but later research has cast doubt upon it. Considerable research effort has been directed towards testing market efficiency, Kothari's fourth point. As research results threw doubt on the EMH, researchers introduced corollary assumptions in an attempt to 'save' the explanatory power of the EMH. These were usually referred to as anomalies; for example, if prices tended to rise at the end of the day's trading it was referred to as the 'day-end effect' and research to support this would examine the stock market in the very short term—intra-day trading—in search of patterns or 'regularities'. So many anomalies have been uncovered that researchers in finance have tended to reject the EMH. However, many accounting researchers have attempted to retain it as it directly impacts on the interpretations that can be placed on observed associations between security prices and accounting numbers (cf. Beaver 2002). In fact, as Lee (2002) clearly states, 'The degree to which markets are efficient affects the demand for accounting research in investment decisions, regulatory standard-setting decisions, performance evaluations, and corporate disclosure decisions' (p. I-234).

The EMH is useful to capital markets researchers who are interested in examining the effect of *new* information releases. For example, Ball and Brown's (1968) study was concerned with the effect on security prices of income announcements and they found a sufficiently high correlation to declare support for EMH. However, subsequent studies questioned this conclusion because they found that abnormal returns continued after a profit announcement, suggesting that the new information was not fully incorporated into the security prices. This is referred to as the 'post-earnings announcement drift' and research in this area became an important sub-area of capital markets research in an attempt to explain this anomaly. The post-earnings announcement drift anomaly is just one of many unresolved issues in respect of market efficiency.[4] Lee (2002) inquires: why do we believe markets are efficient? And he responds that:

> The answer boils down to a visceral faith in the mechanism of arbitrage. We believe markets are efficient because we believe arbitrage forces are constantly at work (p. I-236).

Lee's response is somewhat paradoxical in that if markets are efficient then arbitrage is not possible. For him arbitrage is 'information trading aimed at profiting from imperfections in the current price' (p. I-236). Generally speaking, arbitrage is taking advantage of different prices of an asset in different markets; thus, information trading aimed at exploiting (overall) market imperfections.

Many capital markets research studies seem more appropriate to the disciplines of finance or financial economics than accounting. However, a recent form of this research attempts to investigate the association between specific accounting variables and security prices. It seeks to enable researchers to predict how accounting variables relate to the market value of equity. It has attracted the name **value relevance research**, the fifth item on Kothari's list: an 'accounting amount is defined as value relevant if it has a predicted association with equity market values' (Barth et al. 2002, p. I-79). Value relevance research has become popular since the early 1990s. Its exponents claim that the essential concerns with this type of research are the qualitative characteristics of relevance and reliability.

Value relevance research is different from other capital markets research in that it requires the researcher to have a very sound knowledge of accounting and its institutional setting. It attempts to determine whether accounting numbers relate to value in the predicted manner. Underlying it is a valuation model, so it could be argued that the research is only as good as the valuation model adopted. For example, some use the balance sheet as the basis for valuations. This is surprising because research for more than 50 years has questioned whether balance-sheet figures represent any 'value'. Nevertheless, value relevance research employing the balance-sheet model assumes that the market value of the equity is equal to the market value of severable assets less the market value of liabilities; hence the name, the balance-sheet model. The market value of the component whose incremental association is being assessed is separated from the other items in order that the research can determine the 'value relevance' of that item.

An alternative to the balance-sheet model is an earnings model which, for example, can regress stock returns on alternative measures of earnings, and the regression with the highest R^2 is considered the best performance measure or most value relevant (cf. Holthausen and Watts 2002, p. I-56). There are, however, some problems with this research. Generally, they concern the reliance on accounting numbers to construct the valuation model (see Holthausen and Watts, p. 1-56, or Beaver 2002, p. 464). For example, there are problems associated with the reported measure of income or earnings, such as accounting conservatism. In addition, some items affect retained earnings but are not included in the income statement. Where this happens it is referred to as a 'dirty surplus' as opposed to the situation in which all changes in retained earnings are reflected in the income statement (a 'clean surplus' policy). For Holthausen and Watts value relevance is of very limited relevance to standard setters (as implied in the title of their paper).

Barth et al. (2002), who have undertaken many value relevance studies, have countered some of the criticism. First, they contend that it provides fruitful insights into questions of interest to standard setters who, secondly, have a primary focus on equity investment and are interested in the usefulness of items of information provided to the equity market in financial statements. Third, extant valuation models of valuation can be used despite their often simplifying assumptions. Fourth, conservatism in the accounts is not a problem for value relevance research and can in fact be one of the items for which tests are undertaken. Fifth, although relevance and usefulness are fairly synonymous, the latter is ill-defined, so value relevance research does not test for usefulness. And, finally, there are econometric techniques that can be employed to overcome any problems in the method.

As Beaver (2002) has commented, 'value relevance research is controversial' (p. 460). Nevertheless, there are many well-known researchers engaged in it. They have investigated many reported accounting numbers and issues—for example, pension accounting, non-financial intangible assets and even footnote disclosures. As such it may, as Beaver has suggested, be able to assist in defining and describing accounting issues and lead to some sort of (accounting) theory. Like other forms of capital markets research, it is dependent on market efficiency but it examines questions with respect to valuation differently. It may (Barth et al. 2002) or may not (Holthausen and Watts 2002) assist regulators in formulating appropriate accounting standards.

Market efficiency is essentially about the ability of the 'market' to incorporate information about investment decisions. The 'market' is made up of many economic actors. Some are individuals trading on security markets in their own right or through advisers and/or brokers and some are institutional investors with substantial investment divisions. Assisting in investment decisions are those individuals known as financial analysts, those with expertise in analysing financial and other information that can be used in making investment decisions. On the basis of their analysis, analysts make forecasts on which some investors depend. A major area of accounting research is investigating analysts' behaviour to uncover the reasons why particular forecasts are made, as these forecasts become part of the information available to the market. As Beaver (2002) states, 'Efficient analysts' information processing can facilitate the efficiency of security prices' (p. 464). Much of the research has suggested that analysts' forecasts are optimistic. One cynical reason for this, uncovered in the 1990s, was that some analysts were being compensated for 'talking up' particular investments. However, the research examines analysts' behaviour to determine how and why they arrive at their conclusion, how reliable this information is and what elements of financial statement information they find important.

Noisy trading

In an efficient market, security price movements are like a **random walk**. That is, investors cannot predict what new information might result in changes in security prices responding over time unpredictably—randomly. However, in a strongly efficient market investors will absorb any new information instantaneously and the market will respond accordingly. The actual price of a security will be an estimate of the intrinsic value. Logically, however, it would not really be worth trading as no one could 'beat the market'. However, trading does occur. Efficient market believers respond by weakening the assumption of a *strong* market to one where it is claimed that markets are *semi-strong*. As indicated, market efficiency has been a fundamental assumption of accounting capital markets research. Considerable research energy has been devoted to demonstrating (or saving) market efficiency but the evidence has been mounting against it.

Neimark (1990) has suggested that developments in accounting research mirror developments in the broader academy but 'lag behind other fields' (p. 103). In this statement, she did not have belief in capital markets in mind but her contention seems to be appropriate to capital markets research. Researchers in finance and financial economists have generally accepted that markets are not efficient, yet many accounting researchers persist with it: to them, as Lee 2002 (quoted above) has suggested, it is a gut feeling. An essential assumption of the EMH is that investors act in an economically rational manner—there is rational behaviour.

There has been mounting evidence, as mentioned above, that many investors do not act as rationally as believed; they, in fact, act (economically) irrationally. Accordingly, there has been a distinction drawn between 'smart-money' investors and noise (or liquidity) traders. The former trade on the basis of fundamental information—they utilise the information available quickly and in an unbiased manner. On the other hand, noise traders act on signals that ultimately prove to be 'value-irrelevant' (e.g. unsubstantiated rumours). It has been found that there is a very significant amount of noise trading and it is probably responsible for the volatility in realised returns. As noise trading is irrational, it is not possible to statistically or mathematically model it, which has direct implications for much accounting research.

Behavioural finance

Another financial economist working at the University of Chicago in the same department as Eugene Fama was Richard Thaler. He has long disagreed with his colleague about market efficiency. He has argued that markets are not efficient and that investors respond in an unpredictable and so-called irrational manner. Such a view gave rise to a new way of researching finance, called 'behavioural finance', in which the emphasis is on the study of investor behaviour. Investors' non-rational behaviour has the potential to create problems for markets. For some time Thaler and others noted the anomalies in markets that contradicted market efficiency. For example, they noted that, although the EMH held that investors would only respond to *new* information, trading continued without any new information and prices fluctuated irrespective of any new information. Just because markets are unpredictable (cf. random walk) it does not mean that markets are efficient.

The shift away from the belief in market efficiency to a belief in behavioural finance has implications for how markets are regulated and corporate governance issues, which in turn have flow-on effects for accounting research. For example, the value relevance research seeks to aid accounting regulators by examining the market's response to specific items of accounting information. If markets are not efficient, then it would be virtually impossible to make any predictions based on this type of research. However, some researchers, such as Lee (2002), find that, despite some unresolved issues in behavioural finance, 'capital market research is an exciting place to be at the moment' (p. I-234). For him, there is considerable potential for accounting researchers so long as they 'unshackle' themselves 'from the notion that price is equal to value' (p. I-253).

Positive accounting theory

At the start of this chapter it was pointed out that a distinction is made between positive and normative theorising. This is a distinction that has been made by economists to describe theories based on description and those based on prescription. It is believed that a positive statement is a statement about *what is*, one that contains no indication of approval or disapproval. A normative statement expresses a judgement about whether a situation is desirable or undesirable and is couched in terms of what *should be* or *ought*. On the basis of this distinction there has been a considerable body of accounting research that has claimed to be positive. Actually, all the capital markets research discussed above could probably be described as positive, while it is claimed that the research prior to the 1970 research direction shift was normative. It is a little simplistic to suggest that statements can be categorised as purely positive or purely normative because underlying all statements are unseen assumptions. Similarly, as will be demonstrated later, to classify theories as positive or normative is equally simplistic.

Positive accounting theory (PAT) is an expression of neo-classical economic theory. Fundamental to it is a belief in rational choice theory. That is, material self-interest— usually referred to as **opportunistic behaviour**—is the basis of all economic activity. Therefore, according to PAT, self-interest (opportunistic behaviour) is the reason for the choice of accounting methods and techniques and policy decisions. In PAT the firm (organisation, company or whatever[5]) is described in terms of a collection of contracts—a nexus of contracts. Contracts are necessary in order to get self-seeking individuals to agree to cooperate. For example, there are contracts with managers, suppliers of capital and employees (including the managers). The contracts are necessary to cause individual parties to act to maximise the wealth of the owners (shareholders). However, there are **contracting costs** associated with contracts, for example, costs of negotiating with and maintaining and monitoring the performance of the parties involved. PAT holds that firms will seek to minimise the contracting costs and this will affect the policies adopted, including the accounting policies.

There is a difference between 'positivist' and 'positive' but positive theories are clearly a form of positivist theorising. Therefore, PAT holds to most of the tenets of positivism described in Chapter 1. Accordingly, the aim of theorising is examination, description, explanation and control (prediction). There are three hypotheses around which PAT's predictions are organised: the bonus plan hypothesis, the debt covenant hypothesis and the political cost hypothesis.

The bonus plan hypothesis suggests that managers of firms will be more likely to choose accounting procedures that shift reported earnings from future periods to the current period. To understand the need for this hypothesis it is necessary to look at one of the theories underlying positive accounting research, i.e. agency theory.

Agency theory

Agency theory is an important part of PAT. It has its origins in information economics literature in which information is placed into an explicit decision-making setting; that is, more information leads to better decisions. However, agency theory extends traditional information economics in that it recognises that several forces are at play in organisations that affect how it operates. For example, the notion of **information**

asymmetry is a problem that impacts on resource allocation issues. There is information asymmetry when some parties (managers) have more information than others (e.g. investors). So will managers disclose this additional information to the 'market'? Agency theorists believe there have to be incentives for managers to make additional (voluntary) disclosures.

An agency relationship exists where one party (a **principal**) delegates some decision-making authority to another party (the **agent**). The principal and the agent will enter into a contract that recognises the relationship. According to PAT, both parties will act in their own self-interest which will not necessarily coincide. The classic example of this sort of agency relationship is that between the shareholders and the manager of a company. Shareholders will be interested in maximising their wealth; the manager will want to maximise his or her rewards for managing the firm (material—financial and perquisites, 'reputation' as a good manager, etc.). A principal–agent relationship exists between the shareholders (principal) and the manager (agent). Agency costs will be incurred by the principal to monitor the behaviour of the agent to ensure that the agent operates in the best interest of the principal. Much of these **monitoring costs** will involve accounting—a good example of a monitoring cost is the cost incurred in a financial audit.

On the other hand, the agent will also incur costs to bond himself or herself to act in a manner that serves the interest of the principal. These are referred to as **bonding costs**. Preparing regular (say, quarterly) financial reports for the owners is an example. These are costs of the agent in that there are time and effort involved in preparing such reports and, additionally, such reporting places constraints on any potential opportunistic behaviour of the agent.

A third type of cost is identified as a **residual loss** which will result because, despite the monitoring and bonding costs incurred, the interests of the principal and the agent will still not be fully aligned—the agent does not always act fully in the principal's interests, which results in some unaccounted for costs—that is, residual costs.

Research studies in agency theory have uncovered different types of opportunistic behaviour by agents, including excessive perquisites, empire building, shirking and incorrect investment decisions. Perquisites are the 'little extras' that managers surround themselves with, such as a luxury office, business trips, entertainment and the like. Empire building is increasing the sphere of their responsibility, which will result in greater 'personal satisfaction' and possibly greater remuneration. Shirking is a rather blunt expression to describe the behaviour of managers who do not 'work the full day'—for example, taking long lunches or over-delegation of duties and responsibilities. The fourth example of opportunistic behaviour is slightly more complex. Basically it involves a difference between the risk aversion of the owner and that of the agent. The manager may be less willing to engage in high-risk, high-return investments as it increases the likelihood of loss of job should the investments 'fail'.

Debt-holders and owner-managers

The second hypothesis in PAT, referred to above, is the debt covenant hypothesis. To understand this it is first necessary to know what is meant by a debt covenant. This arises in a contract between a firm and its debt provider(s). The firm agrees to refrain from activities that may increase the debt provider's risk. Some examples would be not to sell assets or raise additional finance (that may affect the debt provider's claims against the assets in the firm) or pay excessive dividends, without the debt provider's approval. There are many other instances where the activities of the firm would not be in the interests of the debt provider and thus require an agreed debt covenant.

The debt covenant hypothesis in PAT is that, other things being equal, the closer a firm is to violating an accounting-based debt covenant, the more likely the owner-manager is to select accounting procedures that shift reported income from a future period to the present period. Any increase in (current) reported income would reduce the likelihood of a technical covenant default. Examples of such accounting-based covenant restrictions may relate the debt to equity ratio, the level of working capital, interest coverage ratios and other similar measures. Remember, however, that PAT assumes opportunistic behaviour, so covenants would usually include the basis on which such measures were made because often there would be slight (and some not so slight!) variations in how certain accounting measures were derived. Therefore, an example of a contracting cost would be the cost of an external audit of the accounting numbers.

A complicating factor in the debt covenant hypothesis relates to who the managers are. If there is a separation of ownership and management then there is an extra agency relationship to be considered. Consequently, in research to test the hypothesis, the case of the owner-manager has often been assumed so as to make it easier to understand why opportunistic behaviour occurs. In addition, the form of debt is a significant factor, for instance, whether it is public debt or private borrowing (for example, see Cotter 1999).

Political costs

The third PAT hypothesis is the political cost hypothesis. This suggests that, other things being equal, the greater the political costs faced by a firm, the more likely the managers will choose accounting procedures that defer reported income from current to future periods. This hypothesis introduces the idea of political implications into accounting policy choice. Some factors attract political attention for some reason or other. For example, in 2005 (and well before) Telstra invoked considerable political attention as the Australian government was contemplating selling its shares in the company. Although much of the political attention was on the level of service to be provided to rural Australia, some accounting policy decisions came to light, for example, the company having paid dividends from its reserves. This could have impacted on the ability of the company to invest in new technologies, which could have affected the service it was to provide to rural Australia customers.

Therefore, this hypothesis of PAT draws attention to the fact that not all policy decisions (including accounting) adopted by a firm will be based on purely economic considerations. When banks announce record profits there will be public pressure on the government to examine their customer charges. Petrol prices are also very susceptible to public attention. In 2004 and 2005 the companies that were the leading profit companies (in countries around the world) were oil companies. This led, in some countries, to special taxes being imposed on petroleum companies, which then (in countries where it was legal, such as the US) switched to LIFO inventory valuations, which led in turn to lower recorded profits and therefore lower taxes. Many firms, because of their sheer size, attract political attention from a variety of 'public watchdogs'. For example, in Australia there is the Australian Competition and Consumer Commission (ACCC), which is charged with ensuring 'fair and competitive' trading policies by companies.

PAT research

Although there had been reference to the need for positive accounting research earlier, it was popularised in the late 1970s by Watts and Zimmerman (1978). Since that time, there has been a tremendous research output claiming to be positive. As indicated above, the earlier neo-empirical accounting research fits the 'positive' description, but it is commonly believed that only research since the late 1970s is positive. Watts and Zimmerman in their earlier work drew heavily on developments in economics and finance and the EMH and other neo-classical assumptions underlying positive accounting. As Kothari (2002) explains, the development of:

> . . . positive accounting theory involves the accounting implications of the concurrent theoretical developments in finance and economics. Watts and Zimmerman then tailored those theories to explain accounting phenomena (pp. I-115–116).

Much of PAT research has focused on the motives of management in making accounting choices when markets are semi-strong—in a strong market accounting loses its relevance as the market is aware of all information—and there are significant costs in drawing up and enforcing contracts, as well as political costs arising out of the regulatory process. The research is often referred to as 'accounting choice research' because the emphasis is on explaining why managers make accounting method changes, given the three hypotheses discussed above. There has been a slight change in emphasis in some PAT research. Originally, PAT researchers assumed that choice was made on *opportunistic* grounds—decisions were based on self-interest. Some later researchers contended that often choices were made on *efficiency* grounds; that is, managers may choose a particular accounting method because it better reflects what they believe to be the underlying economic reality. The majority of positive accounting studies have concentrated on determining post-contracting opportunistic behaviour and use *ex post* data—that is, they assumes managers choose policies after the fact. Other studies assume choices are made before the contracting in order to present a more efficient picture of the firm (say, to a potential lender); choices are made *ex ante* (before the fact) (cf. Healy and Palepu 2002, p. I-418).

The aims of PAT research were clearly set out in early papers by its major initial exponents, Watts and Zimmerman. These aims were summarised by Zimmerman (1978) as he reviewed some earlier research and compared PAT with that. He claimed that PAT sought to 'explain the world in which we live'. As such it attempted to provide answers as to why certain accounting methods were chosen over others, and why (the then) regulation of accounting was left in the hands of the profession rather than direct government involvement. Zimmerman claimed that PAT was essential in identifying the affected parties where questions of accounting choice and policy were concerned.

Watts (1995) claimed that PAT research was an application of the methodology of the sciences (especially those used in economics and behavioural sciences) to the investigation of accounting phenomena. Therefore it was designed to explain (provide reasons for why accounting takes the form it does) and predict (how accounting changes across time and place). Although a wide range of economic and behavioural sciences were used, early PAT research drew heavily on financial economics (finance) for theoretical support. This then extended to other economic theories. A key claim by PAT adherents is that research prior to PAT did not possess an objective function that was independent of subjective preferences. What this means is that the objective function of theory prior to PAT derived an objective function subjectively, as a result of a value judgement. For example, what is the objective of accounting? Some argued for economic efficiency, some for investor protection and so on. There is, PAT adherents argue, no way to establish the correctness of the choice. However, neither can a PAT theory! As indicated, early PAT research was based on the assumption of opportunistic behaviour and later the assumption of desired efficiency. Thus, neither pre-PAT nor PAT theories established an objective function objectively (cf. Zimmerman 1978, p. 610). But implicit in PAT adherents' claim is that, unlike the pre-PAT theorists, they are objective.

As indicated above, there has been a tremendous amount of neo-empirical research undertaken and the results dominate certain journals. Thus, this research has been labelled 'mainstream research'—and there has been a substantial amount of criticism of it. Much of this has been directed at PAT research, although the tenor of the criticism applies to all neo-empirical research. This criticism is of all levels, from the underlying ontological assumptions to the research methods employed. Recall from earlier chapters that it is assumed here that research is undertaken either to generate new theories or to support existing theories. Therefore, the criticism of neo-empirical research can be discussed in terms of how theory, as described in Chapters 1 and 2, is affected.

Ontologically, neo-empirical research adopts a strong realist position and this determines the epistemology and methodology employed. Methodologically, it is positivist, or modernist, meaning that it is committed to employing the method of the physical sciences. Consequently, it is strongly rooted in an empirical epistemology. The method is the hypothetico-deductive methodology. However, this description, although accurate, has to be treated with caution as the advocates and supporters of PAT research do not always use terms and concepts consistently. In fact, an early critic, Christenson (1983), argues that Watts and Zimmerman in their early advocacy of PAT (1978) have totally misunderstood many epistemological and methodological issues. Godfrey et al. (2003), strong supporters of PAT, first argue for the importance of falsificationism in (all) research (p. 270) and then later agree with a suggestion in the literature that falsificationism is inappropriate for PAT (p. 353).

PAT derives its name from economics, specifically the work of two economists, John Neville Keynes (writing in 1891) and Milton Friedman, neither of whom referred to positive theory but rather **positive science**. Keynes was echoing a sentiment popular in the 19th century regarding positive statements which contributed to *positivist* science. Friedman took up the idea of positive science being concerned with 'what is' but his theorising is best described as **instrumentalism**, in which theories are useful only as instruments for generating successful predictions about observables. PAT theorists claim to admit only statements of 'what is', which suggests that they are clearly aligned with positivism (which holds a hard line on this matter) and not instrumentalism (which accepts the slightly more liberal view that such statements are necessary and useful but not always able to be established). Therefore, despite its origins in Friedman's neo-classical economics, it seems that PAT adopts a stricter positivist view than his instrumentalist one. This is borne out by PAT's leading exponents' insistence on the belief that they are truly scientific (e.g. Watts 1995, p. 297; Zimmerman 2002, p. II-418).

The epistemological foundation of PAT is empiricism—that all knowledge is derived from sensory experience. However, there are problems with a purely empirical epistemology and it has generally been rejected by philosophers of science. Christenson (1983) describes some of the problems. Knowledge cannot be derived from pure empiricism as it will have to be described in a language and use concepts which must be *a priori* (cf. the attempt by Nelson (1973) to denigrate some research by describing it as *a priori*, which is discussed in the previous chapter). However, the most significant practical problem is the problem of induction. This is the belief in the uniformity of nature (phenomena) and is based on past observations. In other words, an inductivist argues that he or she will be able to make predictions based on knowledge derived from past observations. This presumes things remain the same such that the past observations are a guide to the unobserved things in the past *and* the future, but the presumption is based only on (past) observed phenomena. Hence the reasoning is circular: we justify reliance on induction by relying on induction. However, in respect of science, Popper claimed that this did not matter because the method of science was hypothetico-deductive. This, as was explained in previous chapters, is to start with an hypothesis and a set of conditions, deduce what follows from them and then test the conclusions to determine whether they are in fact correct. However, in practice, it is not as straightforward as this as there are often many assumptions involved and there are always questions about the testing, including the problem of induction. As it is generally not possible to observe every instance, there will always be some doubt. To overcome this, Popper introduced the notion of falsification, which holds that so long as a statement is falsifiable it can be part of scientific theorising. An example of a falsifiable statement is profit announcements do not affect share prices. An example of a non-falsifiable statement is share prices either respond to or ignore profit announcements. In the first case it is easy to prove or disprove the statement; in the second case the statement is couched in such a way as to make it impossible to prove or disprove.

It is difficult to avoid the conclusion that PAT is in fact not a theory but a methodological prescription. Zimmerman (2002) has given a clear statement of what PAT advocates believe a theory is:

> Succinctly stated, a theory explains what has been observed, tests empirically the hypothesis derived from the theory, and then predicts what is yet to be observed (pp. II-417–418).

He then proceeds to quote Hempel who, along with Popper, is the leading exponent of the hypothetico-deductive process. However, he draws some seemingly contradictory conclusions. For example, he suggests that 'testing hypotheses derived from theory allows knowledge to accumulate'; 'Theories seek to explain systematic regularities'; and 'Theories suggest hypotheses that help guide scientific investigations') (p. II-418). Normally it is claimed by hypothetico-deductivists that hypotheses lead to theories. He agrees with Hempel that without hypotheses data collection is blind, but Zimmerman is suggesting a circular process, which seems to lead him to the same difficulty as the problem of induction, yet he claims that 'theories make predictions about facts that have not yet been collected' (p. II-418)! Theories do *not* make predictions; predictions are used to test a theory. In Popper's terminology, the explanans (the initial hypothesis and the conditions) are tested by serious attempts to falsify them, and where they remain unfalsified theory results. This Zimmerman illustrates by stating that the notion of random walk behaviour of stock prices, together with 'principles from economics', enabled the EMH to be deduced. As indicated above, the EMH has been subjected to a variety of tests and the great bulk of evidence suggests that it has been falsified. Yet many PAT and other researchers in accounting seem to ignore this fact and continue to operate on the basis that the EMH is an established 'theory'. Zimmerman may not be confused about the definition and place of theory but his description certainly is.

The sociopolitical critique of PAT

The above has attempted to demonstrate that there are many unanswered technical and philosophical problems with much neo-empirical, especially PAT, research. Despite these problems, many researchers are still committed to PAT and claim to be engaged in appropriate accounting research. Kuhn (see earlier chapters) suggested that continued adherence to a way of thinking (he used the word 'paradigm') was ultimately a matter of faith. However, there are probably many sociological and political explanations for this faith. The history of human knowledge contains very many examples of where sociological and political power has caused ideas to remain when logic, reason and 'evidence' would show otherwise. For example, the Christian Church for many years persisted with beliefs such as the earth being the centre of the universe when researchers such as Galileo Galilei demonstrated that in fact the earth revolved around the sun as part of a much greater universe. The power and ideology of the Church enabled it to maintain its position despite evidence to the contrary. Galileo was forced to recant or be burned at the stake. Some would suggest that many accounting researchers in US business schools, with an ideological commitment to maintaining neo-classical economic dogma, are the modern-day equivalent of the mediaeval Church in maintaining 'knowledge' which preserves an ideology even though it has been demonstrated to be mistaken!

As with any theory, underlying neo-empirical and PAT research are assumptions. Zimmerman (2002) has alluded to some of these as 'principles of economics', by which he means the assumptions upon which neo-classical economics rests. These include economic rationality—resulting in opportunistic behaviour—a view that holds that all action is driven by the desire to maximise wealth. This is a core assumption for other assumptions such as the free operation of unfettered markets and, consequently, the possibility of efficient markets. It is extended to firms which are said to organise themselves in the most efficient manner to maximise the chances of their survival.

PAT advocates have been very successful in maintaining it as the dominant force in accounting research. They have done this by exercising power to shape the discipline of accounting (research). They have changed the old adage of knowledge is power to power is knowledge—they have strategically defined PAT as the *only* form of worthwhile accounting knowledge. In order to do this they have exercised various political and other techniques such as language.

Watts (1995, p. 299) has described one reason for the shift towards neo-empirical and positive accounting research in the late 1960s and early 1970s. This is the fact that US business schools were encouraged by industry groups and corporations to engage in more 'business oriented' research and to make greater use of the 'underlying disciplines'. This call was backed up by resource support (more than US$30 million in grants). It is reasonable to infer from this that business wanted accounting research that supported business enterprise—to justify their activities. By 'underlying disciplines' it seems they were referring to economics and finance which were already imbued with a strong business (capitalist) ideology (such as neo-classical economics).

As the wealth of developed economies has increased over the last 50 years there has been increased interest in economic and financial matters. Such interest has been brought into everyday living and economic metaphors have become part of everyday language. It is difficult to see that accounting has greatly influenced this, as the advent of PAT research seemed to signal more concern with methodological issues than with everyday practical matters. A great many accounting articles addressed esoteric theoretical issues rather than problems facing the practising arm of the profession. As Lee (2002) suggests, 'Too many academic studies read like chain letters to other academics' (p. I-247). There was a wholesale rejection of all research that did not fit the prescribed PAT pattern. Journal editors acted as gatekeepers and refused to publish non-PAT research papers. This may be excusable in privately sponsored journals specifically set up to publish such research (e.g. *Journal of Accounting and Economics*) but it happened even in the journal of the major academic accounting body, *The Accounting Review*,[6] and later in the Canadian academic journal (*Contemporary Accounting Research*) and its Australian counterpart (*Accounting and Finance*), as well as outlets in other parts of the world. This is one illustration of the power that can be exerted by specific interest groups. It is an attempt to create and shape 'a discipline'; those who do not conform to the prescription are marginalised or 'excluded'.

Rhetoric is a linguistic device by which people persuade others to their point of view. PAT supporters have subscribed to the rhetoric of a particular economic ideology. Mouck (1992) has written on how PAT advocates employed rhetorical devices to convince others that theirs was the only way to accounting truth. The rhetorical devices they used, Mouck suggests, were appeals to the authority of science, including 'economic science', claims to being the only neutral way to knowledge and the disparagement of alternative views.

There is a strong belief in Western societies that science sets the standard for intellectual rigour and this partly explains why those engaged in disciplines of social concern choose the title *social science*. Despite considerable evidence that indicates otherwise, many in economics believe Lazear's statement that 'economics is the premier social science' (quoted in Zimmerman 2002, p. II-423). PAT advocates continually claim to be scientific largely because they 'rely on economics-based theory' (Zimmerman 2002, p. II-423). PAT derives its scientific status through economics unaware that many economic thinkers have rejected the claim to the status of science because they realise it is quite inappropriate.

Equally misguided are the claims by PAT advocates that they are neutral in their research. They do this because, since the time of Plato, objectivity has been held as a desirable aim of reliable knowledge. Obviously PAT researchers are making value judgements in deciding what are researchable problems, what is relevant evidence and how this is to be incorporated into their conclusions. This is the second rhetorical device, Mouck argues, that is used by PAT advocates. This topic was addressed early in the development of PAT research by Tinker et al. (1982).

The third rhetorical device Mouck claims is employed in PAT is the disparagement of alternatives: the campaign of a 'strategy of vilification' and efforts to 'degrade and stigmatize the opposition' (p. 51). This has included emphasising the distinction between normative and positive research and claiming that normative researchers were not 'scientific' (see 'The decline of normative theorizing' in Watts 1995, pp. 300–304). This incorrect assertion has been picked up and popularised without question by some textbook writers (e.g. Godfrey et al. 2003) who make claims such as 'They [PAT critics] fail to provide a competing theory which has superior explanatory or predictive power' (p. 353), while ignoring the near total failure of PAT to impact on the practice of accounting. Such is the power of rhetoric on a susceptible community!

Neo-empirical researchers use other rhetorical devices such as the narrative of emancipation. By this is meant the call to researchers to free themselves from the impossible constrictions of past research which sought truths such as true income and to merely concentrate on description, which would lead to new hypotheses and theories. As Watts (1995) claims:

> One difficulty with the normativist alternative is that there are an unlimited number of possible functions that accounting might fulfil . . . (p. 301).

The implication is that by engaging in PAT the researcher is freed from the 'impossible search' among all the alternative functions, presumably to one which supports the dominant economic ideology.

Consequences of the new research

This chapter has described a major shift in the research approach in accounting that took place around 1970. While still modernist in the claim of being scientific, it differed from previous research in some of the assumptions and the research methods. Although some of this new research has provided insights into the possible use of accounting in economic analysis, it has raised many problems to which it has been unable to respond intellectually. There has been considerable evidence refuting one of its most basic assumptions, that markets operate efficiently (EMH). There is also evidence refuting many other assumptions employed in this new research (e.g. CAPM). There are technical difficulties, such as how to interpret the evidence (Healy and Palepu 2002, p. I-419). There are methodological inconsistencies and misunderstandings (such as those raised by Christenson 1983). There is the question of the sociological assumptions (economic rationality). However, despite all these problems, this new research continues to dominate the academic accounting world at the expense of alternatives, making accounting different from other closely associated disciplines (see the Presidential Address to the American Accounting Association's Annual Meeting in San Francisco, August 2005, <www.aaahq.org/AM2005/invitation.htm>).

This domination has been possible because of the power contained and exercised by a certain group of accounting institutions. While a positive consequence of this power has been the flowering of research in accounting academe, the negative aspects are in the control they exercise in denying the discipline accounting research which is different from theirs; that is, it must comply with their prescription, which is strangely inconsistent with their commitment to description as opposed to prescription.

1   *The Wall Street Journal*, Monday, 18 October 2004.

2   A more cynical interpretation could be that people who have built their not insignificant careers on the basis of commitment to a paradigm have a lot to lose if they later reject it.

3   Kothari (2002) provides an excellent survey of capital markets research, but it is not possible here to cover the field as thoroughly as he has. Those wanting a fuller picture of this research should refer to his work. There are other summaries with slightly different classifications (e.g. Beaver 2002) but, generally speaking, they cover the same material. Kothari's work is part of a full summary of mainstream accounting research published in two issues of the *Journal of Accounting and Economics* in 2001, the proceedings of that journal's conference of 2000. Those interested in pursuing an understanding of mainstream accounting research are referred to this material.

4   Those interested in pursuing this topic are recommended to read Beaver's (2002) or Kothari's (2002) papers.

5   In most of the research in this area reference is made to the firm. However, for a more general understanding, the terms 'firm', 'organisation' and 'company' are used interchangeably. While this may not be entirely accurate—most firms are in fact corporations—it is sufficiently so for the present purposes. Similarly, the terms 'owners' and 'shareholders' are used to represent the principals in agency relationships. In addition, managers are the ultimate decision makers in a firm and they report directly to the board of directors which represents the shareholders' interests. Thus the managers are the agents of the owners. This is a simplification as the issue of corporate governance is complex and will be more fully expanded upon in subsequent chapters.

6   This is well detailed in a book devoted to this issue: Tinker, T & Puxty, T 1995, *Policing accounting knowledge: the market for excuses affair*, Markus Wiener Publishers, Princeton.

REFERENCES AND FURTHER READING

Ball, R & Brown, P 1968, 'An empirical evaluation of accounting numbers', *Journal of Accounting Research*, vol. 6, pp. 159–177.

Barth, M, Beaver, WH & Landsman, WR 2002, 'The relevance of the value relevance literature for financial accounting standard setting: another view', in SP Kothari, TZ Lys, DJ Skinner, RL Watts & JL Zimmerman 2002, *Contemporary accounting research, synthesis and critique*, I, pp. 77–104, Elsevier Science BV, Amsterdam.

Beaver, WH 1968, 'The information content of annual earnings announcements', *Journal of Accounting Research*, Supplement, vol. 6, pp. 67–92.

Beaver, WH 2002, 'Perspectives on recent capital market research', *The Accounting Review*, vol. 77, pp. 453–474.

Christenson, C 1983, 'The methodology of positive accounting', *The Accounting Review*, vol. 58, pp. 1–22.

Cotter, J 1999, 'Asset revaluations and debt contracting', *Abacus*, pp. 268–285.

Fama, E 1970, 'Efficient capital markets: a review of theory and empirical work', *Journal of Finance*, vol. 25, pp. 383–417.

Fields TD, Lys, TZ & Vincent, L 2002, 'Empirical research on accounting choice', in Kothari et al., op. cit., pp. I-255–307.

Godfrey, J, Hodgson, A & Holmes, S 2003, *Accounting theory*, 5th edn, John Wiley & Sons Australia Ltd, Milton, Qld.

Healy, PM & Palepu, KG 2002, 'Information asymmetry. Corporate disclosure, and the capital markets: a review of the empirical disclosure literature', in SP Kothari et al., pp. I-405–440.

Henderson, Scott, Peirson, Graham & Brown, Rob 1992, *Financial accounting theory: its nature and development*, Longman Cheshire, Melbourne.

Holthausen, RW & Watts, RL 2002, 'The relevance of the value relevance literature for financial accounting standard setting', in SP Kothari et al., pp. I-3–75.

Jones, S, Romano, C & Ratnatunga, J, eds 1995, *Accounting theory: a contemporary review*, Harcourt Brace, Sydney.

Kothari, SP 2002, 'Capital markets research in accounting', in SP Kothari et al., pp. I-105–231.

Kothari, SP, Lys, TZ, Skinner, DJ, Watts, RL & Zimmerman, JL 2002, *Contemporary accounting research: synthesis and critique*, Elsevier Science BV, Amsterdam.

Kuhn 1962, *The structure of scientific revolutions*, University of Chicago Press, Chicago, US.

Lee, CMC 2002, 'Market efficiency and accounting research: a discussion of "capital market research" in accounting', in SP Kothari et al., pp. I-233–253.

Markowitz, Harry 1959, *Portfolio selection: efficient diversification of investments*, Wiley & Sons, Hoboken, New Jersey, US.

Mouck, Tom 1992, 'The rhetoric of science and the rhetoric of revolt in the "story" of positive accounting theory', *Accounting, Auditing and Accountability Journal*, pp. 35–56.

Neimark, M 1990, 'The king is dead, long live the dead', *Critical Perspectives in Accounting*, pp. 103–114.

Tinker, T, Merino, B & Neimark, M 1982, 'The normative origins of positive theories: ideology and accounting thought', *Accounting, Organizations and Society*, vol. 7, pp. 167–200.

Watts, R 1995, 'Developments in positive accounting theory', in S Jones et al., eds, op. cit., pp. 297–353.

Watts, R & Zimmerman, J 1978, 'Towards a positive theory of the determination of accounting standards', *The Accounting Review*, vol. 53, pp. 112–134.

Zimmerman, JL 1978, 'On the "Statement on Accounting Theory and Theory Acceptance"', *Proceedings of the 1978 American Accounting Association Meeting*, pp. 606–622.

Zimmerman, JL 2002, 'Conjectures regarding empirical management accounting research', in Kothari et al., 2002, pp. II-411–427.

III

Regulation and Theory

CHAPTER 4

Regulation as Accounting Theory

ith the failure of theorists to produce an acceptable accounting theory the discipline has increasingly turned to regulation to provide statements of 'best practice' to improve, and create greater uniformity in, the practice of accounting. However, as with theories, it is important to have a sound understanding of the knowledge that provides the basis for determining the most appropriate regulation. This chapter therefore examines the structure and underlying assumptions of some of the theories of regulation, which are then discussed and compared. If regulation is to be a 'substitute' for theory it is crucial that we have an understanding of the arguments advanced for promoting different forms of regulation, strategies for implementing such regulation and tactics employed for ensuring compliance. It will be demonstrated that there are widely diverging views of what regulation is and how it should be implemented. ■

Over the years there have been many arguments and debates over the necessity for regulation. Those who believe in the efficacy of markets argue that regulation is not necessary as market forces operate to best serve society and optimise the allocation of resources. However, there are many who point out that markets do not always operate in the best interests of society so some form of intervention in the form of regulation is necessary. This is obvious in many aspects of society. For example, if there were no road rules for drivers chaos would result on the roads. If there were no restrictions on some 'economic' activities there would be no need for drug smugglers as the market would indicate the need (demand) for drugs, which would subsequently be supplied. These are obviously extreme examples, but it is not hard to extrapolate from them that there are many instances where regulations protect societies from undesirable activities.

In 19th-century Britain there was considerable optimism over the benefits brought by the Industrial Revolution and it was deemed undesirable for governments to 'interfere' with the operation of 'pure capitalism'. Governments therefore pursued a policy of what was known as 'laissez faire' (French for 'let be', or 'leave alone'). However, people soon came to realise that this created many social ills, some of which are reflected in the novels of Charles Dickens (*Oliver Twist*, for example) and the writings and work of artists and social commentators of the time. Working conditions were often dangerous and inhumane—children were used as labour and workers toiled for extraordinarily long hours—and there was considerable poverty and misery. Governments soon intervened and imposed socially desirable regulations on economic activity.

The issue of the regulation of accounting also arose, most pronouncedly so after the economic crash of the 1920–30s which, amongst other things, led to the search for the accounting principles and theory described in Chapter 2.

A major objective of accounting is to provide information to interested parties who may not have access to complete (or the necessary) information to make economic decisions—they are at an information disadvantage and so there is information asymmetry. Information asymmetry is often used to justify the need for accounting regulation. However, regulation extends well beyond this information to the preparers of the information; that is, to the professional competence of those calling themselves accountants or auditors who are generally believed to be the most able to provide and/or supervise the provision of financial information.

Accounting and accountants are now subject to a wide range of forms of regulation. There are laws governing the operation of corporations, many of which involve the disclosure of financial information. There are taxation laws. There are laws affecting the creation and operation of professional associations, which in turn impose regulations on their members. Regulations, therefore, are very much part of modern everyday life. However, there is disagreement on the extent to which regulation should intervene in the 'free' exchange of goods and ideas. For example, a believer in a strong form of market efficiency would contend that regulation of securities markets is unnecessary as the market is always instantly informed of all relevant information. However, most people would agree that there are few, if any, instances of strongly efficient markets so some level of regulation of the flow of information concerning the operations of securities (and other) markets is necessary.

The above discussion of regulation is necessarily simple, as the issue of the extent to which government should be involved in the day-to-day operation of society is extremely complex and has been the subject of debate by many scholars (and others) for most of our history. Underlying regulation are theories of the state, politics and ideology. For example, we talk of liberal democracy as an ideal form for society. However, liberalism is a doctrine or ideology which emphasises maximisation of individual liberties and minimisation of state involvement in the activities of individuals. This invokes the question of just what individual freedoms mean and also has implications of power—who decides what freedoms are possible?

Views of regulation

While many would see regulation as concerning 'sustained and focused control exercised by a public agency over activities valued by a community' (Selznick, quoted in Baldwin and Cave 1999, p. 2), there are other viewpoints. Regulation can be seen as a specific set of commands, such as those contained in the Corporations Act, as to the appointment of directors of a company. It may be seen as deliberate state influence, which would encompass the first viewpoint and extend well beyond it; for example, to the whole body of corporations law which directs the establishment, management and winding up of companies. Or it may be viewed in even broader terms and include all forms of social control and influence—not only corporations legislative requirements but other rules and directions, such as professional accounting standards and stock-exchange requirements. However, regulation should not be perceived purely in 'negative' terms because it also facilitates and enables activities. For example, the road rules mentioned above are designed to enable people to feel secure when driving, knowing there are rules that other drivers will (should?) follow.

Reasons for regulation

Baldwin and Cave (1999) argue that there are a number of reasons for regulation. One of the best known forms of regulation—anti-trust legislation (e.g. the Sherman Act and the Clayton Act)—was exercised by the US government over the potential growth of monopolies at the turn of the 20th century. Where there are monopolies it is considered that there has been a market failure because competition does not exist. From this it can be inferred that regulation is associated with preserving competition and therefore that it is associated with the ideology of the efficacy of markets and competition, hallmarks of capitalism. In centrally controlled economies many 'monopolies' are created (usually as some form of bureaucratic control). However, in other economies it is generally believed that it is necessary to maintain an environment conducive to competition. In Australia, the Australian Competition and Consumer Commission (ACCC) is charged with ensuring competitiveness and ruling against anti-competitive behaviour (ensuring compliance with the *Trade Practices Act 1974*). However, economies of scale can give rise to what are known as a 'natural monopolies' (for example, utilities such as water, gas or electricity) to ensure that the market is served at the least possible cost. In this case regulation is designed to ensure fair trading.

Regulation is considered desirable where there are **windfall profits**—where, through a fortuitous event, a firm is able to make 'above normal' profits. For example, suppliers of equipment to aid search and recovery may attempt to charge higher than normal prices following a natural disaster (which seems to be happening more regularly these days) because of the urgent need—the immediate demand—and thus generate above normal profits. Similarly, in the past, many costs related to certain productive activities were excluded such that the 'true' cost was not recognised. These costs were defined as **externalities** because they were not included. Of particular relevance in recent times are the costs involved in preventing pollution. An example is the cost borne by society at large for discharge into river systems. In any discussion of environmental or social responsibility accounting (see later chapters) externalities are of considerable importance.

A significant problem central to much of the neo-empirical and positive accounting research was the need for regulation arising from information inadequacies, resulting in information asymmetry. Such research was directed at determining the possible need for regulation in the form of accounting standards to address the problem (as indicated in the previous chapter).

Regulation is sometimes necessary to ensure that **profit skimming** does not occur. This happens when a supplier sells only to those customers that generate the greatest profit returns and ignores supply to others. This was the issue central to the privatisation of Telecom Australia. The government had to ensure that telecommunication services would continue to be provided as equally and fairly as possible to all Australians irrespective of where they lived—city or country. This case, however, is not an isolated one—there are many other less publicised cases where regulation is used to ensure continuity and availability of a service on an equitable basis. Similarly, where there is seen to be anti-competitive behaviour, such as predatory pricing, regulation is used as a preventative measure to outlaw such activities. Microsoft Corporation was accused of this type of behaviour (source codes for the Windows platform) in the US and the government brought law suits to disallow it.

From the perspective of consumers there are instances of what is colloquially known as the **free-rider effect**. This occurs when some consumers benefit from a service without paying for it at the expense of other consumers who *do* pay for the service. A physical example is a business opening next to a large public car park, therefore avoiding the cost of providing car parking to potential customers. The free-rider effect may serve as a disincentive for some producers so governments will intervene and levy a tax on the service. The term is often used in the context of securities markets in respect of the amount of disclosure of financial information a firm must make. If regulators insist on a high level of disclosure, it is argued, some parties will benefit from the disclosure without having to bear the cost of providing the information. A similar situation, referred to as **moral hazard**, occurs where consumers who do not pay for a service or product overconsume without regard to the costs being borne by others. This is a problem in the insurance industry where some people make excessive claims against their policies while others make few or no claims. Insurance is based on the idea of pooling the costs of bearing risk such that all participants benefit. When some make excessive claims they may be benefiting more than others.[1]

Regulation is also necessary in the rationalisation and coordination of economic activity so as to organise behaviour or industries in an efficient manner. An example is the marketing of many primary products through a central marketing agency, such as the wool board, or the marketing of fish or meat. Similar reasoning applies in situations where some central planning is necessary. Once again, this is important when considering the environmental impacts of activities where some people are required to bear more costs than others. In order to have an equitable outcome, regulation can be designed to balance the costs borne by different sectors. For example, preserving forests may lead to timber sectors bearing a cost for loss of jobs or firm closures, so regulation will be needed to ensure a fair and equitable outcome in that such costs will be borne by the broader society (which will benefit from the preservation of the forests).

A not so obvious need for regulation arises in labour markets. This is a highly politically charged area. For example, the ideology of a government may be to limit membership of unions to reduce the bargaining power of labour providers, so it will ban compulsory unionism. This is seen by some as directly reducing the bargaining power of workers, which directly affects their wages and conditions (including their health and safety).

In some countries there are, or have been, shortages of some goods and services so that rationing (limits to the amount of goods or services permitted to be purchased by each consumer) has been necessary. In such situations it has been thought that regulation rather than market forces would enable a more just distribution. For example, a shortage of petrol could disadvantage those furthest from its supply (say, rural consumers). A purely market-driven reaction by suppliers would be to minimise transport costs and sell to those nearer the point of production in the certainty that all of the product would be sold anyway (very similar to profit skimming). Regulation in this case could be used to ensure that there would be a fairer distribution of petrol.

These are some of the reasons for the need for regulation. In reality, a combination of some of the above reasons may be what leads to regulation. As indicated, regulation may be negative in that it prevents or restricts some behaviour or it may be positive in that it serves to encourage or facilitate activity.

Theorising regulation

Throughout history there have been two main approaches to regulation—the European and that of the United States—each based on a different philosophy (perhaps, more accurately, different ideologies) of the need for regulation. In the US, at least since 1887, regulation has been achieved through independent boards and/or commissions charged with monitoring and enforcing regulation. There, there is an implicit belief in the functioning of the market. Consequently, ownership is left in private hands and 'is interfered with only in specific cases of market failure' (Majone 1996, p. 10).

On the other hand, in Europe, up until the Second World War, there was suspicion—even hostility—towards the idea of the market solving all problems. Consequently, public ownership was the main mode of economic regulation, and industries were nationalised. The resultant public ownership of industries 'was supposed to give the state the power to impose a planned structure on the economy and to protect the public interest against powerful private interests' (Majone 1996, p. 11). However, the nationalisation of industries was designed not only to eliminate political power and the economic inefficiency of private monopolies but also to stimulate economic development. But in the last 50 years, for a variety of reasons, attitudes in Europe have shifted more to a US approach—public ownership as a mode of regulation was seen to have failed. Interestingly, regulation has not always achieved its stated aims. Majone (1996, pp. 17–19) has compared the two approaches and found a remarkably high level of correspondence—that is, both have 'failed' in remarkably similar ways! Notwithstanding this, there have been advantages from regulation.

Initially, the main advantage claimed for regulation was protection of the public interest. This applied to both modes of regulation—statutory regulation and public ownership. Regulation was believed to protect against market failure. Markets 'failed' when they were not economically efficient. The notion of efficiency was formalised by an Italian economist and sociologist, Vilfredo Pareto, after which the concept is named. **Pareto efficiency** (sometimes wrongly referred to as 'Pareto optimality') is used by economists to define the efficient organisation of the economy. Pareto efficiency refers to the allocation of resources such that someone can be made better off while no one else is made worse off. Hence there has been an efficient means of production and distribution of resources. When this does not happen, there has been market failure. This notion underlies neo-classical economics and is an important consideration in understanding the notion of economic regulation, which is the topic of consideration here.

As discussed in the previous chapter, a distinction is made by many between positive accounting theory (PAT) and what is called normative accounting theory. PAT emerges from positive economics. In discussing market failure and regulation a similar distinction is made by some; that is, there are analyses of regulation which are derived from positive economics and some which are based on normative assumptions. These are described as theories of regulation. All can be viewed as some type of interest theory—primarily public or private but with some 'in-between' types.

Public interest theories

Advocates of public interest theories of regulation see their purpose as achieving certain publicly desired results which, if left to the market, would not be obtained. The regulation is provided in response to demand from the public for corrections to inefficient and inequitable markets. Thus, regulation is pursued for public, as opposed to private, interest-related objectives. This was the dominant view of regulation until the 1960s and still retains many adherents. It is generally felt that determining what is the public interest is a normative question and advocates of positive theorising would, therefore, object to this approach on the basis that they believe it is not possible to determine objective aims for regulation; there is no basis for objectively identifying the public interest.

Other questions have been asked of the public interest approach, including some directed to the regulators themselves: Is it possible for them to act in a disinterested manner? Are they sufficiently competent? As might be expected, such critics suggest that the reward structure for regulators may be insufficient, or their career structure and training may be inadequate to achieve the desired results. In addition, it is often argued that the public interest approach underestimates the effects of economic and political power influences on regulation.

Interest group theories

An extension of the public interest theory is the interest group theory approach where regulation is viewed as the product of relationships between different groups and between such groups and the state. Advocates of this approach differ from public interest theorists in that they believe regulation is more about competition for power than solely in the public interest. Baldwin and Cave (1999, p. 21) suggest a range of interest group theories, from open-minded pluralism to corporatism. The former sees competing groups struggling for political power, with the winners using their power to shape the form of regulation, while corporatists emphasise the extent to which successful groups enter into partnership with the state to produce 'regulatory regimes that exclude non-participating interests' (p. 21).

The economic theory of regulation

The public interest theory of regulation is regarded as responding to a weakly defined demand for regulation. The positive or economic theory of regulation was introduced by Stigler in an article in 1971. It was later extended by one of his students, Peltzman, and it has greatly influenced thinking on regulation theories. With many slight variations in interpretation, this type of theory goes under a variety of names: economic theory, private interest theory, capture theory, special interest theory, public choice theory—and probably many more.

Emerging from Chicago, it is seen as a positive (economic) theory in which Stigler attempted to provide a theoretical foundation for an earlier notion of political theory that regulatory agencies are *captured* by producers. As a positive theory it assumes that regulators (political actors) are utility maximisers. Although the utility is not specified, it would seem to mean securing and maintaining political power (Majone 1996, p. 31). In order to do this they need votes and money, resources able to be provided by groups positively affected by regulatory decisions. Thus, the regulators have been 'captured' by such (special) interest groups who 'seek to expropriate wealth or income. Income may take various forms, including a direct subsidy of money, restrictions on the entry to an industry of new rivals, suppression of substitute and competitive products, encouragement of complementary products, and price fixing' (Stigler 1971, pp. 3–7).

This approach to regulation is consistent with **public choice theory**, which stresses the extent to which governmental behaviour is understood by envisioning all actors as rational individual maximisers of their own welfare. Analysis is directed towards the competing preferences of the individuals involved—how they get around regulatory goals in order to further their own goals. Consequently, private interests are served rather than the public interest. Public choice theory reconciles political and economic questions. It relies on the neo-classical economic assumption of rational choice (self-interest) to predict the behaviour of politicians (the regulators)—politicians only enact those policies that ensure their re-election which, as described above, will direct them to those with the resources to further this aim.

The economic theory approach to regulation has encountered many problems for which it has been unable to provide solutions. As explained in previous chapters, when a theory meets problems for which it has no response, theorists add 'extensions' or ad hoc hypotheses in an attempt to save the underlying theory. For example, Stigler's theory did not explain the phenomenon of cross-subsidisation—where the economic benefits of regulation extend from the intended group to other groups of producers and consumers. His student, Peltzman, attempted to extend the original analysis but he also failed to provide convincing conclusions to critics. However, another Chicago colleague, Gary Becker, did reach a more acceptable explanation but he did so by combining elements of positive and normative theories, or the economic theory and the public interest theory![2] Another major problem of economic theories is that they are unable to explain regulation—that is, there is no converse of their explanation for regulation.

Majone (1996) concludes that 'positive and normative theories of regulation should be viewed as complementary rather that mutually exclusive' (p. 34). However, neither includes an explanation for the institutional framework of regulation. Institutions were regarded as 'black boxes' from which regulation emerged.

Institutional theories

A group of regulation theorists who reject the rational actor model argue that institutional structure and arrangements, as well as social processes, shape regulation and therefore need to be understood. They contend that it is much more than individuals' preferences driving regulation, and that it is the organisational and social setting from which regulation emerges:

> Regulation is thus seen as shaped not so much by notions of the public interest or competitive bargaining between different private interests but by institutional arrangements and rule (legal and other) (Baldwin and Cave 1999, p. 27).

Institutional theorists (often called 'new institutionalists'[3]) come from a wide variety of disciplines and a wide range of political and social predilections, but all share a disbelief in atomistic accounts of regulation, that is, those explanations that focus on the individual. One form of institutional theory in the socio-legal literature draws on agency theory. The principals are the elected officials who have to ensure that their 'agents', the bureaucrats, design regulations that preserve the thrust of the original policy position (to avoid bureaucratic drift). As with the agency theory in PAT, there is information asymmetry in favour of the agents so the elected officials need to design procedures that reduce the informational disadvantages faced by them in order to ensure that there are sufficient 'dependable' administrators involved in the design of the regulation[4] (cf. Baldwin and Cave 1996, p. 28, who describe the work on this undertaken by McCubbins, Noll and Weingast; or see Majone 1996, pp. 35–37, for a discussion of other agency approaches to institutional theories of regulation and some of the difficulties involved).

Institutional theorists in political science have concentrated on the way that 'political structures, institutions, and decision-making processes shape political outcomes' (Baldwin and Cave 1999, p. 29), while institutional organisational theorists have focused on organisational structures and processes. Yet other institutional theorists question the assumption of conflict between public authorities and private interests (such as the agency theorists believe) and concentrate on the interrelation between public and private interests and the ever-changing character of these relationships.

The political-economic theories

Most, but not all, of the above theoretical approaches have a tacit assumption of a capitalist system based, sometimes loosely, on neo-classical economics. There are some 'radical' theories which reject the neo-classical assumption, and some of these are discussed by Tinker (1984). Capitalism is a social system in which there is interplay between the political and economic realms. In neo-classical theory it is assumed that the political realm is shaped by economic interests. Employing the work of Lindblom, Tinker argues that there are many social inequalities among the social classes that arise from the degree of access to and use of property and reliance on the marketplace. Regulation is necessary to move towards balancing some of these inequalities and, in effect, to ensure the survival of capitalism. Such regulation serves 'to protect the general or collective interests of capital and the requirements of the capital accumulation process' (p. 66). Tinker contends that the neo-classical economic framework is inadequate for characterising the need for regulation. Such economics is reductionist in that its advocates hold that it is universalistic—it applies to all places at all times. Tinker claims that there are many other social factors that need to be included in any analysis of regulation.

The analysis of regulation by Puxty et al. (1987) also appears to take a political-economic approach, although it is different from that of Tinker. Their approach is more specifically directed to the how and the why of accounting regulation and they discuss this in respect of four countries, the then Federal Republic of Germany, the UK, Sweden and the US, all of which are described as advanced capitalist countries. Despite the similarities in the countries discussed, the authors note that regulation will be shaped 'according to the contrasting histories, cultures and paths of development of different nation states' (p. 275). Thus, their analysis also rejects the reductionism of the neo-classical economic approaches. They build their argument from the work of Streeck and Schmitter who suggest that regulation emerges from the interplay of the three principles of social order—market, state and community. The original authors' analysis sees regulation as part of a 'composite order in which [there is] a delicate balance between three formally incompatible, yet substantially interdependent, guiding principles of coordination and allocation' (p. 277). What is important to note is that regulation is viewed as going much beyond the purely economic (as in the neo-classical approaches) to reflect broader cultural and societal values.

It is essential to understand the different approaches to regulation. Traditionally, discussions of regulation in accounting texts have merely mentioned the private and public interest theories in the context of accounting standards. However, regulation extends well beyond standard setting and has implications for how professions are organised, how they operate and what broader social expectations there are of them. For example, the nature of the regulatory framework will affect perceptions of social responsibilities and ethical behaviour. There are many more implications of regulation than those discussed above. There are implications of power, the dominant ideologies that shape that power and the consequent economic activity within a society. For example, what are the societal expectations of the governance of the major institutions of economic activity—the corporations? Why are there spectacular corporate failures? How is it that corporations can shape the economic activity within a state?

Regulatory strategies

The right choice of regulatory strategies by regulators will avoid debates over the need for the regulation if the relevant objectives can be achieved in ways other than the particular regulation. In fact, there are a number of basic strategies that regulators may employ and Baldwin and Cave (1996) describe several of them, as outlined below.

Command and control

This is where regulators take a clear stand on which activities are considered acceptable and which are not, with strictly enforced and severe penalties imposed on the latter. Examples would include work and safety regulations with which businesses must comply and by which strict standards are imposed. There are some issues with this regulatory strategy. First, it has been shown that because a close relationship develops between the regulator and the regulated, the regulators may be captured by the regulated. Walker (1987) has suggested that this is what happened in the case of the early development of the Australian Accounting Standards Review Board. Second, this strategy often leads to overly strict and inflexible rules—and even to a proliferation of rules. Third, it is often extremely difficult to decide which standards are appropriate. In such situations, standard setting should be balanced against the potential for anti-competitive behaviour, as insisting on such uniform standards could make it difficult to distinguish providers. Finally, there are issues surrounding enforcement. For example, enforcement might involve the appointment of many inspectors by bodies charged with enforcing the many rules, which might lead to the question: how can equity be maintained and complaints avoided?

Self-regulation

This is a less severe regulatory strategy than command and control. It is usually employed in relation to professional bodies or associations. Such organisations develop systems of rules that they monitor and enforce against their members. This is what the accounting profession fought hard to maintain and it was briefly described in Chapter 2. Generally acceptable accounting principles and later accounting standards were developed by professional accounting bodies to avoid government control of accounting practice. Some people are not convinced about the effectiveness of self-regulation, such as the ability of a body to enforce regulation directed against certain behaviour of its members. For example, can a body overseeing honesty in marketing rule against an advertising agent on the basis of its prepared marketing material? Here, there are questions of openness, transparency, accountability and acceptability of the process. In addition, the rules written by self-regulators may be self-serving and it may be difficult to show them as having been contravened. Criticism of this sort has been levelled against many accounting standards or principles. For example, the question of inventory valuation which required assumptions about inventory flows (LIFO, FIFO, etc.) led to several thousand permissible techniques of inventory measurement.

Incentive-based regulation

Although it is usual to think of taxes being used as a penalty to discourage certain activities, taxes can be used as a positive incentive. For example, for many years firms in

Australia were allowed a tax incentive for the purchase of some items of plant and equipment or expenditure on research and development or the cost of employment of apprentices. These can be general (nationwide) or localised (for items used in certain areas or industries). The advantage of such an approach to regulation is ease in enforcement (the regulated have to make claims for the incentive) but the disadvantages include difficulty in predicting the effectiveness of the incentive schemes.

Disclosure regulation

Advocates of the disclosure of information mode of regulation claim it is not heavily interventionist. It usually refers to the requirements of product information, such as the food value of a pre-packaged food, whether the product is organically produced and environmentally friendly, the country of manufacture/origin, and so on. Arguments could be made that this could also relate to the disclosure of financial information, although this is not the usual connotation.

Once again, the above are just a few of the many possible regulatory strategies. A full understanding of regulation would require a much deeper analysis of the many aspects associated with the imposition of regulation.

Regulation is used to direct a society's actions in a way considered best for that society. Just how this 'best' is determined involves many deep questions of power and ideology. 'To decide whether a system of regulation is good, acceptable, or in need of reform it is necessary to be clear about the benchmarks that are relevant to such an evaluation' (Baldwin and Cave 1996, p. 76). A typical economist's reaction would be to associate good regulation with efficiency and wealth maximisation. This does not give any indication of ethical efficacy or the appropriateness of the distribution of that wealth. It may be couched in terms of a time frame such that what may produce maximum wealth in the short term may cause significant environmental damage costs in the long term, which have to be borne by others. Such analyses may rely on artificial and abstract concepts such as utility, happiness or justice.

The term **hegemony** refers to power exercised by one social group over another. It is the capacity of a dominant group to exercise control through the willing acquiescence of others in society to accept subordinate status by their compliance with cultural, social and political practices and institutions that are unequal and unjust (cf. Johnston et al. 2000, pp. 332–334). The word was originally used in more radical sociological critiques but is now used to refer to dominant political and economic interests. Therefore, if wealth distribution is on the basis of wealth maximisation, there is a given distribution pattern which reflects the past and thus reinforces the interests of an economic hegemony. This is part of capitalism. Even though 'All over the world there is a concern that governments are captured by organised business interests' (Mitchell et al. 2001, p. 3), capitalism emphasises the hegemony of business interests, and accountants have long tacitly complied with and reinforced this state of affairs. Some even claim that accountancy associations have 'a long history of opposing reforms, which have sought to make corporations accountable' (Puxty et al. 1994, quoted in Mitchell et al. 2001, p. 10). This antisocial conduct, Mitchell et al. continue, is 'highly visible in relation to auditor obligations for detecting/reporting fraud'. The authors show how accountants, even those in the largest multinational accounting firms, have designed tax schemes to enable their business clients to avoid paying taxes[5] and have also been complicit in schemes of money laundering.

The 'justification' of an even more cynical approach of business to regulation emanates from the University of Chicago law and economics movement. This is that regulation will only be obeyed when the costs of disobedience exceed the benefits. Thus, compliance becomes a business decision not a societal decision: it is an application of strict cost–benefit analysis irrespective of the societal implications. There are many instances in the daily media of business interests ignoring environmental, health and safety, employment and other regulations knowing their non-compliance will attract a fine which they seem content to bear. The fine simply becomes a cost of production which can later be transferred to the consumer! It is this type of thinking that has led to such spectacular corporate collapses as Enron, World Com, Parmalaat, HIH and many others (see Clarke et al. 2003).[6]

It is for these and other reasons that many commentators argue that regulation cannot be assessed on purely economic grounds. Tinker (1984) argues that the current economic hegemony—neo-classical economics—cannot fully resolve issues relating to regulations:

> . . . the inability of the economic-finance literature to say anything definitive about the appropriate form of accounting regulation highlights the need to augment neo-classical economic analysis with sociopolitical considerations (p. 55).

That is, there are much wider social implications of regulation which neo-classical economics simply ignores (cannot answer, according to its theoretical percepts).

Similarly, Puxty et al. (1987) have turned to broader theories of the state in order to assess the accounting regulation in their four-country case study because:

> The institutions and process of accounting regulation in different nation-states cannot be understood independently of the historical and political-economic contexts of their emergence and development (p. 275).

Over the years commentators have not been unaware of the need to view regulation in a broader framework. Some, while recognising the political implications in the process of regulation, have argued that political considerations should be excluded and that accounting should remain concerned only with measuring the 'facts' (Solomons 1978). In light of the above discussion, taken at face value this sentiment would seem unduly naive. However, over the years it has been the hallmark of much accounting debate: that is, the false belief that accounting is value neutral and concerned only with reporting the economic facts!

For most of the 20th century the accounting profession sought to maintain a regime of self-regulation. Accounting professional bodies worked hard to avoid the imposition of regulation on the discipline. For this reason the professional bodies have attempted first to develop generally accepted accounting principles (GAAP) and then a conceptual framework that would serve as the basis of an accounting theory. Most of the developments took place in the United States and therefore the approach to regulation was the US approach described above: that is, confidence was maintained in the operation of the market, with regulation seen as necessary only to provide rules to correct the slight imperfections in the workings of the market. There is a paradox here in that the principles, standards and other associated factors were viewed by many as necessary for the development of an accounting theory, yet accounting practice was seen as only needing 'minor corrections' to be able to work efficiently (in the market).

The search for GAAP and a theoretical framework has been a struggle for both the discipline and its members. Widely differing viewpoints on the necessity and form of regulation have resulted in considerable tensions. The involvement of accounting and accountants in spectacular corporate collapses and major cases of business fraud has ensured the need for accounting regulation. Public interest concern—pressure from various sections of society—has therefore created, or demanded, regulation.

This was similar to what happened in the 1930s when the US government (regulation) created the Securities and Exchange Commission (SEC). The background to this was the economic depression and more particularly the stock market crash of 1929, which hurt many people. A first reaction would be to suggest that the regulation was a result of 'public pressure' and hence in response to public interest. However, as Tinker (1984) has shown, there are diametrically opposed interpretations of this event. Benston, quoted in Tinker (1984), adopts a free-market, economic approach and argues that the legislation damaged capitalism (investment) and should have been repealed (to permit the free operation of the market). His argument assumes a group-interest interpretation as he attributes the 'responsibility for the continuance of securities legislation to self-serving journalists, academics, lobbyists, and government officials' (p. 67). He believes the legislation should have been repealed in the (private) interests of capitalism. On the other hand, Merino and Neimark, quoted in Tinker, claim that the legislation served to 'protect' capitalism. They employ a public interest perspective, arguing that there was considerable public pressure for the legislation which was 'essential to the preservation and reproduction of capitalist social relations' (p. 66)— that is, the growth in public investing in US corporations.[7]

After some heated debate the SEC delegated the development of accounting principles to the profession, and from then on there was self-regulation by the profession. However:

> All has not been smooth between the SEC and the private-sector standard setter. During the 1940s and early 1950s, when the two parties were learning how to relate to each other, the SEC took issue with the Committee on Accounting Procedure on several matters: interperiod tax allocation (i.e. deferred taxes), all-inclusive v. current-operating-performance concept of the income statement, stock options, and upward asset revaluations. During the 1960s, the SEC succeeded in pressing the APB to 'narrow the areas of difference' in accounting practice on such topics as pensions, extraordinary items, and deferred taxes (Zeff 1995, p. 52).

The heated debate between the SEC and the accounting professional bodies continued throughout the rest of the 20th century, which raises questions about the appropriateness of self-regulation. There are specific problems in the discipline of accounting and they concern the issue of independence. In fact, there are many interrelated concerns in respect of independence. Initially, accounting firms earned most of their income from fees for auditing. The first concern, then, is that the accounting firm is investigating its employer so there is an initial conflict of interest here. The accounting professional bodies through their agencies are supposed to ensure that the possible conflict of interest between auditor and client does not arise— that the highest standards of 'professionalism' are maintained. However, the professional bodies comprise members of the accounting firms whose work is being monitored and regulated by the professional bodies—another potential conflict of interest which is rendered acute if the accounting firm has any power over the professional body. This has clearly been shown to be the case in very many instances—the big accounting firms have heavily influenced the professional (private) regulators.

Many of the problems associated with these conflicts of interest have come to light with some of the corporate failures early this century.

The Sarbanes-Oxley Act

This was especially true in the US after the dramatic corporate scandals involving Enron, Tyco International and World Com. Public pressure on the government resulted in the passing of the *Public Company Accounting Reform and Investor Protection Act of 2002*, commonly referred to as the Sarbanes-Oxley Act (often abbreviated to SOX) after the politicians who were instrumental in establishing the Act.[8] The Act established the Public Company Accounting Oversight Board (PCAOB) which, interestingly, is not an agent of the government but an independent non-profit corporation. However, there are many requirements that ensure the PCAOB works with and reports to the SEC.

Section 103 of the Act states that:

The Board shall:

(1) register public accounting firms;

(2) establish, or adopt, by rule, 'auditing, quality control, ethics, independence, and other standards relating to the preparation of audit reports for issuers';

(3) conduct inspections of accounting firms;

(4) conduct investigations and disciplinary proceedings, and impose appropriate sanctions;

(5) perform such other duties or functions as necessary or appropriate;

(6) enforce compliance with the Act, the rules of the Board, professional standards, and the securities laws relating to the preparation and issuance of audit reports and the obligations and liabilities of accountants with respect thereto;

(7) set the budget and manage the operations of the Board and the staff of the Board.

Thus, despite the 'official status' of the PCAOB, it means that the government has become involved with regulating (some) accounting activities. In fact, as paragraph (6) states, the PCAOB is required to be involved in regulation, most specifically, auditing standards (especially those relating to internal control procedures). It is also interesting to note that, despite the Act, in 2005 a survey by *The Wall Street Journal* (21 October) found that 55% of US investors (77% males between the ages of 45 and 54) believed that financial and accounting regulations governing publicly held companies were too lenient.

The Sarbanes-Oxley Act resulted from public pressure and is therefore an example of the public interest approach to regulation. Similar pressures were in place prior to the passage of the US Securities Act in 1934, which resulted in (amongst other things) the creation of the SEC and this seems to add weight to the Merino and Neimark interpretation rather than that of Benston described above. In addition, Sarbanes-Oxley was a blow to the accounting profession's extensive efforts, since the passage of the Securities Acts of the 1930s, to maintain a regime of self-regulation.

Enforcing regulation

A criticism often levelled at self-regulation concerns enforcement. Professional accounting bodies have disciplinary committees designed to enforce the relevant regulations. But how effective is this process? Here, there are issues of politics and power. For example, would accounting bodies take action against major accounting firms if there was evidence of some of their members acting inappropriately? Some suggest had they done so there might have been fewer corporate scandals.

There are various approaches that have been used to ensure enforcement of regulations. These vary from **compliance** to **deterrence**. With the former the aim is to encourage conformity with the regulation; with the latter, prosecutions are used to deter future infractions. The US approach to accounting standards is said to be **rules based** so its emphasis is on deterrence. However, the issue is not that simple. If a system is rules based, then it is important to have rules that are sufficiently precise, extensive and understandable. This may well be why the US has so many accounting standards and why there is an emphasis on standards education! (This matter is further elaborated on in Chapter 6.) In other countries, such as Australia, the approach is said to be **principles based**, which is also the position adopted by the International Accounting Standards Board. The emphasis is on ensuring that users can theoretically justify use of an accounting technique: does it comply with the intention of the regulation?

Deterrence approaches are said to be more direct and definite and more effective in eliminating errant conduct. They are 'tougher' than compliance approaches and it is therefore more rational to comply. Compliance approaches are, it is argued, more susceptible to capture and a lack of sufficient enforcement resources. On the other hand, compliance proponents argue that they are more efficient and less costly because the process of prosecution is extremely costly. They are also more flexible and less confrontational, which in turn encourages compliance. Ayres and Braithwaite have suggested that 'The trick of successful regulation is to establish a synergy between punishment and prosecution' (quoted in Baldwin and Cave 1999, p. 99).

From the comments in 2002 by the then Chairman of the SEC, Harvey Pitt, it is clear that in the US there is the intention of a deterrence approach. He said that the

SEC 'should be empowered to perform investigations, bring disciplinary proceedings, publicize results, restrict individuals and firms from auditing public companies' (Pitt 2002).

Regulation, research and theory

The subject of regulation is very wide ranging and very important. There are very many viewpoints as to the purpose, the need for and the operation of regulation. Not only can regulation be viewed as market failure, it can also be seen as 'theory failure'.

The accounting profession strenuously pursued the search for an underlying theoretical structure through GAAP, standards and a conceptual framework. Had the profession been successful there would have been less need for the intervention of the state in regulating the discipline; so, in this sense it was the failure of those in the discipline of accounting to provide a theory that necessitated intervention—at least to the extent that there has been. Economic purists argue that there should be no need for regulation as the market operates to ensure the fair distribution of resources. However, there is a paradox in the free-market argument as history has shown that considerable regulation has been necessary to ensure that the market operates reasonably efficiently.[9]

Both of these positions—'theory failure' and totally free markets—are simplistic in that they ignore the broader social setting of the discipline. Once again, history demonstrates that no amount of theory or regulation will prevent some people engaging in inappropriate activities. For example, complex income tax legislation does not prevent tax evasion schemes being devised by some accountants. Accountants will still be involved in corporate fraud and collapses. Accounting is a social discipline and cannot be isolated from the broader implications of the actions of those who prepare accounting information and those who use it. Very simply stated, there will always be ill-intentioned accountants and users of accounting information who will not act in the interest of society. This of course is true of most professions—for example, medical doctors taking drugs, lawyers devising criminal schemes to avoid justice, engineers using inferior materials to cut costs of projects. Therefore, whether we like it or not, societies have seen fit to impose some safeguards against such actions—professional and other sanctions—in the form of regulation.

With rapid societal changes brought about by advances in information technology and the pressures of globalisation the need for systems that safeguard social interests has become more acute and there have been greater demands for them from the public. This would suggest a reversion to the regulation in the public interest motive. However, the situation is more complex and, whereas there are many instances of the public interest motive for regulation, there are also many examples of all the other approaches described earlier in this chapter—group interest, private interest, and for institutional reasons. In fact, it is difficult to discern which approach is relevant to much of the regulation as it seems to be a combination of many.

There is also difficulty in determining the public interest. So, while the American Institute of Certified Public Accountants (AICPA) Code of Professional Conduct describes a public interest approach in general welfare terms,[10] one official of that same body argues that the public interest of the AICPA should focus on investors and creditors in capital markets (a neo-classical economic approach) (Baker 2005, pp. 693–695). However, there is little doubt that any regulation is a political process, but there are very different interpretations of what this means. Watts and Zimmerman (1978), in examining the need for accounting regulation (standards), argued that this political process worked to serve the interests of individual academics and groups of academics. Or as Tinker (1984) states, 'academics are reduced to intellectual mercenaries who advocate greater regulation to maximize their own wealth' (p. 59). Thus, Watts and Zimmerman adopted a private interest or group interest approach to regulation.

Irrespective of the approach adopted, there is little doubt that regulation is the result of the interplay of political forces. How these manifest will vary from situation to situation. Over the years, these forces have impacted—and will continue to directly influence—the practice of accounting through the various forms of regulation that have been imposed on accounting and accountants. The next chapter will examine these in relation to the development of accounting standards in Australia.

NOTES

1 But there is always the possibility that they are suffering more than others!

2 See Majone (1996, pp. 32–34) for a fuller explanation. Baldwin and Cave (1999, pp. 24–25) describe other instances such as the work of Bernstein's 'life-cycle' theory which, interestingly, also encompasses both economic and public interest theories.

3 They are referred to as *new* institutionalists' to distinguish them from the institutional economists of the early 20th century (e.g. Veblen).

4 A very popular television program in the 1980s and 1990s, *Yes Minister*, illustrated the difficult relationship between the politician and the bureaucrat.

5 See also, Mitchell, A, Sikka, P, Christensen, J, Morris, P & Filling, SF 2002, *No accounting for tax havens*, AABA, Basildon, Essex, UK.

6 Certainly not all businesses act this way. Consider this statement from the 2004 HSBC Corporate Social Responsibility Report (p. 4): 'While our strategy involves growing revenues by meeting customer needs, our goal is not, and never has been, profit at any cost. We know that tomorrow's success depends on the trust we build today.'

7 By 1940 there were about 4 million investors; by the 1950s investors totalled about 7 million; and by the 1960s the number had grown to 20 million.

8 The full Act can be accessed at: <http://news.findlaw.com/hdocs/docs/gwbush/sarbanesoxley072302.pdf>.

9 This is emphatically demonstrated in the regulation of employment introduced by the Australian government in 2005 in which, for example, there is a highly complex system of employer fines if they contravene how the government views the operation of the 'free' market!

10 Section 53.02: 'The public interest is defined as the collective well-being of the community of people and institutions the profession serves.'

REFERENCES AND FURTHER READING

Baker, CR 2005, 'What is the meaning of "the public interest": examining the ideology of the American accounting profession', *Accounting, Auditing and Accountability Journal*, vol. 18, pp. 690–703.

Baldwin, R & Cave, M 1999, *Understanding regulation, theory, strategy and practice*, Oxford University Press, Oxford, UK.

Clarke, F, Dean, G & Oliver, K 2003, *Corporate collapse, accounting, regulatory and ethical failure*, 2nd edn, Cambridge University Press, Cambridge, UK.

Johnstone, RJ, Gregory, D, Pratt, G & Watts, M, eds 2000, *The dictionary of human geography*, 4th edn, Blackwell Publishers Ltd, Oxford, UK.

Majone, G 1996, *Regulating Europe*, Routledge, London.

Mitchell, Austin, Sikka, Prem, Arnold, Patricia, Cooper, Christine & Willmott, Hugh 2001, *The BCCI cover-up*, Association for Accountancy and Business Affairs, Basildon, Essex, UK.

Peltzman, S 1979, 'Toward a more general theory of regulation', *Journal of Law and Economics*, vol. 19, pp. 211–240.

Pitt, Harvey 2002, 'Regulation of the accounting profession', Public statement by SEC Chairman, 17 January, <http://www.sec.gov/news/speech/spch535.htm>.

Puxty, AG, Wilmott, H, Cooper, D & Lowe, T 1987, 'Modes of regulation in advanced capitalism: locating accountancy in four countries', *Accounting, Organizations and Society*, vol. 12, pp. 273–292.

Solomons, D 1978 'The politicization of accounting', *Journal of Accountancy*, vol. 146, November, pp. 65–73.

Stigler, GJ 1971, 'The theory of economic regulation', *Bell Journal of Economics and Management Science*, vol. 6, pp. 3–21.

Tinker, A 1984, 'Theories of the state and the state of accounting: economic reductionism and political voluntarism in accounting regulation theory', *Journal of Accounting and Public Policy*, vol. 3, pp. 55–74.

van Lent, L 1997, 'Pressure and politics in financial accounting regulation: the case of the financial conglomerates in The Netherlands', *Abacus*, vol. 33, pp. 88–114.

Walker, RG 1987, 'Australia's ASRB: a case study of political activity and regulatory capture', *Accounting and Business Research*, vol. 17, pp. 269–286.

Watts, R & Zimmerman, J 1978, 'The demand and supply of accounting theories: the market for excuses', *The Accounting Review*, vol. 54, pp. 273–305.

Zeff, Stephen A 1995, 'A perspective on the U.S. public/private-sector approach to the regulation of financial accounting, *Accounting Horizons*, vol. 9, pp. 52–70.

CHAPTER 5

Regulation: Standardising Accounting Practice

This is the practical extension of the previous chapter where now the actual attempts to regulate accounting are described and discussed. A most important element of this is the attempts to establish a conceptual framework by the various professional bodies. In Australia, much of the thrust for regulation has been captured by the law—the Corporate Law Economic Reform Program (CLERP)—although there has been an attempt to integrate the professional and the legal regulation of the discipline, with considerable cooperation between those involved. ∎

As previously discussed, there was in the United States in the 1920s, in keeping with the spirit of the times, tremendous optimism, leading to the widespread purchasing of shares (stock) in companies. Shares were purchased like many other commodities rather than as a result of careful investment planning. As a result, in the stock market crash that precipitated the 'Great Economic Depression' of the 1930s, many people lost vast sums of money and consequently suffered extreme economic hardship; some, to the extent that it led to their suicide. Part of the reason for the massive corporate collapses was that the accounting for these companies was directed more towards satisfying management whim than to attempting to portray any perceived underlying economic reality. Often the motive of management was the sale of the shares rather than the long-term survival of the company through prudent planning and careful administration.

Principles for practice

One consequence of the stock market crash was a strong call for the discipline of accounting to produce financial information on which interested parties could rely—information that bore some correspondence with economic reality and uniformity of practice by practitioners. These calls came from at least two quarters. First, the New York Stock Exchange (NYSE) called on the accounting profession to develop a list of accepted accounting standards. Second was the government creation of the Securities and Exchange Commission (SEC) in 1934. It was important for the NYSE to restore public confidence in investing in corporations and, in response to its call, the American Institute of Accountants (now the AICPA) produced a list of five principles:

1 Unrealised profit should not be credited to net income. Profit is realised when a sale is completed.

2 Additional paid-in capital should not be charged with items that are more appropriately charged to net income.

3 Retained earnings of a subsidiary should not be added to consolidated earnings.

4 In rare circumstances, treasury stock may be considered an asset of the firm, but dividends on such shares should not be considered as revenue.

5 Officers', affiliates' and employees' notes receivable should be separately disclosed.

The listing of these principles marked the beginning of the attempts by the profession to regulate the practice of accounting. It was the start of moves by the profession to establish a regime of self-regulation. Serious self-regulation was seen as necessary to prevent the state intervening to enforce regulation on accounting practitioners. Thus, it was seen as necessary to maintain the integrity of the profession of accounting as the capacity to effectively self-regulate was viewed as one of the hallmarks of a profession. The accounting profession therefore continued to be a very private enterprise in keeping with the ideology of capitalism.

But the state did intervene in creating the SEC, and one of its functions was overseeing the published accounting information of publicly listed corporations. However, after much debate between the SEC and the profession, it was decided that the SEC would leave the profession to develop principles of accounting practice which would eventually become generally acceptable as standards of professional performance. As indicated in the previous chapter, there have been various interpretations placed on the reasons for the state's intervention in creating the SEC and the delegation by the SEC of its accounting responsibility to the profession. Taken together, the creation of the SEC and the profession's serious attempt at effective self-regulation would tend to suggest that they were necessary to preserve capitalism from the public disenchantment that marked the great depression.

These developments in the 1930s greatly affected the processes of accounting regulation in the US, and questions surrounding the issues involved continued for many years. Forty years later, another period of major change in attitudes to and practices of accounting regulation began.

'New' accounting

There were many changes in the perceptions of accounting in the decade of the 1970s. As indicated in previous chapters, there was a major shift in the approach to accounting research, which ushered in the era of neo-empirical research. There was also a major change in the approach to accounting regulation in the US. There was significant dissatisfaction with the operation of the Accounting Principles Board (APB) which had been set up in 1959 to replace the Committee on Accounting Procedures, and which had been seen as failing to develop any theoretical foundations for accounting. The professional body (AICPA) established two committees in the early 1970s. One was The Study Group on the Objectives of Financial Statements (Trueblood Committee) and the other, The Study Group on the Establishment of Accounting Principles (Wheat Committee), both referred to by the names of their chairmen.

The Trueblood Committee issued its report towards the end of 1973 listing 12 objectives of financial reporting. A central theme of these objectives indicated a major (stated) shift in the perception of the use of accounting (financial statements). This was greater recognition of the importance of accounting to decision making, especially investment decisions. It seemed to reflect a general perception in the community and was certainly consistent with the conclusions of the American Accounting Association's ASOBAT (see Chapter 2) and the thrust of neo-empirical accounting research. Consequently, the conclusions were not seen as being a dramatically new development.

On the other hand, the conclusions of the Wheat Committee did signal a major change. This was in respect to the manner by which accounting self-regulation was to be maintained. The most radical development was the creation of a body independent of the AICPA, charged with the responsibility for regulating accounting practice: the Financial Accounting Standards Board (FASB). Actually the Wheat Committee established three bodies. There was, first, the Financial Accounting Foundation (FAF), which had 16 trustees, and then the FASB and the Financial Accounting Standards Advisory Council. Still in existence today, the FAF funds the other two bodies, appoints their members and oversees the operations of the FASB. It is the FASB that is responsible for the issuance of accounting standards. Unlike the other bodies, FASB's seven members, not all of whom are practising accountants, are full time, as mentioned in Chapter 2, serving a maximum of two five-year terms. It also employs staff to work on its projects.

The FASB issues several types of publications, including **Statements of Financial Accounting Standards** (which form GAAP), and **Interpretations**, which explain, clarify and elaborate on GAAP. It also has undertaken a major project to establish a theoretical foundation for accounting known as a **Conceptual framework**. This is an ongoing project and the FASB, from time to time, issues **Statements of Financial Accounting Concepts (SFAC)** as elements of the overall conceptual framework. There is a due process for issuing accounting standards, which has not always been followed by the FASB, and this has been a major criticism levelled at the Board. The issuing of SFACs has been a painful and protracted process for the FASB and the project seems to have stalled. Reactions to these pronouncements were similar to those that followed the issue of Accounting Research Bulletins by the Accounting Research Division of the APB—debate and controversy.

Regulation of accounting outside the United States

The brief outline above of the attempts to develop principles, and then a conceptual basis for accounting, has centred on developments in the US. The major reason for this is that, undoubtedly, the US led the world in such developments. While similar attempts were being made outside the US, often these were replicating much of what had occurred there. Not only does this suggest the US was leading accounting thought, but also it is interesting to speculate as to why this was so.

Most people would agree that the political, economic and social environment in the US was much more conducive to the development of accounting. Accounting was more readily accepted into university education there than elsewhere.[1] In the United Kingdom there were social barriers to its acceptance. It was necessary for those wishing to pursue a career in accounting to start as an articled clerk. This was a form of apprenticeship and usually the clerk would pay for the position rather than be paid. Thus, only those who could afford to pay became accountants. Completion of the period of clerkship and passing professional examinations entitled a person (usually male) residing in England or Wales to apply for membership of the Institute of Chartered Accountants of England and Wales (ICAEW). Similar arrangements existed for those living in Scotland, but they became members of the Institute of Chartered Accountants of Scotland. A university education played no (necessary) part in achieving professional accounting association membership. However, by the middle of the 20th century there was much greater 'democratisation' and more professional bodies were recognised. These bodies had different entry requirements, although they still maintained the passing of professional examinations as a prerequisite of membership. But despite the 'recognition' of these 'other' bodies there was very little professional interaction and perceived 'class distinctions' persisted. Even relations between the two main institutes of chartered accountants were not that cordial![2] It is important to be aware of this because it had direct implications on the processes of accounting self-regulation.

In the US professional organisation was more ordered and the different accounting bodies represented different functions undertaken by accountants—financial reporting and auditing, management accounting, financial analysis, and so on. This was initially so also in the UK, but subsequently there was considerable broadening of the membership base of many of the organisations so that often the different accounting bodies were in competition for membership. The development of accounting principles therefore tended to be much slower in the UK (cf. Zeff 1971).

It is also important to note that the British environment had an impact on the development of the profession in the countries that had been subject to British colonisation—the previous colonies, dominions or members of the Commonwealth of Nations.[3] In both Canada and Australia, there is more than one professional body representing accountants, and any move to develop accounting principles has necessitated cooperation between them. (Richardson, 2007, has produced an excellent account of the problems encountered by the profession in Canada to establish a regulatory [standards] regime.) In New Zealand there has generally been only one professional accounting body, and it is arguably the country that has most closely followed the UK. In the UK and the other countries mentioned here there was for many years a much greater reliance on statute, especially the companies (corporations) laws, than in the US. In most of these countries the push for accounting principles did not start in earnest until around the middle of the 20th century.

Accounting was regarded very differently in most of the Continental European countries. Recognition of accountants as independent professionals was much slower coming. In France, the first accounting regulation was contained in the Code Savary of 1673. However, accounting was seen as a technical practice whether it involved preparing financial reports (financial accounting), auditing or management accounting, and was regarded as part of overall governance of business. Accounting in France, along with many other aspects of life, was affected by the Second World War and additional laws were drafted. After the war, in 1947, an accounting plan was devised that would apply to every sector of the economy. The plan, known as the Plan Comptable Général, included a chart of accounts with which all accounting in businesses was to comply. With certain developments in the second half of the 20th century, the plan gradually lost its relevance. These included the growth of different forms of business transactions and information technology, and the establishment of the European Union (EU)—the last mentioned increasingly directing the course of accounting regulation.

In Italy, the Collegio dei Raxonati of Venice was the first professional society of accountants, founded in 1581. This body closely regulated the activity of those offering accounting services and can probably be seen as the first (Western) accounting regulator. There were many developments in accounting thought in Italy, from the teaching of accounting to the practice of it, over the centuries. Many 'theories' were suggested. Fabio Besta published a three-volume treatise around the turn of the 20th century which included the definition of accounting as 'the science of economic control'. Thus, in Italy, as in France, accounting was viewed as part of the overall business control environment, and accounting regulation was gradually subsumed by EU directives towards the end of the 20th century. German accounting was influenced by developments in Italian accounting thought. Similar attitudes to accounting existed there, but with obvious local differences.[4]

The Netherlands stands alone in having experimented with an accounting court in which disputes about the most appropriate accounting practices were settled 'legalistically'. Thus, until very recently, accounting in the non-English-speaking world seems to have been perceived very differently from that in the English-speaking countries.

In respect of the process of economic regulation, there were for many years different ideologies in Europe and the United States, as indicated in the previous chapter. Accounting practices in Europe were seen as part of the broader business environment. However, as many of the attempts to regulate business there were perceived of as failures, there was a switch to emulating what was seen as succeeding—those in the United States. Ironically, any analyses of developments in the US will show that such attempts were also 'failing'. Nevertheless, the economic success and strength of the US economy seemed to indicate otherwise. This was despite the spectacular economic successes of other countries in the second half of the 20th century, notably Japan and Germany (prior to the 1990s reunification). Both of these economies had significantly different approaches to regulating business than the United States! Perhaps it was also because of the enormous political power wielded by the US, together with its demonstrated economic strength, that many felt it desirable to follow US practice. This was evident in the Indonesian accounting profession adopting the US principles enunciated by Paul Grady in ARS7. Similarly in Australia, where John Kenley (1970) was commissioned by the accounting professional bodies to adapt Grady's work to Australia, and this was followed by an adaptation of APB Statement No 4 (Kenley and Staubus 1972).

Internationally, there are three broad types of accounting regulatory regimes, two which are private and one which is government controlled. First, there are those countries in which the professional accounting body (bodies) assumes (assume) responsibility for developing accounting standards (for example, Canada, Hong Kong, New Zealand and Taiwan). Second, there are independent bodies established to develop accounting standards, with the accounting professional body (bodies) being one contributor (for example, in the UK and the US). Many of the countries with this type of regulatory arrangement evolved from the first form, as the discussion of regulation in the US has indicated. The third form is where the government assumes responsibility for accounting regulation, including accounting standards (for example, Australia, China, Malaysia and France). Some of these countries (Australia, for example) have evolved from the first type. The expression 'self-regulation' is used in respect of the first two types; with the third type, regulation is invariably developed through government legislation.

The development of standard setting in Australia

Early accounting principles issued in Australia merely mimicked those previously issued by the ICAEW. The first recommended accounting principles were issued by the Institute of Chartered Accountants in Australia (ICAA) in 1946. They had little impact on accounting practice and there was a high degree of non-compliance. This attempt illustrates the two points made above: the influence of the UK, and the presence of more than one professional body and the lack of cooperation between them. Two main accounting professional bodies dominated accounting in the second half of the 20th century. The first was the ICAA, incorporated by Royal Charter in 1928, and the second was CPA Australia, formed in the early 1950s by the amalgamation of a number of accounting bodies. CPA Australia was initially known as the Australian Society of Accountants (ASA). It then changed its name to the Australian Society of Certified Practising Accountants (ASCPA) and finally, in 2000, to CPA Australia. Over the years several attempts have been made to rationalise this situation and amalgamate the two bodies, but all have failed. As a consequence there has been a waste of resources and, at times, a lack of united professional body action on issues that have emerged. Unlike the US, where the various bodies are generally distinguished by the function their members fulfil, in Australia both bodies cover the same ground—members occupy positions as public, private or government accountants (and other senior management positions).

However, like in the US, crisis led to change. In the 1960s there were many company failures that prompted public concern, media pressure and even the threat of government intervention, which resulted in far greater cooperation between the two accounting bodies in respect of setting accounting standards. They jointly formed and sponsored the **Australian Accounting Research Foundation (AARF)**. The primary function of this body was to carry out and sponsor research and then issue, through the medium of its **Accounting Standards Board (AcSB)**, proposed accounting standards which would be confirmed by the councils of both bodies and which would require members' compliance with them. The process of accounting standard setting essentially involved identifying a problem area, undertaking research which led to the publication of an **exposure draft**, inviting public comment and debate, and after that issuing the standard. The topic could have been identified by observing inappropriate practices, research by individual researchers or the AARF, noting problems identified by overseas professional bodies or through changes in the law. The above description is a simplification of the process but highlights the major steps involved.

Despite the good intentions of the professional bodies in creating the AARF there were constant problems with enforcing accounting standards. Inappropriate accounting practices persisted and played a part in many corporate scandals in the 1970s. Although the professional bodies desired a continuation of self-regulation, in 1984 the government created through Ministerial Council (that is, not statute) the **Accounting Standards Review Board (ASRB)**, whose responsibilities included reviewing and approving accounting standards. The ASRB had legislative support, yet worked very closely with the AcSB, and in September 1988 the two bodies merged, with the AcSB ceasing to exist on the basis of the AARF having greater representation on the ASRB. This, Walker (1987) claims, can be interpreted as a case of regulatory capture—the profession (the regulated/interested party) 'taking control' of the regulator.[5]

The life of the ASRB was short lived and it was soon replaced by the **Australian Accounting Standards Board (AASB)**. This body was established by the *Australian*

Securities Commission Act 1989. Section 226(1) set out the powers and functions of the new body—basically full responsibility for setting and reviewing accounting standards in Australia.

In the early stages of developing accounting standards a large part of the problem was their enforcement. This is always likely to be a problem where there is self-regulation. Statutory backing was seen by some people as desirable if accounting regulation was to be successful. The most logical place for such backing would be in the corporations legislation. However, in Australia, each state was responsible for its own company law. This was a possible barrier to proper enforcement of accounting regulation as, although the state laws were similar, it would have been possible to avoid the jurisdiction of one state's laws by moving interstate. Anyway, a considerable part of business activity was national rather than within a particular state. In the last quarter of the 20th century several successful moves were made by the various levels of government to unify company law, culminating in a national uniform code coming into effect on 1 January 1991. One consequence was that the decade of the 1990s saw the government undertaking a major reform of company law, initially with the intention of simplifying it and then (from 1997) implementing more radical reform through the procedures known as the **Corporate Law Economic Reform Program (CLERP)**. A major item on the CLERP agenda was accounting standards. These moves virtually put an end to the accounting profession's self-regulation.

In the broader picture, accounting regulation is an integral part of the overall issue of **corporate governance**. Recall that the dubious business and accounting practices in the US in the 1920s and the subsequent depression led to the call for improved and more uniform accounting practices. Similar circumstances in Australia in the late 1950s and 1960s, the late 1970s and 1980s, and the late 1990s also led to calls for greater control over corporate management, including the financial statements they published. Movements towards greater and different accounting regulation can be observed as one response to these calls. However, it would be wrong to suggest that this was the only reason for the change in the accounting regulation process—there were many. For example, in the second half of the 1990s, there was pressure by business interests (such as the Australian Stock Exchange) to more strongly align Australian accounting reporting practices with international practices—a consequence of greater economic globalisation. This was necessary, it was claimed, in order to gain greater access to global financial markets.

Two pieces of legislation were significant to the establishment of a 'new' AASB. These were the *Corporate Law Economic Reform Program Act 1999* and the *Australian Securities and Investments Commission Act 2001* (ASIC Act) (especially Section 236B). Under previous legislation the government had created the Financial Reporting Council, with responsibility for overseeing corporate governance matters. This meant that it was responsible for both the AASB and the Australian Securities and Investments Commission (ASIC). On its webpage it indicates that:

> The Financial Reporting Council (FRC) is a statutory body under the *Australian Securities and Investments Commission Act 2001* (ASIC Act), as amended by the *Corporate Law Economic Reform Program (Audit Reform and Corporate Disclosure) Act 2004*. The FRC is responsible for providing broad oversight of the process for setting accounting and auditing standards as well as monitoring the effectiveness of auditor independence requirements in Australia and giving the Minister reports and advice on these matters (<http://www.frc.gov.au/about>, accessed 11 February 2006).

ASIC is an independent government body set up to enforce and administer Australian Corporations Law. It is not responsible for the issuing of accounting standards, but can lobby for (or against) standards, and has, from time to time, issued practice notes which in effect are its interpretations of accounting standards. As all Australian companies must comply with accounting standards, ASIC is definitely involved in the regulation of financial information provided by corporations.

Following the example of the EU, on 3 July 2002 the AASB issued a statement that Australia would adopt international accounting standards to be applied to financial statements issued on or after 1 January 2005. The EU had earlier decided to follow this path and this probably influenced the Australian decision. Thus, Australian accounting standards are now determined by the **International Accounting Standards Board (IASB)**.

Australian accounting regulation

The discussion above has briefly detailed how attempts to regulate the accounting information provided by companies—in financial statements—has changed in Australia from tentative steps by individual professional bodies to having the full force of statutory backing. It has been a complicated path that has seen professional self-regulation replaced by statutory regulation. This clearly demonstrates that accounting is seen as a very important part of the overall economic framework of the country and it has become heavily politicised. Various governments have chosen not to let the development of accounting standards be part of a regime of professional self-regulation and market forces. They have been heavily influenced by various lobby groups such as business groups and the stock exchange. The efficient operation of financial and investment markets is an important feature of late capitalist economies and effective regulation (including its enforcement) has been seen as crucial to this. There are other important factors, too, such as economic globalisation, the development of information technology and the growth of new financial instruments, which have all contributed to the increased complexity of contemporary business practices. The reliability and timeliness of financial information are essential in facilitating contemporary business, and this has been a major factor in the changes in the process of accounting standards formulation. The irony is that in order to facilitate the efficient operation of markets accounting regulation has become increasingly technical and at times highly complicated.

Evidence of this was the creation in late 1994 of the **Urgent Issues Group (UIG)** by the AARF. The intention was to enable public discussion of accounting issues that confronted practitioners from time to time. As its name implies, an objective was to quickly resolve accounting difficulties that arose, usually from differing interpretations of accounting standards. Therefore, the UIG was not involved in the development of accounting standards but they were central to its work. Initially it issued *Abstracts* of consensus views, thus assisting the AASB by dealing with 'minor' problems that arose from accounting standards.

Consistent with the practice of international harmonisation of Australian accounting standards, recent CLERP legislation has made the UIG a subcommittee of the 'new' AASB which now issues *Interpretations* (not Abstracts). The predecessor of the IASB, the International Accounting Standards Committee (IASC), had a Standing Interpretations Committee (SIC) which issued SICs. With the restructure of the IASC and the creation of the IASB, this committee is now known as the **International Financial Reporting Interpretations Committee (IFRIC)** which, as could be expected, issues IFRIC *Interpretations*. The Australian UIG *Interpretations* are required to be consistent with IFRIC *Interpretations* (and the previous SICs).[6] Accounting regulation is clearly quite complicated: the regulations are subject to official interpretations! Maybe the process of regulation is flawed in that it produces regulations that have to have official interpretations.[7] Regardless, it clearly demonstrates that there is a need for a greater theoretical foundation for accounting that would obviate the need for additional explanation. This, in fact, was one of the original charges of the AARF.

A conceptual framework

One of the initial tasks of the FASB, as indicated above, was the development of a conceptual framework. In one its first statements on this project the FASB defined a conceptual framework as:

> . . . a coherent system of interrelated objectives and fundamentals that is expected to lead to consistent standards and that prescribe the nature, function and limits of financial accounting and reporting (FASB 1978, SFAC 1, p. 1).

The development of a conceptual framework was an item on the first agenda of the FASB in 1973. This signalled the (US) accounting profession's continued concern with developing a theoretical basis on which accounting principles could be based (this is clear from the above quotation). The project was to take a building-block approach, starting with 'fundamentals' and then building up from there. In this sense it was similar to what Chambers had advocated and the theory construction process described in Figure 2.1 in Chapter 2.

The conceptual framework project proceeded through the FASB issuing Statements of Financial Accounting Concepts (SFACs). To date seven of these have been issued:

1 Objectives of Financial Reporting by Business Enterprises (1978)
2 Qualitative Characteristics of Accounting Information (1980)
3 Elements of Financial Statements of Business Enterprises (1980; but superseded by SFAC 6)
4 Objectives of Financial Reporting by Nonbusiness Enterprises (1980)
5 Recognition and Measurement in Financial Statements of Business Enterprises (1984)
6 Elements of Financial Statements (1985)
7 Using Cash Flow Information and Present Value in Accounting Measurement (2000).

These statements are not accounting standards but statements of concepts which can be used as the basis for developing accounting standards.

The idea of a conceptual framework was adopted in several other countries, including the United Kingdom, Canada, Australia and New Zealand. In addition, the (then) International Accounting Standards Committee (now IASB) also started work on a type of conceptual framework project. While the titles of these efforts vary slightly, they essentially have the same objective, but none of the projects have been spectacularly successful. In the UK a document entitled *The corporate report* was commissioned and published in 1976 by the ICAEW. One of the major authors of that report (Professor Edward Stamp) was commissioned by Canada to produce *Corporate reporting: its future evolution* (1980), known as the Stamp Report. The IASC's document is entitled *Framework for the preparation and presentation of financial statements*.

Australia followed the US more closely[8] and in 1979 the AARF set about developing an Australian conceptual framework. In so doing, it commissioned a series of *Accounting theory monographs* on which Statements of Accounting Concepts (SACs), after initial publication in exposure draft form, could be based. To date four SACs have been published:

SAC 1 Definition of the Reporting Entity
SAC 2 Objectives of General Purpose Financial Reporting
SAC 3 Qualitative Characteristics of Financial Information
SAC 4 Definition and Recognition of the Elements of Financial Statements.

The first three were published in 1990 and, after controversy resulting in withdrawal, then reissue, the fourth was published in May 1995. However, now that Australia has adopted IASB statements, SAC 3 and SAC 4 have been abandoned in favour of the IASB's *Framework for the preparation and presentation of financial statements*. SAC 1 has been retained because it is fundamental to determining which Australian entities need to apply accounting standards and the IASB has no equivalent, and SAC 2 is also essential to the application of Australian accounting standards.

It is important to be aware of the conceptual frameworks because they are designed to be the basis of accounting regulation, namely accounting standards. As Stevenson (1986) indicated, 'The Standards will be concerned with the application aspects of the concepts' (p. 5). Refer back to Figure 2.1 in Chapter 2 and note that the statements that form part of the conceptual framework would be placed on the left-hand side. That is, it is from *concepts* that theories develop. Therefore, despite being called theory monographs, the works so labelled would form part of the initial explanations of the 'everyday world' in order to derive the concepts. The regulators involved with developing conceptual frameworks have consciously elected to follow a particular process in theory construction. This has led to such projects attracting considerable criticism. Much of this has come from the fundamentalist position adopted by neo-empiricist researchers who seem to believe that the outcome should be specific, incontestable rules for practice. Criticism has also come from 'non-theory' communities—practitioners who, history has shown, are likely to challenge any procedure that restricts the freedom with which they have been accustomed to operating. However, this is not to suggest that the projects should not be criticised, but theory development depends on professional goodwill where possible. One of the strongest arguments in favour of conceptual framework projects is that they force accountants to consider what they are doing and how they go about it. For example, it may well be that accountants are attempting to produce and communicate financial information that is useful to decision makers, or those who rely on the information in making everyday decisions. These matters are obviously open to wide interpretation: for example, who are the users and what information do they 'need'? Conceptual frameworks *may* be able to reduce the uncertainty—that is the main aim in developing them.

Conceptual framework construction

In 1995 the (then) AASB issued a policy statement that included a diagram showing what it referred to as the building blocks of a conceptual framework. It comprised seven levels which would lead to the development of accounting standards and a further level addressing monitoring compliance with the accounting standards. The approach depicted a top down process starting (at the top) with the definition of (general purpose) financial reporting followed (below) by the definition of the reporting entity and then the objectives (in financial reporting). The four issued SACs (above) related directly to the 'building blocks' detailed in the diagram. However, the AARF and the AASB had considerable difficulty in issuing a fifth SAC on measurement as it was impossible to obtain a consensus or an acceptable viewpoint. And now subsequent events have overtaken the need for any further SACs as convergence with the IASB's *Framework for the preparation and presentation of financial statements* has rendered them unnecessary.

SACs 1 and 2 have been deemed to be necessary elements of Australian general purpose financial reporting but SACs 4 and 5 have been abandoned in favour of the *Framework* (now referred to as the AASB's *Framework*). What is interesting is that the AARF made a clear statement as to what it believed to be the process of theory construction. As stated above, this process is similar to that described in Figure 2.1. It is also consistent with the work of some of the individual theorists discussed in Chapter 2, notably Chambers (as evident in his *Accounting, evaluation and economic behavior*) and Moonitz (ARS 1 and 3), but probably many more. The Australian version differs from that of the FASB in that its first two building blocks were concerned with definitional issues, and it is interesting that the two SFACs devoted to them have been retained as pertinent to Australian financial reporting. Once these were established the next stage was to determine the objectives of financial reporting from which the qualitative characteristics and the elements could be deduced.

Reporting entities

Traditionally, financial reporting has generally been in the context of annual reports of public companies. However, SAC 1 recognises that there are many instances where decision makers need to rely on financial statements. Therefore it has defined a reporting entity as:

> . . . all entities (including economic entities) in respect of which it is reasonable to expect the existence of users dependent on general financial reports for information which will be useful to them for making and evaluating decisions about the allocation of scarce resources (SAC 1, para 40).

Therefore reporting entities would include public sector and not-for-profit entities.

Users of general purpose financial reports

SAC 2 states that the objective of financial reporting is 'to provide information to users that is useful for making and evaluating decisions about the allocation of scarce resources' (SAC 2, para 26). Obviously, in order to satisfy this it is necessary to know who the users are. However, determining who the users are has been a persistent and prolonged problem for those involved with the discipline. In response to this question posed by Professor Edward Stamp, the then Director of Research of the FASB, Jim Leisenring responded that they were 'investors, creditors, potential investors and potential creditors' (Stamp 1984, p. S/3). In response to a similar question, financial analyst and professor of accounting at New York University Lee Seidler said:

> I know the Board (FASB) members are honest men of integrity. I think the problem is that they don't really know how financial statements are used. And in the past the only work we've had on it has been—unfortunately—academics setting questionnaires to analysts which are garbage in garbage out type research (Stamp 1984, p. S/11).

In Australia, the question is addressed in SAC 2 (paras 16–20), which claims there are three categories of user groups and then lists four: resource providers, recipients of goods and services, parties performing a review or oversight function, and management and governing bodies.

Determining who the users of financial statements are has been the subject of a great number of research studies over the last 80 years. Is it really necessary to know who the users are? Many argue that users have to be identified in order to develop standards that would lead to the satisfaction of their needs. The logic of this is questionable as the resulting standards may very well privilege certain groups (of users). The consequences of this were discussed in the last chapter.

The AASB's *Framework* recognises that there will be a wide range of users. Financial statements will not meet all the needs of all users but should meet the 'common needs of most users' (para 13) so they can, in particular, assess the stewardship and management of management.

Qualitative characteristics of financial reports

SAC 3 was designed to define the qualitative characteristics of financial reports. Similar sentiments are contained in the *Framework*. These characteristics are the attributes that make information useful to users, and there are four of them: understandability, relevance, reliability and comparability.

Understandability

Obviously, if information is to be provided to interested parties it is important they understand it. However, this does not mean that complex but relevant information should not be disclosed. Rather, it is beholden on the preparers to make this information as understandable as possible. This implies that investors (and other users) who do not have training in accounting should be able to understand the financial statements included in a company's annual report.

Relevance

Financial reports should disclose all relevant information. However, there is again circular logic here: even if users were known, how could all their needs be met? This is similar to the problem of induction that Popper resolved to overcome (see Chapter 2). Seidler's critique went even further when he claimed that:

> Only someone who had never taken a logic course at university would attempt to develop a conceptual framework (quoted in Stamp 1984, p. S/12).

The question of relevance is further complicated by the idea of *materiality*: 'Information is material if its omission or misstatement could influence the economic decisions of users taken on the basis of the financial report' (*Framework*, para 30). The issue of relevance has been behind the value relevance (and other) research discussed in Chapter 3. Determining materiality is a highly subjective decision and will impact on the issue of relevance.

Reliability

Intuitively, reliability would seem to be the most important qualitative characteristic of information in financial statements. It has generally been a hallmark of all professions—dependability and expertise in special forms of knowledge (knowledge 'provides the basis for professional practice'—Macdonald 1995, p. 161). However, when it comes to specifying just what it means difficulties arise. In the *Framework* it is defined as information that is:

> . . . free from material error and bias and can be depended upon by users to represent faithfully that which it either purports to represent or could reasonably be expected to represent (para 31).

The *Framework* states that there are several 'sub-components' of reliable information: faithful representation, substance over form, neutrality, prudence and completeness.

The first, whilst being difficult to pin down the exact meaning, is in accordance with its title. The second states that the information should represent the economic reality rather than merely be included just because of some legal or regulatory requirement. Neutrality refers to a standard of objectivity to which preparers of financial information should comply. The selection and presentation of information should not influence the making of a decision in order to meet a predetermined outcome. Unfortunately, numerous violations of these criteria have led to corporate scandals and frauds.

Prudence is similar to what used to be called 'conservatism'. Here, too, over-zealous accountants have used this to perpetrate dubious accounting practices. Completeness requires that all information within the bounds of materiality and cost be disclosed as exclusion of items may lead to the wrong impression.

Comparability

Users of financial statements are often interested in comparing a reporting entity's performance over time. Therefore, it is important that the basis for accounting for items included in the financial statements remain consistent from year to year. However, this does not mean that an entity should not change its accounting policies when better and improved (more relevant and reliable) methods arise. In situations where policies have changed this fact should be disclosed. Of course the law requires corporations to include two years' statements, so it is important that proper comparison of these is possible. Prospective investors and analysts would usually be interested in more than the two years.

The conceptual framework as a theory of accounting

Regulation is a substitute for theory. In an ideal world theories would exist to explain and lead practice. However, generally some direction for practitioners is necessary where no acceptable theory exists. This has been the story of accounting. Despite the efforts of theorists and researchers, there is no acceptable theory of accounting. Therefore, in order to overcome inappropriate and even deviant behaviour of accountants in practice, it has been necessary to make statements of considered *best practice*—that is, accounting standards with which accountants should comply. Accounting regulators such as the FASB, AARF, ISAB and others have recognised that the standards they issue should be based on sound theoretical considerations. The conceptual framework and other similar projects are attempts to provide this theoretical basis. However, after a promising start, most of these projects have slowed or even stopped. Various reasons—political, economic, sociological, methodological, epistemological—have been provided in the accounting literature as to why this has occurred. For some, the attempts to produce a conceptual framework are means of maintaining a regime of professional self-regulation and avoiding government intervention. Self-regulation, as discussed above, is often seen as a signifier of professional status. If this is true, there is nothing 'sinister' in this motive as it seems quite natural to want the profession to want to self-regulate. However, a less charitable interpretation is that the regulators are concerned with self-preservation—maintaining their prestigious positions, and the power that comes with them, and other associated benefits.

Others have argued that there have been epistemological and methodological deficiencies in the process of developing the frameworks. There are also ontological considerations. Positive theorists have suggested that the procedures have been normative and that not enough attention has been paid to extant practices. At one level this criticism is simply not true, and there have even been those who have suggested that the conceptual frameworks are mainly descriptions of existing practices (similar to Grady's *Inventory of GAAP* in ARS 7 discussed earlier). However, it would be more accurate to say that positive theorists' criticism of the conceptual frameworks is that they conflict with the fundamental assumption of positive theory of market efficiency. This, of course, is true of all regulation as it can be seen as an externally imposed constraint on free-market activity, and the question is fundamental to the arguments about the need for regulation discussed in the previous chapter.

Regulators have made (and continue to make) epistemological and methodological assumptions because of their realist ontological presuppositions. These are apparent in the claimed qualitative characteristics of financial information—for example, faithful representation, neutrality and, to a lesser extent, relevance and reliability and a true and fair view. The epistemology is positivist and the methodology supposedly hypothetico-deductive (described in Chapter 2). The problems with this methodology (and positive theorising) have been described above. In constructing a theory it is necessary to start with basic assumptions such as the context, the need for the theory and the behavioural implications of the theory. These assumptions are always subject to interpretation so invariably it is difficult to get agreement from those affected by the theory. This is true in respect of financial statements. For example: What use will be made of them? Who will use them? The designers of the conceptual frameworks (including the *Framework*) have consciously adopted a user emphasis, a decision-making perspective. In so doing they have had to make assumptions and these are contestable.

There are other methodological problems in the approach adopted in the conceptual framework projects. An excellent example of the use of hypothetico-deductivism in accounting is found in Chambers' *Accounting, evaluation and economic behavior* (1966) in which he develops his theory of continuously contemporary accounting (CoCoA). Chambers sets up conditions and every subsequent statement follows from those stated conditions. This is not always the case in the conceptual framework projects, the stated purpose of which is to lay the theoretical foundations from which accounting standards can be developed. In fact, in the Australian *Framework* the statement is made that it does not define standards and that sometimes there may be a conflict (paras 3 and 4). Further, in CoCoA the technical features follow consistently from the initial conditions. The main reason for the slow progress in the conceptual framework projects is the non-acceptance by, and disagreement with, practitioners as to the technical aspects, most especially over the recognition and the types of measurements to be used, yet these should be the deduced consequences of the prior theorising.

There are very few who would argue that the conceptual framework projects are examples of successful theorising. However, there are probably many who would argue that the projects serve a useful purpose. With the *Framework* being the basis on which accounting standards are devised, there will be more consistency in accounting standards. Previously accounting standards were developed individually and were often ad hoc, and at times there were contradictions between standards. Now, the *Framework* defines the elements of financial statements so it will be easier to relate requirements of one standard to those of other standards. With more countries adopting IFRS and, consequently, the *Framework for the preparation of financial statements*, there will be greater international uniformity.

Cynical commentators have argued that frameworks are devices for establishing professional and personal legitimacy and therefore for creating power relations. This may well be so but, if it is, developments this century have been detrimental to such aims. In Australia, there is no longer professional self-regulation. In the US, the spectacular corporate collapses and frauds have resulted in the creation of greater government regulation—for example, the establishment of PCAOB (Public Company Accounting Oversight Board) and the Sarbanes-Oxley legislation.

One thing is clear from the very unsatisfactory story of accounting so far, and that is that there has been a complete lack of success in all of the attempts to create a theoretical foundation for accounting. Individual theorists, committees and regulators have all failed to develop an acceptable theory of accounting. In the absence of any theory, the various regulations imposed on the discipline can be viewed as policies substituting for rigorous theory. One problem may be that people have an incorrect view of what a theory is and what theory can provide. The issue has been complicated by the growing globalisation of most aspects of contemporary life, especially economics and business. The next chapter discusses the implications of internationalisation and globalisation.

NOTES

1   The first university accounting course was offered by the Wharton School of Finance and Economics, University of Pennsylvania, in 1883.

2   The title 'chartered' derives from the granting of a Royal Charter, which has some social implications! By 1887 there were five chartered accounting bodies in the UK—Edinburgh, Glasgow, Aberdeen, England and Wales, and Ireland. The first three later combined to form the Institute of Chartered Accountants of Scotland. Although a predecessor body was founded in 1919, the (now) Chartered Institute of Management Accountants (CIMA) only received its Royal Charter in 1975. CIMA, as its name suggests, has concentrated on promoting management accounting. The Association of Certified and Corporate Accountants (ACCA) was for many years seen as a body of 'lesser professional status' than the ICAEW and only received its Royal Charter later in the 20th century. Early attempts at developing accounting regulation in the UK did not include these two bodies, although other non-accounting bodies (for example, the London Stock Exchange, the City Panel on Take-overs and Mergers, etc.) were consulted!

3   This is not only true of ex-British colonies but other countries as well (e.g. France). This proposition is supported by Nobes (1998, p. 170).

4   Germany after the First World War was dramatically affected by extreme inflation and German accountants and economists had to tackle the problem of how to produce financial statements that bore some semblance of economic reality.

5   Walker's article is an excellent presentation of the circumstances surrounding the attempts at that time to regulate accounting in Australia.

6   'All Australian Interpretations have the same authoritative status and those that are equivalent to the IASB Interpretations must be applied to achieve compliance with the International Financial Reporting Standards (IFRSs) of the IASB' (*AASB 1048*, Preface).

7   Some standards deal with difficult issues and end up being quite complicated, for example, the US standard on accounting for derivatives: 'SFAS 133 is the most difficult and confusing standard ever issued by the FASB. It is the only standard to be followed by an FASB standard implementation group that addresses the many implementation concerns of companies. That group known as the Derivatives Implementation Group (DIG) publishes issues and conclusions . . . SFAS 133 is also the only standard for which a CD-ROM study guide was prepared by the FASB' (Hubbard and Jensen).

8   Stevenson, then director of AARF and the person in charge of the project, in speaking of the development of the Australian conceptual framework, said, 'we would maximise our use of FASB thinking' (1986, p. 4).

REFERENCES AND FURTHER READING

CPA Australia 2008, *Accounting Handbook 2008*, Pearson Education Australia, Frenchs Forest, NSW.

Kenley, J 1970, *A statement of Australian accounting principles*, AARF, Melbourne.

Kenley, J & Staubus, GJ 1972, *Objectives and concepts of financial statements*, AARF, Melbourne.

Macdonald, KM 1995, *The sociology of the professions*, Sage Publications, London.

Financial Accounting Standards Board 1978, 'Objectives of financial reporting by business enterprises' *Statement of Financial Accounting Concepts*, no. 1, FASB, Norwalk, US.

International Accounting Standards Board 1989, *Framework for the preparation and presentation of financial statements*, IASB, London.

Nobes, Christopher 1998, 'Towards a general model of the reasons for international differences in financial reporting', *Abacus*, vol. 34, pp. 162–187.

Richardson, Alan 2007, 'Standards wars versus regulatory competition in accounting: a case study of the Accounting Standards Authority of Canada', paper presented to Accounting History Conference, Banff, Canada, August.

Stamp, E 1984, 'Accounting regulation in the US: the growing debate', keynote interviews by Professor Edward Stamp, *International Accounting Bulletin* (Special Report: January 1984).

Stevenson, KM 1986, 'The role and nature of a conceptual framework', AAA/KMG Conference on Standard-Setting for Financial Reporting, Princeton, US.

Walker, RG 1987, 'Australia's ASRB: a case study of political activity and regulatory "capture"', *Accounting & Business Research*, vol. 17, pp. 269–286.

Zeff, Stephen A 1971, *Forging accounting principles in five countries: a history and an analysis of trends*, Stipes Publishing Company, Illinois, US.

CHAPTER 6

Accounting in the Global Environment

Internationalisation has been an important consideration for business practice for some time, and accounting has attempted to facilitate this through the creation of an international regulatory framework. Notions of internationalisation have now been superseded by those of globalisation. However, there has been resistance to globalisation, and the impact of this on accounting is discussed in this chapter. ■

Joseph Stiglitz, the 2001 recipient of the Nobel Prize for Economics, has suggested that 'Almost overnight, globalization has become the most pressing issue of our times' (2002, p. 4). There are several dimensions to globalisation but all too often the discussion centres around 'the emerging global economic system, its history, structure, and supposed benefits and failings' (Steger 2003, Preface). This discussion has greatly affected accounting and we are now in an era where there are serious attempts to develop global regulation of the financial information in financial statements. As Tweedie has stated:

> The International Accounting Standards Board (IASB) is committed to developing, in the public interest, a single set of high quality, understandable and enforceable global accounting standards that require transparent and comparable information in general purpose financial statements' (Foreword, Alfredson et al. 2005).

The major stated reason for these international accounting standards has been the need for the free movement of funds to accompany the globalisation of capital markets. As a one-time Chairman of the US Federal Reserve Board of Trustees has said:

> If markets are to function properly and capital is to be allocated efficiently, investors require transparency and must have the confidence that financial information accurately reflects economic performance . . . In a rapidly globalising world, it only makes sense that the same economic transactions are accounted for in the same manner across various jurisdictions (Paul Volcker, quoted in Alfredson et al. 2005, p. 5).

The last quotation is a little ironic as the United States has been one of the few countries not to wholeheartedly accept the move towards International Financial Reporting Standards (IFRS). Maybe Volcker had another option in mind? However, these are the sentiments that led the Australian Accounting Standards Board (AASB), after consultation with the Financial Reporting Council (FRC), to move to the complete adoption of IFRS, as have many other countries.

History of the International Accounting Standards Board

The IASB started its life in a different guise. In the late 1960s representatives of the accounting professional bodies of the United Kingdom, Canada and the United States formed the Accountants International Study Group (AISG). Their intention was to try and seek some harmonisation of accounting and auditing practices in their countries with a longer term view that some day combined accounting standards could be issued. The AISG had a life of about 10 years and issued 20 studies before it was disbanded (in 1977). At the 1972 World Congress of Accountants in Sydney representatives of the Group met to discuss a proposal to form an International Accounting Standards Committee (IASC). It was agreed, and representatives of six other countries (Australia, France, Germany, Japan, The Netherlands and Mexico) were invited to join, and in 1973 the IASC commenced operations with its inaugural meeting of 29 June 1973 at its headquarters in London. Each of the nine members had a representative on the IASC Board.[1] A year later several countries were admitted as associate members (Belgium, India, Israel, New Zealand, Pakistan and Zimbabwe) and, subsequently, additional associate members have been admitted.

Prior to the formation of the IASC, a worldwide federation of professional accounting bodies had existed—the International Federation of Accountants (IFAC). It was agreed between the two bodies that the IASC would assume responsibility for all matters relating to international accounting standards, while the IFAC would continue as a 'federation' of professional accounting bodies and would be concerned with other matters affecting accounting. All members of the IFAC were invited to join the IASC.

Like accounting, the world's securities markets regulators have an international 'federation', called the International of Securities Commissions (IOSCO).[2] This body has proved to be an extremely important 'lobby' group for the establishment of international accounting standards. It has been, Parker and Morris (2001) argue, 'a demanding critic of the IASC's harmonization efforts' (p. 298). Its concern over the last two decades of the 20th century has been (was) that inconsistent nationally imposed accounting standards have hindered the international flow of financial investment due to the uncertainty which investors have faced in reading the different financial reports. There have been, it argued, inefficiencies between capital markets as a result of the differing accounting policies and enforcement. The IOSCO, together with many other significant world financial and economic bodies (e.g. the World Bank), have pressured member countries for the creation of effective international accounting standards.

International accounting standards

The IASC, since its establishment in 1973, had issued international accounting standards, and member countries were obliged, insofar as it was practicable, to comply with these standards. This took the form of national accounting standards consistent with these international standards, or a clear indication of how they differed. It is probably fair to say that, initially, while there was considerable willingness to comply with the spirit of these international accounting standards, it was the national accounting standards to which more attention was directed. It was the recognition of this state of affairs that led to the pressure from the world bodies described above, such that towards the end of the 20th century the emphasis had shifted to harmonisation and then convergence of national standards with international standards.

The issuing of accounting regulations (standards) is a costly process. Therefore, to avoid the cost of developing national standards, many smaller countries adopted the international accounting standards as their national standards. Other countries have adopted international standards for more ideological reasons—the growth and expansion of efficient global financial markets. The move to adoption of the international accounting standards has not been easy as in some countries it was seen as surrendering sovereignty—handing economic regulation to organisations outside the state. In addition, there were cultural factors (infrastructural and institutional) to be considered. Nevertheless, there has been quite considerable success.

The process of issuing accounting standards by the IASC was similar to that in many member countries:

1. A project was recognised as needing attention, and a steering committee of experts were appointed.
2. Usually a discussion (or issues) paper was published, as well as a draft statement of principles (DSOP).
3. An exposure draft was published to solicit public comment.
4. Then standards were issued.

Also, as in some member countries, the IASC felt it was necessary to establish a Standing Interpretations Committee (SIC) whose responsibility was to settle any implementation issues that arose. For example, in the United States, the standard on accounting for financial instruments (FAS 133) had been seen as especially difficult and in need of extra guidance for members so guidelines were published. Similarly, for the international accounting standard, IAS 39 Financial Instruments: Recognition and Measurement, the IASC created an Implementation Guidance Committee (IGC). This committee addressed several issues surrounding the standard, most of the outcomes of which were later incorporated in the revised accounting standard.

In addition, like many member countries, the IASC developed a statement explaining the conceptual basis for the accounting standards it was to issue. This resulted in 1989 in the adoption of the *Framework for the preparation of financial statements*—essentially the IASC's conceptual framework. The *Framework* signalled the intention of the IASC to develop **principles-based standards** rather than (as in the US) **rules-based standards**. The major difference in the two approaches is that the principles-based approach proceeds from underlying principles (such as expressed in the *Framework*) whereas a rules-based approach attempts to specify actions for each instance—that is, rules with which to comply in specified situations. The principles approach relies on professional judgement in applying the principles relevant to the transaction(s) rather than stipulating the procedures to be followed. The differing philosophies have been cited as a major reason for the less than wholehearted acceptance by the US of international accounting standards. However, they also account for there being far fewer international accounting standards than US accounting standards.

International Financial Reporting Standards

History repeats itself. The problems faced by regulators in the US some three decades earlier also arose in respect of the IASC, which resulted in the restructuring and reconstituting of the IASC from a part-time body to a full-time one in order to cope with the extensive amount of work needed to develop effective standards. Early in this century the IASC was replaced by a smaller but mainly full-time International Accounting Standards Board (IASB). This body was to operate under a governing foundation of trustees representing different part of the world—the International Accounting Standards Committee Foundation (IASCF). The new IASB was to be assisted by an advisory body called the Standards Advisory Council (SAC). The previous SIC was to continue in revised form as the International Financial Reporting Interpretations Committee (IFRIC). International accounting standards were to be known as International Financial Reporting Standards (IFRS). The IASB was also to be assisted by members with liaison responsibilities. These members were Australia, Canada, France, Germany, Japan, New Zealand, the UK and the US, and their responsibility was to meet with other members to ensure that all members' interests were fully represented.

The IASC had issued 41 international accounting standards and the SIC had issued 33 interpretations. Although the new standards were called International Financial Reporting Standards (IFRS), the previously issued standards were to remain as international accounting standards until they were amended or replaced. Similarly, the SICs would also remain in force until replaced. (As mentioned above, standards issued under the IASB are called IFRS and interpretations are called IFRICs.)

The structure of the IASB is shown in Figure 6.1.

Adoption of IFRS

As yet, not all countries have adopted IFRS as their standards. Australia is one country that has adopted IFRS, which are effectively the national accounting standards with the provision that the letter 'A' is placed in front to indicate that the AASB has resolved

Figure 6.1 Structure of IASB

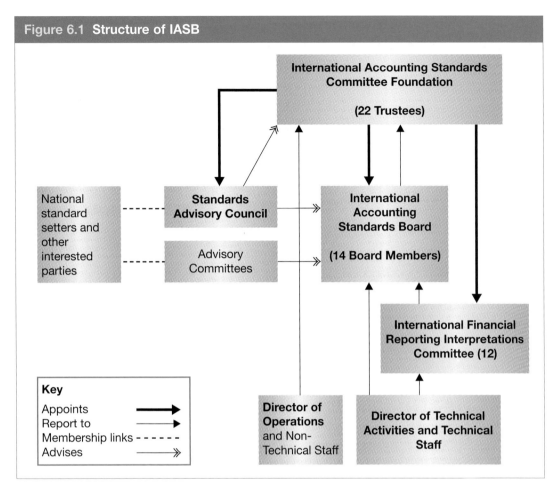

to adopt the IFRS as the Australian standards.[3] The European Union also requires all listed companies to employ IFRS in their consolidated accounts. However, unlike Australia, where there is one securities regulator, there are several in Europe, so enforcement of compliance will be more complex in Europe than in Australia. Other countries have adopted IFRS as their national standards (e.g. Bangladesh). Some countries (e.g. New Zealand) are moving towards this position, while others remain further away from full-scale convergence (e.g. Canada).

The accounting and business communities have long argued the case for and against the harmonisation of accounting standards. Harmonisation is necessary, as some commentators have argued, in order to improve 'the allocation of goods, labour and capital in international markets to reduce firms' costs of capital and operating expenses, and to facilitate social control of multinational companies' (Parker and Morris 2001, p. 299). However, as two past presidents of the Australian accounting professional bodies have stated, 'care needs to be exercised that in the pursuit of common accounting rules the resulting standards do not become overly prescriptive, and lack economic reality and understandability' (Kropp and Johnston 1996, p. 289). The notion of harmonisation has also been the subject of debate. While it can be seen as 'a process of increasing the compatibility of accounting practices by setting bounds to their degree of variation' (Nobes, quoted in Parker and Morris 2001, p. 302), there is a difference in what is legally required in regulations (*de jure* or formal harmony) and what is actually done by companies in practice (*de facto* or material harmony). Some researchers have even provided measures of the degree to which some national accounting standards are in harmony with IFRS (e.g. Fontes et al. 2005).

One 'cost' to the Australian accounting profession will be the loss of influence it will have on the international accounting community. Some years ago, Peter Agars, then a partner in a major international accounting firm, argued that Australia played an important role in international accounting practice. He claimed that:

> Australia helps to keep the international profession in balance in four ways:
> - by the influence it exerts in standard setting
> - by the influence it exerts on behalf of the Asia-Pacific region
> - by the equilibrium it engenders between the major powers
> - by the resources it contributes (Agars 1996, p. 362).

The relationship of the IFRS to the FASB's standards (US) is complicated. The ISRB and the FASB have been negotiating convergence but it still seems it will be some time before this will occur as there are a few deep differences. The situation is actually quite a paradox. As indicated above, the IASB has stated that it will adopt a principles-based approach, unlike the rules-based approach used in the US. However, at the same time, the IASB has a stated policy of moving closer to FASB standards to encourage full convergence! To be fair, the SEC and the FASB have started discussions on the appropriateness of a principles-based approach which, no doubt, would make full convergence easier. The matter is quite complex, relating to where companies are registered. For example, in Canada, foreign securities issuers are permitted to use IFRS in place of and with reconciliation to Canadian GAAP, but domestic companies are not permitted to do so. The position in the US is not quite so clearly stated and has been complicated by the recent creation of the Public Company Accounting Oversight Board (PCAOB) by the Sarbanes-Oxley Act.[4] And the situation is constantly changing. It is obvious that supporters of global accounting regulation would welcome the acceptance of IFRS by the largest and strongest economy, the US.[5] In fact, the IASB and the FASB on 29 October 2002 signed a memorandum of understanding (the Norwalk Agreement) that they would work together towards complete convergence of US standards with international standards. Currently there are several joint projects under way; for example, the Conceptual Framework—Joint Project of the IASB and FASB. Regular public conferences on the progress towards convergence are held, in addition to joint meetings of representatives of the two bodies.

A question of principle?

Many commentators have questioned whether in fact the US does adopt a rules-based as opposed to a principles-based approach to standard setting and whether such a distinction can really be made at all. As was described above, the common belief is that a rules-based approach is one in which detailed authoritative prescription prevails,[6] reducing the opportunities for managers and auditors to make professional judgements. It would seem that the main advantage of a rules-based approach is to assist preparers of financial reports and auditors to avoid potential litigation. That is, if they can claim that the financial statements are prepared in accordance with (the rules of) accounting standards, then they are cleared of any responsibility should something 'go wrong'. However, too many things do 'go wrong' and, as a result of corporate collapses such as Enron, the US Congress ordered the SEC to study principles-based accounting as part of its program for corporate reform.

Thus, the debate over rules-based and principles-based accounting regulation has largely resulted from the perception that the US has rules-based accounting standards and should move to a principles-based regulatory basis. This is important for those outside the US because of the desire to have international accounting standards in the preparation of which the US fully participates. Currently the US does not accept the IFRS, but for supporters of global accounting regulations it is obviously important that the world's largest economy be a part of the process. The IASC has always claimed that it adopts a principles-based approach to developing IFRS. It is somewhat ironic, given that for most of the 20th century the US accounting regulators sought the underlying principles (or theory) of 'good' accounting practice, that accounting regulation (GAAP) in the US has not been based on principles. However, Schipper (2003) claims that US GAAP *is* based on principles—those developed in the FASB's Conceptual Framework—but that there are elements that lead people to believe that rules are the basis of the standards. Her perspective is not consistent with the majority of those involved in the debate, including the regulators themselves. However, her argument is persuasive.

Although some would suggest that the distinction is not important (e.g. Bennett et al. 2006), there are considerations of great significance in the debate. First, there is the question of professionalism. As West (2003) has indicated, if compliance with accounting standards is merely a technical process of crossing the boxes, then there is little room for what would be considered professional judgement, leading to questions of whether accounting is in fact a profession at all.

Second, the distinction is important because it can lead to different accounting treatment of the same transaction. For example, when a company enters into a lease, it has to decide how to report the lease. It has to decide whether the lease is a capital or an operating lease and, if it is the former, it will have to disclose the lease on its balance sheet. The company may then follow accounting rules which enable it to circumvent the intention behind the transaction. It was argued that Enron technically followed GAAP but was able to 'get around the rules' and this seems to be a reason why the US government, in the Sarbanes-Oxley Act of 2002, required the SEC to examine the feasibility of principles-based accounting regulation. A problem with attempting to establish rules to guide practice is that there is always the potential that not all situations will be covered by the rules. This can be dramatically illustrated in taxation legislation where legislators try to cover all contingencies, yet 'creative' accountants and lawyers seem to come up with schemes that bypass the legislators' intentions. As a result, taxation laws have become increasingly complex and detailed. This is also true with rules-based accounting regulation. Alexander and Jermakowicz (2006) have suggested that the 'Increasing detail and complexity of US Generally Accepted Accounting Principles have been attributed to a rules-based rather than principles-based approach to standard setting' (p. 133).

The principles-based approach has nowhere been clearly defined but basically the intention is to provide a conceptual basis for accountants to follow rather than a list of detailed rules. Or, as Alexander and Jermakovicz state, it is 'an attempt to tell preparers and auditors not what to do but how to decide what needs doing' (p. 134). It is sometimes referred to (for example, by the SEC) as an objectives-oriented approach to standard setting,[7] which highlights why the distinction is important: it resurrects the question of what are the objectives of financial reporting. These objectives are usually expressed in terms of reporting the underlying economic substance (representative faithfulness) for a reporting entity rather than the form of transactions. It also involves the emphasis taken in financial reporting—does the balance sheet assume more importance (the asset/liability model) or the income statement (the revenue/expenses model)? The implications of this are discussed by Schipper (2003) and by Benston et al. (2006) and include valuation and measurement issues. For example, what is the meaning of the fair value of financial instruments and how is it best measured?

The debate over principles-based and rules-based standard setting is complex and has many implications for accounting practice. The IASC has consciously set out to determine principles-based standards but the reality is that it has often had to explain some requirements of the standards in the form of 'rules' to follow. From a theoretical perspective, a principles-based approach is preferable. The matter can be perceived as a matter of something in the minds of accountants. However, a rules-based approach would seem safer for accountants in a litigious environment. That is, the accountant has to demonstrate that the rules have been followed to avoid any possible claim of negligence. There are echoes here of West's (2003) concern with professionalisation. A principles-based approach necessitates professional judgement by the financial statement preparer and the auditor. If such judgement is avoided, then just how professional is the accountant? There is ample evidence to show that seemingly attractive rules-based accounting standards can very easily lead to abuse of the professional status that societies tend to accord accountants.

International dimensions of accounting

There have always been international dimensions to accounting but they have become more evident in the last hundred years. These dimensions can be usefully considered from three perspectives, although they all overlap. First, individual firms have been engaged for a long time in international trade but gradually they have become larger and larger until the revenues for several of those corporations have risen to be more than the gross domestic product of many of the countries in which they operate. These firms have come to be known as multinational corporations (MNCs). Second, there is the comparison of factors that shape the accounting practices in different countries, sometimes referred to as comparative accounting. Finally, there is the perspective of accounting in the context of an increasingly globalised economy—the most recent phenomenon—which will prove to be by far the most important consideration in examining the international dimensions of accounting. This is the major motivation for advocates of international accounting standards.

Obviously all three aspects are closely interrelated. By definition, a globalised economy refers to the increase in transactions across national boundaries, resulting in a need for an examination of the accounting practices in those countries in order to develop meaningful financial reporting. However, initially it is useful to consider each of these aspects separately if we are to develop a meaningful genealogy of current accounting practices.

Multinational corporations

The first problem in examining MNCs (also referred to as transnational corporations—TNCs) is defining them. Economists have not resolved this issue. One international economist has suggested that an MNC is a corporation that:

- engages in foreign production through its affiliates located in several countries
- exercises direct control over the policies of its affiliates
- implements business strategies in production, marketing, finance and staffing that transcend national boundaries (geocentric).

Various criteria have been suggested, including the location of ownership or orientation (home country, host country or world). However, insofar as accounting is concerned, the final financial reporting is significant. In respect of financial reporting, it is significant to know *which* financial reporting requirements are to apply. Therefore, ownership or whereabouts of headquarters become important considerations. Issues that arise include: How are transactions in different currencies to be treated? What measures for assets and liabilities are to be used in compiling final reports? What methods and processes of consolidation are to be used? These issues have been the subject of many, often highly debated accounting standards.

An example of a reporting question faced by MNCs would be: at what foreign currency exchange rate should a transaction be translated for inclusion in the financial statements? This problem arises because exchange rates fluctuate during the normal accounting period and the exchange rate at the time of the transaction might be significantly different at the time of reporting. Another problem results from the holding of long-term depreciable assets: what should be the basis for depreciation? Most corporations try to avoid the effects of fluctuating exchange rates by engaging in various hedging schemes—where an MNC uses another transaction to reduce the risk that it will incur a loss on the foreign currency involved in the original transaction. The problem then is how to account for the benefits and/or costs arising from the hedging transactions. The nature of the foreign operation also poses a potential problem: was the overseas transaction part of a self-sustaining foreign operation or was it part of the normal operations of the company? These are just some of the issues that are involved in reporting transactions that involve more than one currency.

Accounting in and for MNCs also involves management accounting issues revolving around costing procedures. An example would be where a developing country allows a foreign corporation to operate in the country because of the benefits to be derived from the operation (such as employment and taxes). In this instance, what costing structure should be used by the MNC? Many MNCs were criticised for loading costs on to their operations in developing countries such that no profit was earned and no taxes were payable. This is known as **transfer pricing** and considerable research has been undertaken on this issue. It is now part of a larger problem associated with the benefits of globalisation.

Comparative accounting

Over the years there have been many research studies into factors deemed to be the cause of national differences in accounting—referred to as **comparative accounting**. The reason for the differences has been ascribed to many factors; Nobes (1998, p. 163) has listed 17 reasons he found in the literature, including colonial inheritance, age and size of accounting profession, legal system, culture, history, language and religion. Other international accounting researchers have produced smaller 'lists'. However, a difference that has dominated much of the research has been that referred to as *culture*. Herein lies a problem because, even across disciplines, no one has successfully defined culture. Some have tried, notably Geert Hofstede (1980), who claimed to have uncovered national cultural characteristics despite most cultural theorists having agreed that this was not possible; 'Culture is neither a particular kind of practice nor practice that takes place in a particular social location' (Sewell 1999, p. 48). And as Johnston et al. have stated:

> . . . it is widely recognized that culture is best understood contextually and historically. It is broadly accepted that the idea of a 'superorganic' culture as an active force . . . is untenable (p. 141).

Sadly, several accounting writers have adopted Hofstede's ideas without critically thinking about their tenability. Gray (1988) has even extended and developed the ideas to present an explanation for differences in accounting practices in different countries. Fortunately, other accounting writers such as McSweeney (2002) have clearly shown Hofstede's work to be epistemologically and methodologically fatally flawed.[8] The work is based on 'data extracted from a pre-existing bank of employee attitude surveys undertaken around 1967 and 1973 within IBM subsidiaries in 66 countries' (McSweeney 2002, p. 90). The data was statistically analysed and the result was four dimensions of culture (with a fifth added in his later work to accommodate Chinese 'culture'). McSweeney demolishes most of Hofstede's arguments on the basis of the methodology employed.[9] Further criticism can be levelled at the ontological position adopted—it is clearly a realist position and hence there is the possibility of the reductionist claim of there being identifiable national cultures (contrary to the work of the majority of cultural researchers, as indicated above). The fact that Gray and other accounting writers can unquestioningly accept Hofstede's work and attempt to relate it to accounting is a sad commentary on much accounting research.

Culture is socially constructed and is ever changing so it is not possible to claim that fixed cultural dimensions exist. Knowledge of a culture is acquired through complex social understanding. Cultures are characterised by their historical nature—they constantly change with changes in the social, economic and political organisation of society. There is little doubt that accounting practices, as socially defined activities, are greatly affected by culture but it is not possible to prescribe fixed dimensions as to how culture impacts on those practices. The consumption of food is a culturally defined activity and changes in food consumption patterns in different parts of the world are well known, as large food TNCs, with considerable marketing (rather than culinary) expertise, affect these patterns.

Comparative accounting cannot rely on the simplistic cultural dimensions Gray (1988) has described and must involve a much broader compass if it is to have any meaning. In fact, the movement for the convergence of financial reporting regulation and practices will reduce the impact of national cultural differences—this is a characteristic of globalisation.

Globalisation

Currently, one of the most topical subjects for debate is globalisation. However, there are at least two common misconceptions of globalisation: first, that it is a recent pheno-menon[10] and, second, that it concerns only economic factors. But what is it? No one definition has proved to encompass all the dimensions of globalisation. It is certainly a subject that stirs up vigorous debate and at times strong physical reactions, as the protests outside the World Trade Organization (WTO) and other international organisations' meetings in cities such as Seattle (WTO), Melbourne and Davos, Switzerland (World Economic Forums), Gothenburg, Sweden (European Union Summit), Quebec City (Summit of the Americas) and Gleneagles, Scotland (G8 Summit) have clearly demonstrated; at the G8 Summit in Genoa, Italy, there were 100 000 anti-globalist demonstrators, one of whom was killed. As we move towards a global economy, we also now have global terrorism, very dramatically highlighted in New York and Washington on 11 September 2001 (referred to as 9/11). And, as Giddens (2004) has indicated, such worldwide terror 'can only be combated through worldwide collaboration, both among nations, and between nations and other agencies' (p. xvii).

There is no clear and accepted definition of globalisation and in fact there is some confusion over the condition and the process. That is, there is a process of globalisation, and there is a state or condition of globalisation, so it is important to know to which reference is being made. Despite the lack of acceptable definition there are some qualitative characteristics of globalisation (the process). Steger (2003) has detailed four characteristics. The first is that it involves:

> . . . the *creation* of new and the *multiplication* of existing social networks and activities that increasingly overcome traditional political, economic, cultural, and geographical boundaries [emphasis in original] (p. 9).

The second is reflected in the expansion and stretching of social relations, activities and interdependencies. The third characteristic refers to the intensification and acceleration of social exchanges and activities, and the fourth, to peoples' growing awareness of the second and third characteristics.

From the first characteristic it is clear that globalisation involves more than economic considerations, although often people concentrate on this aspect. However, as mentioned above, to concentrate only on economic considerations overlooks many other major threats and changes in social dependencies (for example, worldwide terrorism and international ecological degradation). Given these characteristics, then, despite popular belief globalisation (the process) is not a new phenomenon. It is through the processes of globalisation that the invention of writing, money, Arabic numbers, items of food, the spirit of modernity and very many other aspects of everyday living spread to other parts of the world. These 'social exchanges' were similar to the use of the Internet today in that they represented the creation of new networks that overcame traditional boundaries. However, despite the process of globalisation having a very long history, it is more commonly associated with the period that witnessed the growth of industrialisation, improved transportation, development of communication technologies and the population explosion of the last 200 years. This process has become even more dramatically evident in the last 40 years.

There have been many gains from the process of globalisation. Improved communication has reduced the sense of isolation felt in many of the world's poorer countries. There have been improvements in health systems leading to higher life expectancies and the reduction in the spread of many diseases (e.g. AIDS) and illnesses. There have been some improvements in the rates of employment in many developing countries. Many social injustices, such as the use of child labour, have been diminished. There has been increased foreign aid and the forgiveness of debt (e.g. the Jubilee Project), which have benefited some developing countries. As Stiglitz (2002) states, 'Those who vilify globalization too often overlook its benefits' (p. 5). However, he continues:

> . . . the proponents of globalization have been, if anything, even more unbalanced. To them, globalization (which typically is associated with accepting triumphant capitalism, American style) *is* progress: developing countries must accept it, if they are to grow and to fight poverty effectively. But to many in the developing world, globalization has not brought the promised economic benefits (p. 5).

Despite the many dimensions of globalisation, it is largely the *economic aspects* that have been the subject of controversy and, because of this, accountants have to be aware of the role they play in the process. However, it is not really possible to discuss the economic aspects of globalisation without also considering political processes and the institutions that play such an important role in furthering the 'aims' of globalisation.

International economic institutions

Much of the angst over the economic aspects of globalisation has arisen from the actions of three international economic bodies, namely the International Monetary Fund (IMF), the International Bank for Reconstruction and Development (the IBRD, or as it is better known, the World Bank) and the World Trade Organization (WTO). All of these organisations have been important tools in enabling promoters of globalisation to wield tremendous political power. The first two institutions arose from a meeting at Bretton Woods, New Hampshire, in the US, in 1944 to rebuild Europe after the Second World War and prevent a recurrence of the economic depression that had preceded it. Put simply, they were created to ensure global economic stability. The Great Depression, the economic depression of the 1930s, was seen as evidence that markets often did not work well. The IMF was founded on the belief that there was a need for *collective action at the global level* for economic stability' (Stiglitz 2002, p. 12, emphasis in the original), just as the United Nations was necessary for collective political action at the global level to preserve political stability.[11] The IMF worked for about 30 years on the basis that markets often worked badly, but in the 1980s, with Thatcher in the UK and Reagan in the US preaching free-market ideology, it, along with the World Bank, changed to champion 'market supremacy with ideological fervor' (p. 12).

In 1990 the IMF, the World Bank and the US Treasury produced what is referred to as the Washington Consensus, which formed a major part of 'the free market mantra' (Stiglitz 2002, p. 16). There are several points worth noting. First, it was originally designed to relate to distressed Latin American economies but was later used to relate to all countries wishing to borrow from the IMF or the World Bank. Second, although these institutions were supposedly global, this policy emerged from the US—as its name graphically signifies. Third, it marked a definite shift in the agenda of the IMF and the World Bank to further neo-liberal interests to deregulate markets around the world.

The 10 points of the Washington Consensus are:

1 Fiscal discipline to curb budget deficits
2 A redirection of public expenditure priorities towards fields offering both high economic returns and the potential to improve income distribution, such as primary health care, primary education, and infrastructure

3 Tax reform (to lower marginal rates and broaden the tax base)

4 Financial liberalisation, with interest rates determined by the market

5 Competitive exchange rates, to assist export-led growth

6 Trade liberalisation (including abolition of import licensing and reduction of tariffs)

7 Liberalisation (promotion) of inflows of foreign direct investment

8 Privatisation of state enterprises

9 Deregulation of the economy (to abolish barriers to entry and exit)

10 Protection of property rights.

The conditions imposed by these three financial institutions on a borrowing nation are referred to as **conditionalities**. Supporters of the new direction taken by them point to statistics indicating an overall increase in global wealth and employment in developing countries, and there is little doubt that, taken at face value, these are indicators of an improving global economy. However, very often these are macro-measures, or averages, which ignore the micro-level inequalities and other damaging consequences of so-called 'trade liberalisation'. There is considerable evidence supporting Chomsky's claim that these

> . . . 'reforms' restore colonial patterns, bar national planning and meaningful democracy, and undermine programs which benefit the general population, while establishing the framework for a world of growing inequality, with a large majority consigned to suffering and despair in the interests of narrow sectors of privilege and power (Chomsky, quoted in Fox 2001, p. 57).

The effects of the enforcement of the new ideology within the IMF and the World Bank are graphically illustrated in the documentary film, *Life and debt*, by Stephanie Black. The film describes how the economy of Jamaica was transformed from one with a strong agricultural base to one now almost totally dependent on tourism. For example, as conditions of a loan from the IMF, fresh milk supplied by local farmers was replaced by cheaper US powdered milk, destroying the local milk farming industry. Bananas had to be imported from Ecuador where they were grown by large US banana corporations. Justification for these (and other similar) conditions was on the basis of trade liberalisation. They were imposed by the World Bank, which was charged with reconstruction and redevelopment, and consequently the generation of economic stability has destroyed the lives of many citizens.

There has been considerable hypocrisy in the application of the Washington Consensus ideology. Debtor countries are required to remove barriers to trade (to liberalise global trade), yet in many instances the developed countries (especially the

US) protect their own industries with considerable subsidies. An outcome has been increasing the debt of debtor countries rather than 'developing' (or structuring) stronger economies.

There is strong empirical evidence for countless other injustices imposed on developing countries and these are detailed in many places in material presented by those of various political perspectives. For example, the effects of the conditionalities imposed on Indonesia during the Asian financial crisis of the late 1990s are well detailed by Graham and Neu (2003). As a highly respected economist (Nobel Prize winner) and someone who has been involved in the governance of the World Bank, Stiglitz (2002) is difficult to argue with. He suggests that, underlying all this, there is one basic structural problem. It is that, while the market system may work relatively well in developed economies where there is near 'perfect' information, it cannot in most developing countries as many of the preconditions for its operation do not exist. Reforming one area of the country without the necessary reformation of other areas has created only imbalance and (social) chaos and inequities. For example, 'The IMF forced one African country to abandon its uniform pricing before an adequate road system was in place' (p. 75). So, who bears the cost of transportation?

The role of accounting in globalisation

Globalisation has raised many questions in which there are strong implications for accounting and accountants. This is especially true if one adopts a broader, more social and transformative view of accounting, as many authors have suggested.[12] For example, issues of corporate governance, anti-corruption measures, financial codes and standards, general standards of accountability and regulation of large international corporations, as well as many other concerns, involve accounting. Some have argued that 'Globalization destabilises our understanding of accounting with associated effects on empire, the environment and the social sphere in which accounting is conducted' (Cooper et al. 2003, p. 359).

There is a popular belief that globalisation has made individual states powerless to regulate the flows of capital. This is an argument supporting globalisation by showing how open financial markets have become. Arnold and Sikka (2001), however, demonstrate that if a longer view is taken of the so-called growth of global financial markets it can be seen that the reverse is in fact true. Paradoxically, financial markets have become increasingly dependent on the state. What goes unnoticed is that political interests within the state exert considerable power over financial markets in order to further their own interests. Arnold and Sikka illustrate this by examining the case of the Bank of Credit and Commerce International (BCCI), a bank that operated in

73 countries before its spectacular collapse amidst charges of fraudulent management and money laundering. They argue that a state–professional relationship (with a large accounting firm) had empowered the growth of the bank through banking regulations and audit technologies. It is also interesting to note that the Australian federal government had forced the Australian accounting profession to engage in the (accounting standards) harmonisation process (see McCombie and Deo 2005).

However, the importance of accounting in the globalisation debate is clearer when the broader social, political and economic implications of accounting are considered. There is little doubt that accounting impacts on organisations and society. Despite the traditional belief that accountants present a neutral economic reality, it is now generally realised that accounting presents an economic reality shaped by the dominant economic power groups. However, because of its technical nature, this is not at first obvious to many. Thus, it provides organisations with a seemingly objective basis for decision making. While this may more easily be recognised in respect of large international corporations, it is also true of other international institutional organisations such as the IMF and the World Bank. If the conditionalities imposed by these institutions create misery, then accountants must be aware that their discipline contributes to this.

Accounting has long been used by large international corporations to create a 'convenient economic reality'. For example, costs within these corporations are allocated to show that no profits have been made in countries in which they have been operating, resulting in no taxes being paid in those countries. This is referred to as the transfer pricing problem, as discussed above, and it has been a concern for many years. It is now just one way in which TNCs, with revenues larger than the GDPs of many countries, yield massive economic power. There has been a considerable growth in the number of TNCs, from about 7000 in 1970 to well over 50 000 by the turn of the century. They account for over 70% of world trade. All maintain headquarters in North America, Europe, Japan or South Korea. A recent development is that these TNCs now wield what is known as 'monopsony power' in addition to the traditional power of the monopoly or oligopoly; that is, they dictate to suppliers the prices they are prepared to pay, and failure to meet these prices often results in cancellation of contracts for supply and inevitably the ruin of the supplying company. For example, the world's biggest retail corporation, WalMart Inc, has demanded prices for products that were below the suppliers' costs. Failure to meet these prices resulted in suppliers going out of business, causing massive social disruptions, especially, for example, where the supplier company was a town's major source of employment, with proportionally massive unemployment virtually destroying the economic base of the town. Accounting plays a significant role in such practices as such decisions are based on accounting generated numbers. It is well known that companies are increasingly seeking sources of cheap labour costs, resulting in shifting labour and production to areas where this is obtainable! Again, the analysis which forms the basis for such decisions is based on accounting numbers. Therefore, accountants are not acting neutrally or (usually) in the best mid- to long-term societal interests (unless this simply means the lowest prices for commodities).

However they choose to act, accountants should be fully aware of the active role they play in the furtherance of the (profit-oriented) goals of TNCs, which have become extremely important agents that affect the economic, political and social welfare of many states.

Regulation, globalisation and accounting

The stated objective of the Australian government in requiring the adoption of IFRS by the accounting profession was to facilitate the global flow of investment funds. Taken at face value, this motive was admirable. However, a deeper examination reveals this to be yet another example of false consciousness—that is, there are serious implications which are not at first obvious. In facilitating the global movement of investment funds, the accounting regulators have also enabled many social, political and economic inequities to emerge. There seems little doubt that globalisation has improved the lot of many, especially (but not only) those in Western developed economies. However, questions have been raised as to the distribution of these advantages. While some developing economies have had considerable economic benefit, great political power imbalance has so often resulted in the economic benefits flowing only to a corrupt political hegemony—a few individuals with the political power, often supported by military might. Too often, also, those wielding economic power in the developed nations have been content to ignore these factors to preserve their own economic interests, including TNCs, international financial institutions and governments with close ties to these institutions. Supporting the decisions of these bodies are accounting measures.

NOTES

1 The UK representative also represented Ireland.

2 Membership includes ASIC, the SEC and similar organisations of many other countries. There are three classes of members—ordinary (national bodies); associate (other non-national securities commissions in some countries, e.g. Alberta, Canada, and other authorities with interests in financial securities); and affiliate (organisations with similar concerns, e.g. Australian Stock Exchange). They (plus other information) can be found at the organisation's website <www.iosco.org>.

3 There are many sources for specific details of Australian accounting standards (e.g. CPA Australia 2008).

4 Domestic firms that are registrants with the Securities and Exchange Commission (SEC) must file financial reports using US generally accepted accounting principles (GAAP). Foreign firms filing with the SEC can use US GAAP, their home country GAAP, or international standards—although if foreign issuers use their home country GAAP or international standards, they must provide a reconciliation to US GAAP.

5 There are many publications which compare US standards with IFRS as well as detailing the adoption of IFRS in other countries. An excellent source is that created by the accounting firm, Deloitte. They very generously make a wealth of material available on their website which educators and students are allowed to access without charge: <http://www.iasplus.com/dttpubs/pubs.htm>. They even provide foreign language versions (e.g. Chinese) of their publications. In addition, they permit access to an IFRS e-learning website within their Resource Library.

6 The term 'bright line law' is often used. It refers to a law in which its application is very clearly stated, leaving little or no room for interpretation.

7 To add even more confusion, the FASB (and the American Accounting Association) refers to it as a concepts-based approach to standard setting.

8 Hofstede has not only influenced accounting writers but also other management disciplines, such that he has made 'a reputation' on his work despite the successful critiques of a large number of writers!

9 Hofstede did respond and McSweeney replied in a later issue of the journal.

10 In an article published in *The Australian Financial Review* ('The end of globalism', 20 February 2004), John Ralston Saul even claims that globalisation is over!

11 There was a hidden political agenda to the establishment of the IMF and the World Bank—to prevent the spread of communism. Therefore, with the fall of the Soviet Union, the way was clear to pursue a more extreme free market ideology.

12 This encompasses the social, cultural and political, as well as the economic dimensions of a society on which accounting impacts. This point is expanded upon in Chapter 7.

REFERENCES AND FURTHER READING

Agars, P 1996, 'Keeping a global balance from Down Under', *Accounting Forum*, vol. 19, pp. 361–372.

Alexander, D & Jermakowicz, E 2006, 'A true and fair view of the principles/rules debate', *Abacus*, vol. 42, pp. 132–164.

Alfredson, K, Leo, K, Picker, R, Pacter, P & Radford, J 2005, *Applying international accounting standards*, John Wiley & Sons Australia Ltd, Milton, Qld.

Arnold, PJ & Sikka, P 2001, 'Globalization and the state–profession relationship: the case of the Bank of Credit and Commerce International', *Accounting, Organizations and Society*, vol. 26, pp. 465–499.

Bennett, B, Bradbury, M & Pragnell, H 2006, 'Rules, principles and judgments in accounting standards, *Abacus*, vol. 42, pp. 189–203.

Benston, GJ, Bromwich, M & Wagenhofer, A 2006, 'Principles- versus rules-based accounting standards: the FASB's standard setting strategy', *Abacus*, vol. 42, pp. 165–188.

Cooper, C, Neu, D & Lehman, G 2003, Globalisation and its discontents: a concern about growth and globalization', *Accounting Forum*, vol. 27, pp. 359–364.

CPA Australia 2008, *Accounting Handbook 2008*, Pearson Education Australia, Frenchs Forest.

Everett, Jeffery 2003, 'Globalization and its new spaces for (alternative) accounting research', *Accounting Forum*, vol. 27, pp. 400–424.

Fontes, A, Rodrigues, LL & Craig, R 2005, 'Measuring convergence of national accounting standards with International Financial Reporting Standards', *Accounting Forum*, vol. 29, pp. 415–436.

Fox, J 2001, *Chomsky and globalisation*, Icon Books, Cambridge, UK.

Giddens, Anthony 2004, *Runaway world*, Profile Books Ltd, London.

Graham, Cameron & Neu, Dean 2003, 'Accounting for globalization', *Accounting Forum*, vol. 27, pp. 449–471.

Gray, SJ 1988, 'Towards a theory of cultural influence on the development of accounting systems internationally', *Abacus*, vol. 24, pp. 1–15.

Hofstede, G 1980, *Culture's consequences: international differences in work-related values*, Sage, Beverly Hills, CA, US.

Johnston, RJ, Gregory, D, Pratt, G & Watts, M, eds 2000, *The dictionary of human geography*, 4th edn, Blackwell Publishing, Oxford, UK.

Kropp, Jim & Johnston, Bryam 1996, 'International convergence of accounting standards', *Accounting Forum*, vol. 19, pp. 283–290.

McCombie, Kellie & Deo, Hemant 2005, 'The international harmonization of accounting standards: making progress in accounting practice or an endless struggle?', *Journal of American Academy of Business*, vol. 7, pp. 154–163.

McSweeney, Brendan 2002, 'Hofstede's model of national cultural differences and their consequences: a triumph of faith—a failure of analysis', *Human Relations*, vol. 55, pp. 89–115.

Nobes, Christopher 1998, 'Towards a general model of the reasons for international differences in financial reporting', *Abacus*, vol. 34, pp. 162–187.

Palast, Greg 2001, 'World Bank conditionalities', *The Observer*, 10 October 2001.

Parker, Robert H & Morris, Richard D 2001, 'The influence of US GAAP on the harmony of accounting measurement policies of large companies in the UK and Australia', *Abacus*, vol. 37, pp. 297–328.

Root, Franklin 1994, *International trade and investment*, 5th edn, South-Western Pub. Co., Cincinnati, US.

Schipper, K 2003, 'Principles-based accounting standards', *Accounting Horizons*, vol. 17, pp. 61–73.

Sen, Amartya 1999, *Development as freedom*, Anchor Books, New York.

Sewell, William H, Jr 1999, 'The concept(s) of culture', in Victoria E Bonnell & Lynn Hunt, eds, *Beyond the cultural turn*, pp. 35–61, University of California Press, Berkeley and Los Angeles, US.

Shortridge, RT & Mayring, M 2004, 'Defining principles-based accounting standards', *The CPA Journal*, <http://www.nysscpa.org/cpajournal/2004/804/essentials/p34.htm>, accessed April 2007.

Steger, Manfred B 2003, *Globalization: a very short introduction*, Oxford University Press, Oxford, UK.

Stiglitz, Joseph E 2002, *Globalization and its discontents*, WW Norton & Company, New York.

West, B 2003, *Professionalism and accounting rules*, Routledge, London.

IV

P A R T

Extending the Boundaries of Theory

CHAPTER 7

The Critique of Accounting Theory

In the last 40 years there has been an increasing interest in alternative approaches to developing accounting theory. Rather than drawing heavily from dominant economic theory, accounting theorists have been looking at knowledge developed in other disciplines in the hope that it may contribute to a fuller understanding of the complex demands on and uses of accounting information. This chapter introduces some of those alternative perspectives on what constitutes meaningful knowledge of accounting in the expectation that they could lead to improved accounting practice—practice more sensitive to the wider demands of society. ■

To this point in the book, the discussion has focused on three perspectives of accounting: accounting as a science, together with attempts to employ a scientific methodology; as a purely technical expression of economic theory, heavily dominated by research in finance; and as part of 'law', albeit law (regulation) heavily influenced by the dominant economic and political ideology. The discussion has revealed that all of these perspectives suffer from severe shortcomings. Fortunately, there are other perspectives on accounting that may prove more fruitful, some of which will be discussed in this chapter. A common element in many of these alternative approaches is to view accounting as a *social* science.

Social science

A few hundred years ago there were disciplines referred to as natural philosophy and moral philosophy. The former evolved into the natural sciences, the latter into the social sciences. However, like so many of the terms we use regularly, the term 'social science' is difficult to define precisely and this has been the subject of much debate. Essentially, social science is the study of aspects of human society. It has been heavily influenced over the last 200 years by positivism, the underlying assumption being that the study of societies can be undertaken scientifically. Closely associated with this is that the methods of the 'natural sciences' can be applied to the study of human society. Sometimes the term 'social science' has been used to refer to the discipline of sociology, but in a broader sense it includes a variety of disciplines that have evolved very differently and remain so. While collectively the term may be used to imply the use of scientific methodology, several other methodologies have emerged.

Accounting can be included with those disciplines concerned with aspects of human society because, clearly, it is a 'system of thought' designed by humans to assist human decision making and influence (human) behaviour. Therefore, a social constructionist ontology, rather than a realist ontology, would seem to be a more appropriate basis for conceptualising accounting. Consequently, rather than attempting to re-create the methods of the natural sciences, accounting has more appropriately turned to those methods that recognise the human aspects of the discipline rather than those that claim an intellectual status akin to that of the natural sciences. Unfortunately, accounting theorists and researchers have been very slow to recognise this, as is evident from the emphasis on neo-empirical research programs over the last 50 years.

There is some truth in the view that accounting is a fairly 'young' intellectual discipline and has yet to demonstrate the maturity of self-reflection and understanding. To date, it has been happy to accept the position of being a sub-discipline of (and consequently inferior to) economics. As a result, it has relied heavily on economic theories and methodologies. This is not to suggest for one minute that it is not closely associated with economics, because it certainly deals mostly with economic phenomena. But it deals with such phenomena from a very different point of view (otherwise it would simply be part of the discipline of economics). While some would argue that accounting is merely the 'handmaiden of capitalist economics', this reflects a conservative and overly deferential viewpoint. There are several aspects of accounting that are quite separate from simple economic analysis—for example, control systems, information processing and behavioural considerations.

The development of alternative accounting theories

Several different approaches to developing an accounting theory have been discussed in previous chapters. These have included the work of individual theorists such as Chambers and Mattessich. Their work, and that of others, emerged from the desire to employ rigorous research methods and logical analysis to stated assumptions and propositions as to the purpose of accounting, especially the production of general purpose financial statements. As was explained, their writings were classical modernist works in that they advocated the appropriateness of essentially a hypothetico-deductive scientific method for achieving intellectual rigour in accounting. Many of the major works of these theorists were published in the 1960s, but several similar major works on accounting had been published prior to that decade (for example, William Paton's *Accounting theory* (1922), John Canning's *The economics of accountancy* (1929) and Stephen Gilman's *Accounting concepts of profit* (1939)).

Also discussed earlier were the attempts by various professional bodies to develop a theoretical basis for accounting: initially the search was for generally accepted accounting principles, then accounting standards and a conceptual framework on which the standards could be based. At first these attempts were represented by commissions to individual (or groups of) accounting theorists, the best example of which was Paton and Littleton's *An Introduction to corporate accounting standards*, first published in 1940 but reprinted many times through to the 1980s. Later, these attempts developed into commissions to committees and then to officially designated research divisions of the professional bodies to develop 'guidelines for theory development' and later to independent organisations specifically charged with developing 'theoretical statements'. As these attempts evolved, there was a change in the function of the published pronouncements; there was a change in their authoritative scope. That is, the pronouncements became parts of a system of regulation which has now expanded from recommended statements of best practice for members of the professional bodies to a complex international system of required practices. Regulation has been substituted for theory—it has become the 'required theory' underlying accounting practice.

In the latter years of the 1960s decade there were several factors which coalesced to change the face of accounting research and theorising. These included the development of doctoral programs in accounting during which students were given rigorous training in quantitative research methods, neoclassical economic and finance theory, and the use of new information processing technologies (especially the use of computers). Concurrently with this was the growing availability of large-scale stock-market databases initially funded by the business community, with a demand for business research to be directly related to extant business practices. Out of this emerged the seminal articles by Ball and Brown (1968), 'An empirical evaluation of accounting numbers', and Beaver (1968), 'The information content of annual earnings announcements', which were discussed in Chapter 3. From here the floodgates opened and neo-empirical research in accounting, including positive accounting theory, was born and became the dominant basis of research publications in the accounting literature. As indicated above, this research was embedded in a neo-liberal ideology and the unshakeable belief in the power of the market to solve almost all of society's problems.

At the same time, there were major changes in attitudes to research in the social sciences, underlying which was a growing acceptance of the belief that positivistic scientific epistemology was inappropriate for the social and human sciences. Because these disciplines involved human and social aspects of society, it was thought to be impossible to develop objective, value-neutral research methodologies. Thus, there was a rejection of the long-held modernist belief that methods employed in the natural sciences, and held to be the highest standards of intellectual rigour, could be universally applied to all disciplines. Alternative methods were sought—methods which had underlying ontological and epistemological positions different from those of the positivist program that had dominated Western thinking for so long. There was a greater awareness that understanding the processes of knowledge required, in turn, an understanding of language and cultural and societal factors which had previously been disregarded in the process of theory development.

Neo-empirical accounting research emerged from a conservative business school environment typically found in the US. It was steeped in neo-liberal ideology for which the rights of the individual and the market mechanism were fundamental beliefs. That is, neoclassical economics, which was central to this ideology, sought to explain the actions of independently minded individuals interacting with one another only by means of market competition; the rights of individuals were supreme and their interaction was achieved through the operation of the market mechanism. The only constraints were provided by nature. Therefore, there was no need of social institutions or government intervention—that is, no form of externally imposed regulation. This implied that the individual or decision-making unit had full knowledge of what was best for her/him or it. Neoclassical economics was the cornerstone of the monetarism espoused by Friedman that came to dominate what was referred to as Chicago School (The University of Chicago) economics in which almost all of the early neo-empiricist accounting researchers were trained. These acolytes spread this belief to other institutions as they took up academic positions in them. So effective were they in doing this that it has become a dominant style of research in accounting which, in turn, has been forced by business schools on their students and new colleagues and many journal editors (despite being contrary to the underlying tenets of the movement—individual choice!). This dominance has led to it often being described as **mainstream accounting research**.

Accounting as social science

As indicated above, accounting can be regarded as a social science. Lowe and Tinker, some time ago, clearly agreed with this:

> Accounting as a discipline and accountancy practice should . . . be regarded as integral parts of social science and social behaviour (1989, p. 47).

So did Hopwood:

> Accounting is coming to be regarded as an interested endeavour. Rather than being seen as merely residing in the technical domain, serving the role of neutral facilitator of effective decision-making, accounting is slowly starting to be related to the pursuit of quite particular economic, social and political interests (1989, p. 141).

The social nature of accounting had been recognised much earlier. For example, in 1931 DR Scott had published a book which stressed the historical and social character of accounting. Scott argued that society and its institutions (including the economic) constantly changed, and that if accounting was to be useful in providing an understanding of 'economic realities', then it should be considered from a much broader (than merely technical) perspective. Scott developed his argument on the basis of an economic theory different from most others of the time—the institutional economics espoused by people such as his colleague, economist Thorstein Veblen.[1]

Since that time there have been many others who have expressed similar views. In an article published in *The Accounting Review* in 1963, one of the co-authors of one of the most significant auditing monographs,[2] RK Mautz, argued that accounting met the accepted defining criteria of a social science. Therefore, educators and researchers needed to re-evaluate their approach to the discipline to recognise the rigorous demands of social science. Practitioners could then make better use of research results.

Accounting has understandably been predominantly concerned with the financial reporting of corporations as they are the primary form of business organisation in most societies. There have been many who have demonstrated the significant changing nature of the corporation over the last 200 years. Perhaps one of the best known early works to address this issue was *The modern corporation and private property* by Berle and Means.[3] Ladd (1963) argued that these changes had resulted in a 'new orientation of business responsibilities and new concepts of appropriate business activities and objectives' (p. 2). This re-orientation meant that the responsibility of corporate management went beyond the satisfaction of shareholders' interests to include a much greater social responsibility, yet 'accounting concepts and procedures are firmly based on the premise of the paramountcy of the ownership interest' (p. 2). To Ladd, accounting had clearly not kept pace with business developments partly as a result of 'inertia—from an unwillingness to change procedures which have worked in the past' (p. 31). He cogently argued for a change in accounting method to reflect the very great changes in the nature of the corporation and its activities. This included the added dimension of corporations as 'good citizens' (in societies).

Another person to argue the need for a fundamental change in accounting was the English accounting theorist, Trevor Gambling, described on the dust jacket of one of his books as someone who had 'earned the reputation as an awkward and original thinker in a field where original ideas are not much expected'. In his *Societal accounting* (1974) he attempted to reconcile traditional accounting theory and practice with broader economic accounting such that accounting could be used to signal wider social issues and concerns (based on accepted social indicators). Gambling's major contribution has been to draw attention to the limitations of traditional narrow accounting thought. In many respects, like some of the others discussed above, he was ahead of his time, as it is only recently that many of his ideas have been taken up seriously by other accounting researchers and theorists. There are many other than those mentioned above who recognised the need for a change in the way accounting was perceived if it was to properly serve the needs of a more broadly defined set of users.

One thing that becomes clear is that accounting, as a social science, has to reflect the changed ontological, epistemological and methodological assumptions that occurred in the other social sciences. As reflected in the Hopwood quotation, there has been a growing realisation that accounting is not merely a neutral technical endeavour but reflects the economic, social and political viewpoints of those who are engaged in its practice. Morgan (1983) was even more explicit:

> . . . accounting researchers are obliged to face the dilemma that they are really social scientists . . . and to keep abreast of new developments and be competent at their craft, they will need to devote serious consideration to the nature and practice of what counts as good social research (p. 385).

In recognising the social nature of accounting it becomes clear that the positivist natural science approach to accounting research is not appropriate—it has been rejected in most of the social sciences. The naive assumptions (such as value-free propositions and efficient markets) of the neo-empirical approach are insufficient to reflect the 'real' role of accounting in society and in fact, suggest Lowe and Tinker (1989, p. 48), 'may be disastrous for the practical usefulness of financial accounting statements'. And Tomkins and Groves (1983) argue that adopting an approach other than that claimed to be used in the natural sciences may bring accounting theory and practice much closer together.

From Figure 7.1 it can be observed that neo-empirical research (as demonstrated earlier) is based on a realist ontology. Neo-empirical researchers believe there is an objective reality that exists independent of any human agency (human involvement). Following on from this then, human beings are viewed as interacting with this reality passively—that is, they do not create the reality but have to live around it. Therefore, human behaviour—its response to 'a real world'—can also be objectively observed.

Figure 7.1 (Some) assumptions of neo-empiricism

Ontological
That there is an objective external reality
That human behaviour is purposive
That social order is controllable

Epistemological
Observation is separate from theory and is for either verification or falsification
Causality

Accordingly, how humans respond to external stimuli (their surroundings and their attempts to exist therein) can be predicted. Consequently, social order is controllable; societies can be managed. The means by which knowledge of such an idealised world is obtained follow from this ontological position.

In respect of knowledge claims, empiricism and testability become paramount. However, as Christenson (1983) has demonstrated, in accounting research there is considerable confusion as to the process of empirical testability. Causality is a problematic notion and complex causal modelling and extensive multivariate analysis, designed to demonstrate causality, have had not proved otherwise. It remains a highly disputed concept.

Thus, there are many problems with attempting to employ the methodology of the natural sciences in *any* discipline, let alone one so obviously a social phenomenon as accounting. This led Mautz (1963) to argue that the discipline must 'accept more responsibility for value judgements' because, while the accountant may attempt to adopt an impersonal, disinterested viewpoint, 'the truth is that his [sic] data include value judgements and for him to ignore such considerations is to ignore important aspects of his data' (p. 319).

Alternative research methodologies

Accounting researchers have drawn on a number of theoretical frameworks that have been used in the social sciences. There is a logical difficulty in attempting to describe or classify some of these because 'by definition' they defy classification.[4] However, for pedagogical (instructive) purposes a description of what they involve can be undertaken. They mostly employ **qualitative** rather than **quantitative** research methodologies and this is sometimes taken as a defining characteristic. To varying degrees they are concerned with, for example, notions of language, culture, interpretation, reflexivity, discourse, text, power and history.

The simple differences between quantitative and qualitative research are presented in Table 7.1. One of the major steps in quantitative research is the identification of variables. The variable—a concept that varies—is central to quantitative research. Quantitative research uses the language of variables and is primarily concerned with the relationships between them: the aim is to establish the causal structure of the variables. This is possible because of the realist ontology adopted. Therefore, variables are representations of the real world. They can be objectively determined, so the aim is to observe them and establish a causal relationship, the outcome of which can then be generalised to other (similar) situations (sets of variables). The researcher remains separate from—outside—the data in order to maintain objectivity. In qualitative

Table 7.1 **Research differences**

Quantitative research	Qualitative research
Aims to determine the facts and causes of phenomena	The aim is to determine an understanding of actors' behaviour
Uses controlled measurements	Uses naturalistic and uncontrolled observations
Claims objectivity	Openly admits subjectivity
Seeks verification/confirmation through reduction	Seeks to discover and explore the research environment
Has an outcome orientation	Has a process orientation
Claims to use hard and replicable data	Claims data represents everyday reality and is rich in meaning
Produces generalisable outcomes	Is non-generalisable
Assumes static and stable reality	Assumes an ever-changing, dynamic reality
Assumes an outside perspective	Assumes an insider perspective

research, the interest is in the processes and the behaviour of individuals in response to an ever-changing—dynamic—world. The researcher tends to be intimately involved with the subject under investigation and acknowledges the subjectivity of the results, which are presented as of potential interest to others but are not generalisable because each situation will differ.

For example, a capital markets study will be a quantitative research study. Stock-market data are collected and summarised (reductionism) to indicate evidence, or confirmation of an hypothesis, and the claim will be that this—share price reaction—will always occur in similar situations. The researcher will be committed to a realist ontology whereby the reality is represented by the stock-market prices. The same study can be replicated in another stock market with the same results, which will (again) confirm the results of the original study as a representation of hard reality. On the other hand, a behavioural study might examine stock-market prices resulting from the actions of a group of investors in certain situations. The results would not be generalisable as these circumstances and the behaviour of individuals would never be identical. The qualitative study may well involve the use of quantitative data (share prices) but the significance of them would not be the same as in a quantitative study where they are considered to be hard objective facts.

This example is a simplified one and the differences between the research methods are likely to be much more significant. Whereas there is one methodology (which is privileged) in quantitative research, this is not so in qualitative research. As explained earlier, the methodology in quantitative research will be of a positivist scientific type.[5] For qualitative research, many forms of research (research methodologies) exist, each regarded as the most appropriate to different situations. Some of these will be as positivist as neo-empirical research methodologies, some will retain the essential characteristics of modernism, some will totally reject modernist precepts, and some will be based on very radical philosophies. In the accounting literature there are a plethora of adjectives describing some so-called theory adopted in a particular research study. Many of these are epistemologically extremely dubious!

Subjectivity versus objectivity

A key assumption underlying whether a quantitative or a qualitative research approach should be adopted is a belief, or not, in the neutrality of the resulting knowledge; in other words, is it possible to be objective when researching? As indicated above, quantitative researchers believe objectivity is not only desirable but possible (even essential!). On the other hand, qualitative researchers believe that objectivity is not possible and therefore the researcher should acknowledge his or her subjectivity. These positions can be contrasted in terms of the classification of assumptions described (and terminology employed) in earlier discussion, and as shown in Table 7.2.

In accounting, neo-empirical research adopts the objectivist position. This research is sometimes referred to as **nomothetic**, which means that it sets out to establish law-like generalisations. For example, research examining the effects on share prices of an accounting method choice will claim the result as something that will always occur in similar situations. Such research will tend to use large numerical databases from which conclusions will be drawn. The original research will be replicated using different databases and, after the conclusions have been confirmed sufficiently, it will form a scientific law. Conversely, a subjectivist approach is sometimes referred to as **ideographic**, which simply means that the focus will be on cultural and historical particulars and a description will be made on the basis of the researcher's interpretation

Table 7.2 **Theoretical assumptions underlying objectivist and subjectivist views**

Objectivist view		Subjectivist view
Realist	Ontology	Constructionist
Positivist	Epistemology	Anti-positivist
Intended to create law-like generalisations	Methodology	Intended to provide specific non-generalisable descriptions
Mainly quantitative	Appropriate methods	Qualitative

(e.g. a case study). As indicated, in subjectivist qualitative research no method is privileged over others, so there are many variations, some of which will be discussed below.

Accounting theory as critique

In the accounting literature there has been a tendency to refer to any non-positivist accounting research as critical theory research. Unfortunately, this has also been true in much of the social science research literature where it may refer to a range of theories that take a critical view of society and social processes. Thus, the term has been used quite loosely and can have a very broad meaning. This is unfortunate because, strictly speaking, **critical theory** refers to the work of a group of social theorists and philosophers called the Frankfurt School, working in Germany early in the 20th century. Their work was continued by one their students, Jurgens Habermas, and in turn some of his 'students' have carried on (and developed and extended) his work to the present day.[6]

Frankfurt School critical theory has hugely influenced social theory, largely as a result of the work of Habermas. The theory is complex, and the summary here has, of necessity, been simplified. Some essential characteristics of critical theory are its rejection of positivism as the sole arbiter and generator of knowledge largely because of its lack of self-reflection, leading it to reduce epistemology to a crudely mechanical methodology. Self-reflection requires the acceptance of the importance of human agency in the creation of knowledge. This is necessary because, without it, oppressive power relations may be hidden. Crudely speaking, if you do not think about what you know and how you know it, your actions may be simply reflecting what others want you to do, so you will be reinforcing the dominant and powerful views that exist in society. For example, accountants believe they are acting in a value-neutral and objective manner and are reporting on economic reality. However, it is important to know what 'reality' is being represented—what attributes are being measured and how they are being presented in a financial report. Through self-reflection one is freed from past constraints (such as dominant ideology and traditional disciplinary boundaries) and thus critical theory is emancipatory.

Critical theory was initially strongly influenced by Marxism but 'developed in contrast to the crude materialist, determinist and allegedly scientific Marxism that had become orthodox in the Soviet Union' (Simons 2004, p. 2); rather, it developed as what is often referred to as Western Marxism. Despite Habermas's rejection of the scientism of the positivist program (which he believed was only one of many forms of knowledge), he continued to remain attached to the idea of modernity and viewed the Enlightenment as a worthy but unfinished project.

There have been several accounting studies advocating critical theory. Perhaps the strongest advocate has been Richard Laughlin, who was later joined by Jane Broadbent as well as other co-authors. A more general case for accounting as a critical social science was made by Dillard (1991) who uses the work of two prominent accounting authors to demonstrate the benefits of a more critically oriented approach. To this extent Dillard's work is a good summary of some of the key considerations in adopting a critical theory approach. On the other hand, Laughlin's work is directed more to employing critical theory to solve 'real life' accounting problems and issues. His work examines accounting systems in organisations and he makes a case for a critical theoretical understanding. Previous technical positivist attempts to understand the operation of accounting systems, he argues, have not contributed to our understanding of accounting in practice (Laughlin 1987). Many of the advantages of using critical theory were seen by its advocates as most suited to accounting in organisational contexts and can therefore be said to have improved our understanding of management accounting.

In his later work Laughlin, especially that written with Broadbent (and in her own work), turned his attention to accounting and accountability in the public sector (under the New Public Management). Their work extended their use of critical theory to include the later work of Habermas which examined issues of law (juridification) (e.g. Laughlin and Broadbent 1993) and communicative action (how understanding is communicated).

In a 1999 paper Laughlin argues that there are at least four important characteristics of critical accounting. First, it is always contextual—that is, it recognises that accounting has social, political and economic consequences. Second, it seeks engagement, which means that it is always undertaken to change (improve) the practice or profession of accounting. Third, it is concerned with both micro (individuals and organisations) and macro (societal and professional) levels. And, fourth, it is interdisciplinary in that it engages with and borrows from other disciplines. Thus, critical accounting is much more broadly concerned with the practice, profession and discipline of accounting than are traditional studies.

The work of Prem Sikka clearly illustrates Laughlin's characteristics of critical accounting. He is somewhat of a political activist in accounting and has taken issue with the profession for not having more forcefully aided the fight against issues such as money laundering, fraud and transnational crime, and professional body insouciance (indifference to many of these issues) (see, for example, Sikka and Wilmott 1997).

Critical accounting has influenced research in many countries and in 2002 a special issue of the journal, *Critical Perspectives in Accounting*, was devoted to 'Critical accounting in different national contexts'. In this issue Broadbent asks: why do we need critical accounting? Her response argues that in a world pondering the allocation of scarce resources, 'We need to ensure the use of accounting does not represent certain interests at the expense of others'. And, she continues, 'Constructions and interpretations of accounting information must pay attention to the cultural imperatives of those it seeks to control as well as those who are using it as a tool of control' (p. 444). Thus, critical accounting seeks to unmask the often hidden interests of those who would seek an unjust allocation of a society's scare resources so that all interests in society can benefit. The spectacular corporate collapses and fraud of early this century—and before—clearly indicate that such maladjusted interests exist.

Accounting theory as interpretation

It should be remembered that classifying the alternative methodologies is antithetical to the essence of many of these alternatives. Classification usually presumes a fixed basis for categorisation—a fixed 'reality'—which is the very thing many of these alternative methodologies reject. Therefore, it is restated here that such grouping is done for instruction to those unfamiliar with the philosophical complexities involved with these alternative views of how knowledge is created.

While the Frankfurt School critical theorists adhered to a belief that there were foundations to knowledge, those who hold strongly to a social constructionist ontology deny that it is possible to determine such foundations (or, in fact, deny their existence). This has important implications for how knowledge is perceived. Foundational beliefs are taken as certain and beyond doubt—they exist independent of any human agency. Constructionists believe that knowledge is produced by human societies: we do not discover knowledge so much as make or construct it. We create concepts, models and systems to make sense of our experiences. Accounting, of course, is a good example of constructed knowledge. However, our experiences are constantly changing so our constructions also have to change. Accounting in the 19th century was different from accounting today. Our understanding is therefore dependent on how we interpret our changed experiences. Such interpretation does not exist in isolation but depends on societal norms, social demands, language and other considerations. There is a range of research and theory approaches that concentrates on interpretation. These approaches, like critical theory, are necessarily interdisciplinary, so it is important to understand the political, social, legal, economic, linguistic, cultural and historical context of the interpretations. There are many variations of these interpretive approaches to knowledge, some dating back to just before and after the turn of the 20th century as in the work of Max Weber (a major classical sociologist) and Edmund Husserl (founder of the movement known as modern phenomenology). Other approaches include those known as philosophical hermeneutics, ethnomethodology and symbolic interactionism. While these are rather complex sounding titles, they all share the aim of attempting to enrich peoples' understanding of the meaning of their actions in order that they can change their worlds through such self-understanding.

One of the earliest works to draw attention to the potential of improving accounting practice by using interpretive theories was a paper by Tompkins and Groves, 'The everyday accountant and researching his reality' (1983). Their central intention was to argue that accounting research had traditionally uncritically borrowed models and methods from the natural sciences which were very often inappropriate for studying accounting practice. 'Naturalistic' rather than positivist approaches would result in a better understanding of accounting practice. This is a strange use of the term 'naturalistic', but others have used it, and it is intended to relate to non-positivist methods, including some of the interpretive approaches, namely ethnomethodology, symbolic interactionism and transcendental phenomenology.

Ethnomethodolgy seeks to determine how people go about their daily practices (hence the title of Tompkins and Groves' paper!) and what 'rules' lead them to derive meaning from their actions: in other words, how do they make sense of their world? Tompkins and Groves suggested that it might be applied to determining how accounting influenced the actions of others or their understanding of events. Accounting 'rules' were determined from accounting practice—that is, the significance and meaning of the rules emerged from how accountants (and others) interpreted and acted on them.

Symbolic interactionism was developed at the University of Chicago and is similar to ethnomethodology except it is more concerned with the actions and interpretations of individuals. Meanings do not reside in objects but emerge from social processes. Individuals act on the basis of the meaning they attach to things and this becomes evident as they interact in society. Tompkins and Groves suggested that this research approach could be used to study financial control. By examining how various individuals responded to financial decision information it would be possible to identify 'key people' who were aware of 'the larger macroeconomic determinants of behaviour' (Wilmott 1983, pp. 394–395).

Interpretive approaches have been used more in management accounting than in financial accounting. Chua (1986, pp. 615–617) provides an excellent example of the significance of an interpretive approach by comparing two pieces of research related to budgetary processes, one a traditional approach, the other an interpretive study. She demonstrates that in the former the 'budgetary control system' is seen to exist as 'a facet of reality that is external to the world of the researchers', while in the latter the budget is 'symbolic not literal, vague not precise, value loaded not value free'—in fact that the budget shapes reality through the meanings people place on it and how it influences their actions within the organisation. In another article Chua (1988) shows that management accounting research has used the interpretive approach and points out some of the difficulties with its use in accounting. In the paper Chua explains the difference between symbolic interactionism and ethnomethodology and suggests some new insights that the interpretive perspective can bring to the traditional approaches to management accounting research and how they can continue to be used to advantage.

Accounting theory as structure

Early in the 20th century a French linguist, Ferdinand Saussure, developed an approach to the study of language that concentrated on underlying structures which he argued underpinned all language. Later, his approach was adopted to apply to a form of social analysis in which the structures of social organisation took priority over the human aspects. The term **structuralism** refers to the methodological and theoretical approaches to culture and social analysis which assume that societies can be studied in a manner similar to the Saussurian structural analysis of language.[7] Therefore, the theoretical study of accounting would concentrate on the 'structures' on which accounting was built. The onus would be on the unobservable but structural relations between the conceptual elements to expose the essential logic that bound the 'structures' together—in other words, the object of investigation studied as a system.

The accounting profession's search for GAAP and then a conceptual framework can be viewed as a 'structuralist' approach. However, this has never been consciously considered. Nevertheless, the search for the essential logical elements that bind accounting systems and result in financial reports being prepared is very similar to the structuralist approaches taken in other disciplines (notably anthropology).

It is important to note that economic theory *has* been greatly shaped by structural thinking. In fact, Saussure 'took economic theory as *the* model for his highly influential semiotic theory of language' (Macintosh 2002, p. 9); and, as one commentator has said, 'Economics, be it noted, is the structural study par excellence' (Sturrock, quoted in Macintosh 2002, p. 9). Because accounting has relied so heavily on economic theory, Macintosh goes on to demonstrate that it too has been heavily structuralist and he illustrates this with agency theory: 'Agency theory is prototypically structuralist' (p. 10). However, few accounting researchers have consciously seen their research as being directly shaped by structuralist theory.

Accounting theory as language

The cliché, 'accounting is the language of business', has been around for many years. Knowledge can exist only through communication, and language is the most common medium of communication. Therefore, to understand how knowledge of accounting is established it is useful to study language. And if accounting is the language of business this becomes even more important. However, the study of language is highly complex, and there are several ways by which such study may be undertaken. The Ancient Greeks, for example, saw language as comprised of signs, and a common word for the study of language, **semiotics** (or semiology in Europe), has Greek origins (interpreter of signs). Other bases for the study of language include linguistics, rhetoric, hermeneutics, discourse analysis—and many others.

About the same time that Saussure, in Europe, was developing his semiotics—his theory of language (which was to become the basis of structuralism, as mentioned above)—one of America's most important philosophers, Charles S Peirce, was creating his semiotics, his theory of signs, which he believed extended to a whole system of philosophy. Peirce was also the founder of **pragmatism**, the theory that holds that a proposition is true if holding it to be so is practically successful or advantageous. He also greatly influenced the development of logic.[8]

Saussure was primarily concerned with the development of a theory of language central to which is the notion of the **sign**, which, in turn, is a combination of the paired elements of *signifier* and *signified*. The signified is the concept (for example of 'catness') and the signifier is the sound image (or the sound spoken), 'cat'. One thing to note is that the sign is arbitrary—that is, it can differ from one language to another. It is also important to realise that not only are different signs used in different languages but that this leads to users of the signs thinking differently: the influence of culture shapes the way people think. In 'accounting language' the word 'asset' is a signifier and the concept of asset ('assetness') is the signified, but just what the concept of 'asset' is has been the subject of debate for many years. It can be 'future economic benefit', but on what basis is this measured?

As indicated in the previous section, Saussure's work was primarily intended as a theory of language. However, it was taken up by other disciplines, such as anthropology (by Levi-Strauss), psychology (by, for example, Lacan) and economics. The ultimate aim was to determine the underlying structures. Two other features become evident here. First, if underlying structures are sought, then the individual (human) is no longer relevant because she or he exists independently of the underlying structure. Second, such analysis is *synchronic*—it is ahistorical—as structures are seen as independent of time. The opposite of synchronic is *diachronic*—

changing over time. Structuralist analysis, therefore, ignores history and development. To some scholars who originally subscribed to structuralism this was a naive understanding of how language actually worked. Therefore they rejected structuralism (as it stood) and sought ways of extending or changing it to make it reflect the fact that language changes over time depending on how individuals and societies interpret the signs contextually. These scholars came to be known as **poststructuralists** (because they came 'after' structuralism). However, they developed their ideas in very different directions and all rejected this label. The common features of their work are, first, a recognition that language is viewed as the medium for defining and contesting social organisation and subjectivity, and second, the claim that individuals are knowing, rational subjects and necessary for the creation of knowledge.

These views can be compared to the mainstream positivist notions of knowledge. To the positivists knowledge involves uncovering the elements of a real world and formulating the knowledge into a neutral theoretical language. The individual therefore is just a 'device' for uncovering this knowledge. The poststructuralist view is quite the opposite—it is that knowledge comes into existence through language, and that this language is comprised of a socially derived and accepted set of signs which every individual interprets in their own way. Two of the best known of the so-called poststructuralists are Michel Foucault and Jacques Derrida. Foucault turned to history; Derrida took language and meaning to the extremes, breaking it down—or deconstructing it—to its barest elements. There are several studies in accounting which have adopted a Foucauldian approach but very few that have employed Derrida's analysis.

Foucault was one of the most influential thinkers in the second half of the 20th century and still exerts a strong influence on theory in the social sciences and philosophy. So it is little wonder that some accounting researchers have been attracted to his ideas. Foucault is a notoriously difficult person to categorise but there are three phases of his work. In the first, he referred to his method as 'archaeology', which portrays his structuralist roots (although it had moved well beyond Saussurean structuralism). The method in his second phase he called 'genealogy', and in the third phase it was described as being concerned with discourse ethics. Themes found in his work include history, language, discourse, subjectivity and power.

Although he is often seen as a historian, Foucault's history is not that of the traditional historian. Rather than seeing continuous progress and development he looked for disruptions. He did not seek out simple causality but rather sought to determine the factors that made social institutions and beliefs possible throughout history. Comprehending these helps us understand where we are now.

In accounting, those who have employed his approach have mostly resorted to historical study. Stewart (1992) says that Foucault:

> . . . provided a theoretical schema within which to problematize and question accounting, and break away from a unidimensional picture of its development. Accounting has not been created just by capitalism or industrialization or ownership or organizational structures. Rather, the emergence and functioning of accounting in its various contexts is a complex phenomenon, due to the interplay of many different influences (p. 61).

Stewart cites several works in accounting that have employed a Foucauldian perspective—works that have examined such topics as the professionalisation of accounting, the emergence of administrative power, the development of cost accounting in the UK and the role of the state in developing accounting. The aim in Foucauldian studies is to see 'accounting as transcending time and space considerations and developing into a set of supra-historical accounting techniques that will be better able to meet the needs of the organization' (p. 58). Hoskin and Macve (1986) have argued that double-entry bookkeeping emerged from the context of disciplinary techniques developed by mediaeval monastic orders. Furthermore, accountability and control received an impetus from the universities developing a system of monitoring student performance through examinations—'a power–knowledge framework' (p. 123). Loft (1986) demonstrated that the professionalisation of British accounting was influenced by the need for cost accounting during the First World War. These are only a couple of examples—there are numerous other studies in accounting that employ a Foucauldian perspective.

Accounting theory as rhetoric

Rhetoric is an old discipline dating back to the 4th century BC. Its contemporary meaning is the art of persuasive communications and eloquence. As Arrington and Francis (1989) point out:

> Every author attempts to persuade (or perhaps seduce) readers into accepting his or her text as believable (p. 4).

It is important to note here the words 'author', 'persuade' and 'text'. The author subjectively selects the rhetorical devices he or she feels will be most useful in persuading others of a particular position. The word 'text' is widely used and now means more than a written document—it refers to many other things in which meanings are conveyed, such as films, speeches, advertisements, instruction manuals, conversation and, of course, financial reports.

As indicated in Chapter 3, Mouck (1992) demonstrated how positive accounting theorists employed several rhetorical devices to persuade others that positive accounting theory was the only way to truth. Rhetoric is most commonly encountered in literary studies; however, in 1980, McCloskey published a paper in the *Journal of Economic Literature* entitled 'The rhetoric of economics', which spawned a new movement in economics, consistent with similar movements in other social sciences, which have seen rhetoric as an alternative to positivist epistemology.[9] Whereas epistemology is based on a set of established abstract criteria, rhetoricians hold that truth emerges from within specific practices of persuasion.

One of McCloskey's primary aims was to draw the attention of economists to how they use language and how language shapes their theories. Similarly, Arrington and Francis (1989) sought to show how 'the prescriptions of positive theory function linguistically rather than foundationally and cannot purge themselves of the rhetorical and ideological commitments' (p. 5). Arrington and Francis (1989) moved beyond a simplistic analysis of language and drew on the work of Derrida to make their case. Derrida's work is highly complex and extends the discussion of signs and language to extremes, as mentioned above. His concern is with deconstructing the text—that is, unpacking the text 'to reveal, first, how any such central meaning was constructed, and, second, to show how that meaning cannot be sustained' (Macintosh 2002, p. 41).

Largely due to its complexity and its controversial reception by some quarters of the academic community, very few studies in accounting have drawn on Derrida's work. However, his central message that language cannot be the unambiguous carrier of truth, which has been assumed in many methodological positions, should never be forgotten or overlooked. Like other poststructuralists, Derrida saw all knowledge as textual—comprised of texts. He believed that all Western thought was based on centres. In this sense, a centre was a 'belief' from which all meanings were derived, as that which was privileged over other 'beliefs'. For example, most Western societies are based (centred) on Christian principles. Perhaps it could be stated that accounting is centred on capitalist ideology. Deconstruction usually involves decentring in order to reveal the problematic nature of centres. So, it could be argued that many accounting problems arise from problems with capitalism—it has changed so much over the years, however, that it is hard to be precise. Another example could be that so much accounting thought has been centred on historical cost measurement. In many discussions over the years, until recently, it has been 'assumed' that historical cost was the basis for measuring accounting transactions, and advocates of alternative measurement bases were viewed as if they were heretics.

Accounting theory as hermeneutics

Hermeneutics is the study of interpretation and meaning and, as a formal discipline, was initially used several hundred years ago by biblical scholars interpreting biblical texts. In the mid-19th century it became a discipline for the critique of the attempted application of (natural) scientific method to the human sciences. Hermeneutics, as the interpretation of meaning of texts and other works (e.g. art works), was the recommended methodology. In the 20th century hermeneutics was extended from an epistemological position to an ontological one—that is, from focusing on knowledge to focusing on being (existence), thus making it a valuable approach for understanding social organisation (e.g. accounting). This extended view of hermeneutics resulted in it usually being referred to as 'philosophical hermeneutics'. However, the focus is still on language, meaning and interpretation. It is also common to find reference to the 'hermeneutic circle'. This is because interpretation inevitably requires understanding through language and the interpreter comes to the matter under consideration with an historical understanding—language is developing over time. Thus, it is inevitably circular—'new' understanding is based on previous (historical) understanding: meaning is grasped from past interpretations because that is all there is. Consequently, value-free inquiry is not possible and truth only exists as shared interpretations—knowledge can only be regarded as knowledge when it is accepted by an audience.

There was, in the social sciences, a growing interest in interpretation which has been referred to as the 'hermeneutic turn'. Boland (1989) argues that the hermeneutic turn has also been reflected in accounting research. For him, this was manifest in the work of those researchers wishing to break from the subjectivist–objectivist dichotomy who saw the renewed interest in subjectivist approaches to theory as having considerably more potential for a fruitful understanding of accounting.

Different accounting theory

The discussion above has provided a brief view of some of the many different approaches to accounting theory that have developed over the years.[10] While they are very different in specific orientation, they do share some characteristics. Collectively, they are often referred to as 'critical studies'. While the term 'critical theory' has a specific meaning, it is also used to refer to a heterogeneous set of theories that generally can trace their roots to a European rather than an Anglo-American philosophical tradition. Such embracing of an alternative philosophical framework has served as an antidote to the sterile positive prescription of the mainstream methodological hegemony.

Critical accounting studies take a wide range of stances, from highly conservative to extremely radical (albeit only a few), but they all have the intention of trying to improve accounting practice by making accountants more aware of the wider social, political and economic consequences of their practice. And, as Morgan (1983) has indicated, 'the more one recognizes that accounting is a social practice that impacts on a social world, the less appropriate natural science approaches become (p. 385). Critical studies, then, are united in opposing the use of positivist scientific methodology in pursuing accounting research because it specifically excludes any human or social considerations under the misguided apprehension of producing objective knowledge. One consequence of accepting accounting as a social practice is that it imposes greater responsibility on accountants to be more aware of the social implications of their practice. In order to do this many researchers have turned to research undertaken in the social sciences as exemplars for appropriate methodologies.

A dominant theme in critical studies is an awareness of the role of language in producing knowledge. It is through language that accounting is constructed and constructs a reality. Thus, many of the alternative methodologies have been dependent on the many and varied approaches to the philosophical study of language, including semiotics, linguistic analysis, rhetoric, hermeneutics and deconstuction. Language has always been a central concern of philosophers but there was, according to American philosopher Richard Rorty (1992), a 'linguistic turn' in many disciplines in the later half of the 20th century. Since then, there has been a far greater awareness of the importance of language to the creation and understanding of knowledge. Thus, language plays an important role in most of the methodologies developed in the social sciences and, consequently, in most critical accounting studies.

Other important elements commonly encountered in critical accounting studies are cultural consciousness and awareness of the importance of history. Languages are created in societies and the impact of culture is crucial to any understanding of a language. Languages change over time, despite the position adopted by Saussure and the positivists; there are no universals. Associated with this realisation is that societies are regulated by rules and conventions so it is important to determine how individuals interpret the rules and conventions. Critical accounting researchers have taken up many of these issues in their work. Interpretation is a very individual exercise so subjectivity and reflexivity are important considerations of human behaviour.

All of these epistemological considerations are reflected in the fact that most critical accounting researchers advocate and practise qualitative research methods. Therefore, the research undertaken by critical accounting researchers is very different from that practised by neo-empirical researchers, even though both critical and neo-empirical researchers are attempting to determine a 'truth'. In order to make an evaluation of these truth claims, it is important to appreciate where the researcher is coming from. This chapter has attempted to provide a very brief understanding of where critical theorists are coming from to balance the background to neo-empirical researchers provided in Chapter 3.

1 Institutional economics concentrates on the social systems that constrain the exchange and use of scarce resources. In doing so, it explains the emergence of alternative institutional arrangements and their influence on economic performance through controlling, by various means, access by economic actors to resources. Over the years it has been championed and debated by many very important economic theorists who have continued to try to develop a theory of economic institutions.

2 Mautz, RK & Sharaf, HA 1961, *The philosophy of auditing*, American Accounting Association, Florida.

3 Berle, AA & Means, GC 1932, *The modern corporation and private property*, Macmillan Co., New York. Both authors subsequently wrote several other works individually and with other co-authors.

4 This is because some of them rely on a (social) constructionist rather than a realist ontology. That is, by definition they do not exist as independent objective entities.

5 This will probably be a form of hypothetico-deductivism described in earlier chapters and used in neo-empirical research.

6 It is generally held that there are three phases of critical theory: first, the work of the original members of the Frankfurt School, and the early work of Habermas (up to the mid-1970s); second, the later work of Habermas (post mid-1970s); and third, the work of Habermas's 'students'.

7 Although most usually associated with Saussure, structuralism most likely originated in (the then) Czechoslovakia and Russia.

8 Pragmatism is the archetypical American philosophy and has been dominant in American thinking. While it has probably influenced many accounting theorists, one who admits to being an adherent is Barbara Merino. Most of her research has been in the history of accounting (see, for example Merino (1989).

9 McCloskey later expanded the argument and published a book by the same name: *The rhetoric of economics* 1998, University of Wisconsin Press, Madison, WI. Other economic rhetoricians have criticised that work as being too conservative and deferential to neoclassical economics and have greatly extended the arguments of the rhetoric of economics movement; for example, James Arnt Aune's *Selling the free market: the rhetoric of economic correctness* 2001, The Guilford Press, New York. Arnt Aune argues, like Mouck (1992), that neoclassical economists have resorted to various rhetorical devices to sell the idea of the free market but he goes further and demonstrates that politicians and commentators (including novelists) have also rhetorically contributed to the selling of liberalisation, privatisation, globalisation and transnationalisation (i.e. the free market and minimum political intervention) economic (and social) policies.

10 There have been many other proposed approaches, which have drawn on the work of philosophers or social theorists. For example, labour process studies initially drew on Marxian ideas; actor network theories drew on the work of French techno-scientists, Latour, Callon and others; post-colonial theoretical studies used as a starting point the legacy of colonisation. There have also been historical sociological studies—the new history. See Lodh & Gaffikin (1997).

REFERENCES AND FURTHER READING

Arrington, CE & Francis J 1989, 'Letting the chat out of the bag: deconstruction, privilege and accounting research', *Accounting, Organizations and Society*, vol. 14, pp. 1–28.

Arrington, CE & Schweiker, W 1992, 'The rhetoric and rationality of accounting research', *Accounting, Organizations and Society*, vol. 17, pp. 511–533.

Boland, R 1989, 'Beyond the objectivist and the subjectivist: learning to read accounting as text', *Accounting, Organizations and Society*, vol. 14, pp. 591–604.

Broadbent, Jane 2002, 'Critical accounting research: a view from England', *Critical Perspectives in Accounting*, vol. 13, pp. 433–449.

Christenson, C 1983, 'The methodology of positive accounting', *The Accounting Review*, vol. 58, pp. 1–22.

Chua, Wai Fong 1986, 'Radical developments in accounting thought', *The Accounting Review*, vol. 61, pp. 601–632.

Chua, Wai Fong 1988, 'Interpretive sociology and management accounting research—a critical review', *Accounting, Auditing and Accountability*, vol. 1, pp. 59–79.

Chua, Wai Fong, Lowe, Tony & Puxty, Tony, eds 1989, *Critical perspectives in management control*, The Macmillan Press Ltd, Basingstoke, UK.

Davis, SW, Menon, K & Morgan, G 1982, 'The images that have shaped accounting theory', *Accounting, Organizations and Society*, vol. 7, pp. 307–318.

Dillard, Jesse 1991, 'Accounting as a critical social science', *Accounting, Auditing and Accountability Journal*, vol. 4, pp. 8–28.

Gaffikin, Michael 2005, 'The idea of accounting', in Funnell, W & Williams, R, eds 2005, *Critical and historical studies in accounting*, Pearson Education Australia, Sydney, pp. 1–24.

Gambling, Trevor 1974, *Societal accounting*, George Allen and Unwin Ltd, London.

Hopwood, Anthony 1989, 'Accounting and the pursuit of social interests', in Chua et al., eds, op. cit., pp. 141–157.

Hoskin, K & Macve, R 1986, 'Accounting and the examination: a genealogy of disciplinary power', *Accounting, Organizations and Society*, vol. 11, pp. 105–136.

Ladd, Dwight R 1963, *Contemporary corporate accounting and the public*, Richard D Irwin Inc., Homewood, Illinois, US.

Laughlin, R 1987, 'Accounting systems in organisational contexts: a case for critical theory', *Accounting, Organizations and Society*, vol. 15, pp. 479–502.

Laughlin, R 1999, 'Critical accounting: nature, progress and prognosis', *Accounting, Auditing and Accountability Journal*, vol. 12, pp. 73–78.

Laughlin, R & Broadbent, J 1993, 'Accounting and law: partners in the juridification of the public sector in the UK?', *Critical Perspectives in Accounting*, vol. 4, pp. 337–368.

Lodh, S & Gaffikin, MJR 1997, 'Critical studies in accounting research, rationality and Habermas: a methodological reflection', *Critical Perspectives on Accounting*, vol. 8, pp. 433–474.

Loft, A 1986, 'Towards a critical understanding of accounting: the case of cost accounting in the UK, 1914–1925', *Accounting, Organizations and Society*, vol. 11, pp. 137–169.

Lowe, Tony & Tinker, Tony 1989, 'Accounting as social science: abstract versus concrete sources of accounting change', in Chua et al., eds, op. cit., pp. 47–61.

Macintosh, NB 2002, *Accounting, accountants and accountability: post-structural positions*, Routledge, London.

Mautz, RK 1963, 'Accounting as a social science', *The Accounting Review*, pp. 317–325.

Merino, Barbara 1989, 'An analysis of the development of accounting knowledge: a pragmatic approach', paper presented at the Studies in Accounting as a Human Practice Conference, University of Iowa, US.

Morgan, Gareth 1983, 'Social science and accounting research: a commentary on Tomkins and Groves', *Accounting, Organizations and Society*, vol. 8, pp 385–388.

Mouck, Tom 1992, 'The rhetoric of science and the rhetoric of revolt in the "story" of positive accounting theory', *Accounting, Auditing and Accountability Journal*, vol. 5, pp. 35–56.

Rorty, Richard 1992, *The linguistic turn*, The University of Chicago Press, Chicago, US.

Scott, DR 1931, *The cultural significance of accounts*, Henry Holt, New York.

Sikka, P & Wilmott, H 1997, 'Practicing critical accounting', *Critical Perspectives in Accounting*, vol. 8, pp. 149–165.

Simons, Jon, ed. 2004, *Contemporary critical theory*, Edinburgh Press, Edinburgh, Scotland.

Stewart, Ross 1992, 'Pluralizing our past: Foucault in accounting history', *Accounting, Auditing and Accountability Journal*, vol. 5, pp. 57–74.

Tomkins, C & Groves, R 1983, 'The everyday accountant and researching his reality', *Accounting, Organizations and Society*, vol. 8, pp. 361–374.

Wilmott, Hugh C 1983, 'Paradigms for accounting research: critical reflections on Tomkins and Groves' "Everyday accountant and researching his reality"', *Accounting, Organizations and Society*, vol. 8, pp. 389–405.

CHAPTER 8

The Ethical Dimension

The question of how we should lead our lives was a central concern of Classical Greek scholars and has led to considerable debate and discussion ever since. A central issue is how individuals respond to the broader interests of others within societies: to what extent can we pursue our own interests without impinging on the rights and needs of others who make up the societies in which we exist? These concerns are usually referred to as the moral or ethical responsibilities that all members of society should be aware of in the interests of building a better and more just society. The extent to which such considerations affect the behaviour of accountants is the subject of this chapter. ■

I t has often been suggested that the expression 'business ethics' is an oxymoron—it employs contradictory terms because business seeks to maximise gains from its operations, while ethics implies a very different basis for business practice. Although the more cynically minded would subscribe to this view, there has been a very dramatic upturn in interest in ethical considerations by business leaders and professional business organisations, partly as a result of the demands of societies which have had to bear the costs of spectacular corporate collapses and the unscrupulous business activities of a minority of business practitioners. In fact, the subject has become an industry, spawning books, courses, seminars, workshops, lectures and models, as well as ever-increasing comment and debate in the public media.

All people have some inner understanding of what constitutes ethical behaviour, but problems arise when it comes down to defining ethics, as our definition is shaped by personal, cultural, societal and professional values, all of which are difficult to specify. Some stress the importance of society's interests; others stress the interests of the individual. These conflicting viewpoints have dominated the discussion of ethics for a long time. Most are agreed that ethical belief systems emerge from a community—from a social or cultural context, or what Blackburn (2001) calls 'the surrounding climate of ideas about how to live' (p. 1).

Basic moral considerations

When examining the issue of ethics there are some basic moral considerations on which to reflect. They involve questioning the extent to which the following affect attitudes to determining what constitutes moral behaviour and how this impacts on an understanding of ethics:

1 Religion (divine command theories)
2 Conscience
3 Selfishness
4 Respect
5 Rights
6 Utilitarianism
7 Justice
8 Virtue.

Many people believe that ethical behaviour is shaped by moral principles laid down in religions—that there is an authoritative code of instructions on how to behave. While this seems well and good, history has demonstrated that in most religions the determination of these principles has been subject to considerable debate and has even resulted in practices which seem, to an outside observer, to have little connection with moral behaviour. For example, one of the commandments said to be at the base of Christianity is 'Thou shalt not kill', yet societies throughout history have rationalised this away in times of war and for activities such as burning of witches and capital punishment. Christianity, of course, is not alone in this! Hinduism is built around a caste system which subjects certain groups to what outsiders see as extreme forms of prejudice and disadvantage. Islam has a penal code which seems to the outside observer as involving extremely harsh forms of punishment. There are probably similar apparent inconsistencies in other religions, all of which suggest that the connections between religion and moral behaviour are not necessarily absolute. Also, in Western societies, with the rise of humanism, so much a part of the post-Enlightenment modernist spirit, the influence of religion has diminished. There is increasing secularisation—a breakdown in the influence of organised religion. Yet people still behave according to, and feel the need to abide by, 'moral principles'.

The question of whether humans are innately good or bad has troubled not only religious scholars but philosophers as well in the significant field known as 'moral philosophy'. For example, the 17th-century philosopher, Thomas Hobbes, introduced the notion of **psychological egoism**, which holds that humans are intrinsically nasty entities. Such a notion, of course, is hugely reductionist: is it possible to generalise this view to *all* human beings? To attempt to overcome this difficulty, Hobbes's solution was to develop the notion of the **social contract**. This is an 'agreement' entered into by people in a society in order to avoid social conflict. Everyone consents to a legal agreement not to engage in activities such as killing others or stealing from others because it is in their own best interests. This social contract is enforced by a neutral third party—government. For Hobbes and his followers strong governments are desirable.

Initial questions

Prior to arriving at an understanding of what ethical behaviour is there are some preliminary considerations: issues about which we must have some idea (*a priori*) in order to arrive at a theoretical basis for deciding what is and what is not ethical. These are at least some of the questions a philosopher would need to ask, most of which are closely interrelated:

1 What is the basis of human nature/behaviour?
2 Are some people better at being moral?
3 Do we have the right to dictate morality?
4 Are there acts which are universally wrong (e.g. torturing children)? If so, what are they?

5 Is ethics a special kind of knowledge?

6 Is morality about obeying rules or considering consequences?

7 Is there a difference between society's laws and moral laws? If so what are they?

8 Why should we be better people?

9 When people say they know a thing is wrong (e.g. murder), how do they know this?

As the previous section indicated, the basis of human nature is a big question and involves a great many considerations. Most ethical theorists or philosophers usually start with what they perceive as the defining characteristics of human behaviour. Being such an unresolved area means, of course, that it opens up any subsequent discussion to question. However, it does provide an overall framework for any subsequent discussion. For example, Hobbes was able to develop an argument for the need for strong government because he conceived humans as innately nasty. Other ethicists have different 'definitions' on which they base their arguments. So, if there is some 'definition' of human behaviour, it will be easier to decide whether some people are more predisposed to being moral than others. Some ethicists start with an assumption diametrically opposed to that of Hobbes: that is, that humans are intrinsically 'good', not nasty. Some even believe this to be genetically determined, that we have a 'social gene', so morality is seen as instinctive behaviour.

Whether we have the right to dictate ethics to others involves deciding on the issue of **moral relativism** as opposed to **moral absolutism**. Moral relativism means that morality is determined by the culture or subculture (country, tribe, class, time or whatever) in which one exists. This argument has been used to justify the payment of bribes in some countries to procure business favours on the basis that it is 'acceptable business practice' in those countries. Ethical absolutists (also referred to as universalists or realists) would disagree with that suggestion because there are universal 'standards' or 'rules' of ethical business behaviour that prohibit the payment of bribes. Obviously, both positions are somewhat precarious. There are, of course, much bigger issues than bribery—such as torture, genocide and poverty—so both positions are also very complex. Absolutists have a problem in defining and justifying an adopted stance, while relativists would have us ignore certain behaviours that would be quite abhorrent to most people. The ontological basis for moral relativism is constructionist, for moral absolutism it is realism. Therefore, many of the arguments for and against each position discussed in previous chapters (such as the critique of various ontological presuppositions) are relevant here.

Two people who feature large in any discussion of ethics are Jeremy Bentham (1748–1832) and Immanuel Kant (1724–1804). Bentham was the founder, along with JS Mill, of a movement known as **utilitarianism**, and both have also significantly influenced economic thought. According to utilitarianism, an action is right if and only if it conforms to the principle of utility; that is, it will be more productive of pleasure or happiness or it will better prevent pain or unhappiness than an alternative. Just how right an action is depends entirely on its consequences and this is why this theory is also referred to as consequentialism (or act-utilitarianism). In determining whether a particular act is right, it is the value of the consequences of the act that is important. This sounds dangerously like 'the ends justifies the means', and one of the main criticisms of act-utilitarianism is that the actual act is not considered, just the consequences. The position was therefore reformulated as rule-utilitarianism whereby the value of consequences is considered on the basis of a sort of cost–benefit analysis. Rather than looking at the value of a particular act, rule-utilitarianism is concerned with determining the value of the consequences by following the best *rule of conduct*. One disadvantage of this, of course, is that it works on generalisations rather than on specific situations, because rules are generalisations. Therefore, it might not help in certain specific circumstances. Also, determining what the best rule is is not likely to be a simple process. Nevertheless, rule-utilitarianism has been held for many years to be a valid means of assessing ethical behaviour.

When discussing values and consequences, it is necessary to ask: for whom are the consequences? A Hobbesian position would look at the individual's self-interest—psychological egoism—whereas a consequentialist would wish to determine the consequences for all parties affected by a particular action. Recall from Chapter 1 that psychological egoism—the pursuit of self-interest—influenced economic thought. Consequently, it seems paradoxical that it is also the basis of a perspective on ethics—ethical egoism. However, there are numerous variants of utilitarianism, each differing in the extent to which they emphasise the pursuit of self-interest, pleasure or happiness, or the rightness of actions.

Purposive explanations are said to be **teleological**; that is, they are explanations in terms of final causes. Utilitarianism is teleological because actions are assessed in terms of their consequences—the final or end result. Kant believed that morality rarely had anything to do with happiness. Thus, a moral action is one which is done from a *sense of duty*. Ethics is about what these duties are. Kant's position is known as a deontological one—he was a deontologist, a believer in duties and right conduct. In **deontology** the emphasis is on individual duty, such as telling the truth, acting justly or keeping promises. Kant held that there are two foundational principles. First, always act on a principle that you are willing to have everyone else act upon. Second, always be respectful of others (and yourself). These form part of what Kant referred to as the **categorical imperative**, which is a compulsory moral law designed as a method to guide free human action. These laws are determined by applying the **universability test**—a process of using our reason to ask: what would happen if we 'universalised' what we wanted to do? For example, what would happen if everyone stole from everybody else? So, do not steal. This is an act according to the principle (maxim) that you believe should be a universal rule of behaviour.[1]

Although hugely influential in the field of moral philosophy, Kant's deontological position is at times too inflexible—it is absolutist in its claim that there is a single moral 'truth' to which all people should comply. For example, *always* telling the truth may sometimes be inappropriate, such as at times when the safety or well-being of others is involved. In other words, it may at times be necessary to lie to protect others.

The teleological and deontological theories of ethics are usually classified as normative. Although they are very different they both classify actions as right or wrong and seek to establish standards of rightness or wrongness. Thus, they are concerned with norms of behaviour.

Metaethics

David Hume, who lived around the same time as Kant, introduced a type of moral philosophy known as metaethics. This is the study of moral language and its meaning and certainty. It is an investigation into the nature of ethical concepts and propositions and applies strict rules of deductive logic. Metaethics addresses the following types of questions:

1 Semantic questions, such as the meaning of moral terms (e.g. good, right and ought)
2 Logical questions, such as the (syllogistic) validity of moral arguments
3 Ontological questions, such as the existence of moral facts
4 Epistemological questions, such as the possibility of moral knowledge and, if it does exist, the scope of such knowledge.

An often quoted example of Hume's concept of metaethics lies in the statement, 'murder is wrong'. It is not possible, according to Hume, to 'prove' such a statement because it is not an empirical observation, but a moral belief. Hume was a radical empiricist and, like the positivists, made the distinction between factual and moral statements. The same distinction is made by positive accounting theorists, that is, between 'is' and 'ought' statements. Therefore, someone who says murder is wrong is merely stating that she or he disapproves of murder. Hume argued that moral beliefs were psychological rather than logical or empirical but, unlike the later positivists, he also argued that they were far from trivial or meaningless. This was the position adopted far more aggressively by the 20th-century positivist philosopher, AJ Ayer, for whom moral language was indeed meaningless. For him, moral philosophy was some kind of linguistic and logical error and there was no such thing as moral knowledge. Such discourses he called **emotivism**.[2]

The relationships between the various theories of ethics can be seen in diagrammatic form in Figure 8.1.

Rights and justice

Returning to the deontological positions described above, there are two notions that need to be considered as they underlie more recent developments in deontological thinking (since Kant)—rights and justice. A right is an entitlement and should not be confused with a duty (an obligation). The American political and moral philosopher, John Rawls, was interested in which social and legal agreements would make a more just society. His work has become part of what is referred to as **social ethics** and his book, *A theory of justice* (1971), is generally regarded as one of the most significant works on political philosophy of the 20th century. In the book he attempts to develop

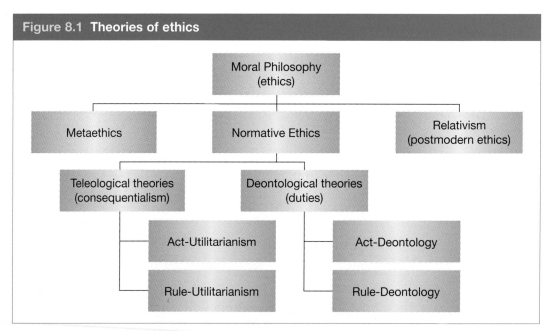

Figure 8.1 Theories of ethics

Source: This diagram was influenced by (but is not the same as) an exhibit in Paul Northcott's, *Ethics and the Certified Practising Accountant*, Australian Society of Certified Practising Accountants, Melbourne, 1993, p. 4.

a justification for a concept of social justice, namely, justice as fairness. He also revives the notion of the social contract—a series of rules that society considers necessary to make a just and fair community. These 'rules' are so created to ensure that the least well-off in a society are protected and, because of an uncertain future (what he calls a 'veil of ignorance'), that societies will preserve these 'rules' to protect themselves (in case they fall into the less well-off category). Two principles emerge—of justice and fairness:

> First Principle: Each person is to have an equal right to the most extensive total system of equal basic liberties compatible with a similar system of liberty for all.
> Second Principle: Social and economic inequalities are to be arranged so that they are both:
> a   to the greatest benefit of the least advantaged, consistent with the just savings principle, and
> b   attached to offices and positions open to all under conditions of fair equality of opportunity.

The first principle takes precedence over the second.

Rawls's theory has been criticised from many angles, ranging from those who argue that he ignores individual property rights (Nozick) to those who argue that he ignores community interests!

Virtue

Another American philosopher, Alasdair MacIntyre, believed that modern ethics was in deep trouble. He argued that the differences between deontology and utilitarianism were basically irresolvable and sterile. There was too much concentration on individuals and their private moral decisions. What was needed, he argued, was attention to the community and its moral health and welfare. Returning to Aristotle's position, he suggested that we should be concentrating on what sort of people we should be rather than the things that we do. This is referred to as **virtue theory**.

The Ancient Greeks spent considerable time pondering what makes a 'good person', and their thoughts have formed part of the background of Western moral philosophy throughout history. For them, generally speaking, a 'good person' was a 'good citizen' who contributed to the state. So there were political undertones to how they envisaged morality. A well-known catchcry of Socrates was 'the unexamined life is not worth living', so it was important that people continually questioned themselves and their motives. His thinking was teleological in that humans had an ultimate purpose and there was a 'real self' inside, which was only discovered through self-reflection and, through this process, what was right and just would become known.

His pupil, Plato, was a rationalist. He believed (basically) that pure forms, including morality, existed and could only be discovered through reasoning. Plato, therefore, was a moral absolutist—he believed that moral facts existed. For Plato, morality of the individual and morality of the state were the same thing. The individual needed to discover this morality, the moral facts, through reasoning.

Perhaps the most important of the Greek thinkers is Plato's student, Aristotle, whose best known relevant work is his *Nichomachean ethics*. Everyone says the good life is about happiness, but it is hard to know what happiness consists of. Aristotle says the answer lies in determining what humans are—or their function—so happiness results when humans function well. He is not interested in abstractions but in the everyday 'goodness' that most people choose. We live in societies and we need to behave morally towards one another. Governments should reflect this and encourage justice, fairness, temperance, courage and so on. This is the virtuous life and people need to be educated to bring out the latent goodness in them. Virtue theory is communitarian.

MacIntyre (1984) resurrected and updated many of Aristotle's positions. In his virtue theory the focus is on personal disposition and character, the moral qualities of a person. In summary:

- The good person knows the right thing to do.
- It is necessary to identify qualities that are virtues.
- Societal virtues arise from community/profession/tradition.
- It is necessary to distinguish between:
  - external goods (e.g. wealth, status, power, pleasure), and
  - internal goods (e.g. honesty, respect).

For the Classical Athenians the notion of a 'good man' had a concrete factual meaning. MacIntyre argued that this position had been eroded by sceptics like Hume and Ayer, while Kant had made morality a cold and unsympathetic exercise in reason and the utilitarians had reduced it to a set of pseudo-scientific calculations. This constant erosion of moral beliefs had led to the emptiness of philosophies such as Ayer's emotivism, which totally ignored all notions of community or communal values. This, according to MacIntyre, had led to societies devoid of moral values in which people were at times utilitarians, at other times Kantians, but generally utterly confused. MacIntyre concluded, however, that we are all essentially communitarian with lives bound by moral traditions and that we should continue to develop these traditions.

Although many philosophers agree that the direction MacIntyre has taken is the most promising for establishing ethical behaviour, one major problem remains: what

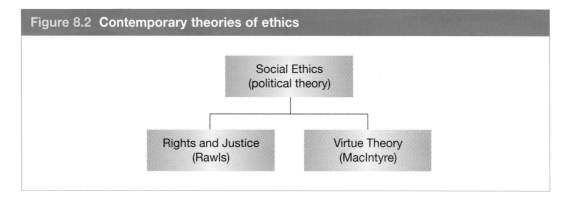

Figure 8.2 **Contemporary theories of ethics**

will the virtues be? Both historically and culturally there have been many differences in what has been considered virtuous.

Figure 8.2 graphically presents the major contemporary theories of ethics.

Moral development

An alternative approach to ethics is to consider the processes people follow in decision making and what level of moral reasoning is involved. Thus, while not a theory of ethics, this approach is useful in discussing business ethical behaviour because decision-making is a central feature of business analysis. This was the approach adopted by American educational theorist Lawrence Kohlberg. Although Kohlberg's interest was in examining the moral development of students, his work has been generalised to other fields where the emphasis is on the moral development of individuals as reflected in the reasoning they employ when making decisions. Kohlberg (1969) identified three levels of development, each with two stages. The levels are hierarchical in that people move from the lowest level to the highest—they progress in their moral reasoning (through social interaction) from pre-conventional (the lowest) through conventional to the post-conventional level. Kohlberg was not concerned with the decision (yes or no) but with the reasoning behind the decision. His work was influenced by, and built on the work of, the Swiss psychologist, Jean Piaget, who had built a two-stage theory. Kohlberg's stages are summarised in Table 8.1 (overleaf).

In the first stage of the pre-conventional level, people behave according to socially acceptable norms because they are told to do so by an authority figure. It is assumed that powerful authorities hand down a fixed set of rules which must be unquestioningly obeyed. This obedience is compelled by the threat or application of punishment. The second stage is characterised by a view that right behaviour means acting in one's own best interests because it is recognised that there is no *one* authority but many authorities, each with a different viewpoint.

Table 8.1 **Kohlberg's stages in moral development**

Level	Stage	Social orientation
Pre-conventional	1	Obedience and punishment
	2	Individualism and exchange
Conventional	3	Good interpersonal relationships
	4	Maintaining the social order
Post-conventional	5	Social contract and individual rights
	6	Universal principles

At the second level of moral thinking there is a shift from unquestioning obedience to a relativistic outlook and a concern for good motives. Stage 3 is characterised by an attitude that seeks to do what will gain the approval of others, while stage 4 is oriented towards maintaining the social order: what would it be like if everyone stole?' is the typical sort of response. Therefore, while the question in stage 4 is the same as in stage 1, the consideration is now for social order.

By stage 5 there is an understanding of social mutuality and a genuine interest in the welfare of others, with a view to creating a good society—envisaged as one having a social contract into which people freely enter, to work towards the benefit of all. The final stage (stage 6) is based on respect for universal principles and the demands of the individual conscience, the pursuit of which could even countenance civil disobedience.

Individuals move through each of the stages—that is, they do not skip a stage but progress through each to the next highest. However, not all (probably very few, in fact) reach the post-conventional stages, despite this being the level which Kohlberg believed to be the most desirable and as having the best outcome (that is, moral development of each individual).

Not all people agree with Kohlberg's analysis. There are epistemological issues: for example, to what extent is the hierarchy universal—does it apply universally (which is probably what Kohlberg believed)? It has also been argued that in developing his theory he ignored cultural and gender issues. Does it have a Western bias? Does it apply in Eastern cultures? Does it apply at the level of traditional village cultures? Is it male oriented? Conservatives do not accept his post-conventional stage because of its implications for possible social disruption by those arguing for universal principles. That is, it may not be desirable to have people put their values above society and the law. His theory indicates moral reasoning and not moral actions. Commentators looking for quantitative indicators are also disappointed because it is very much the result of qualitative analysis. There are also questions surrounding the sequencing, which some have found awkward: how do people proceed through the levels and are the levels in fact hierarchical? And, once someone reaches a higher level, does that mean that the previous levels are inferior?

Despite the criticisms and the fact that he was looking at moral development of children, he has presented a very useful framework for investigating moral reasoning. For example, the independence of auditors requires them to have reached a high stage of moral development in order that they avoid conflicts of interest. A study by Gaffikin and Lindawati (2005) used Kohlberg's framework to investigate the extent to which accountants in Indonesia resist pressure from corporate clients in exercising independence in undertaking auditing responsibilities. Several other studies have investigated the level of moral reasoning by accountants and in public accounting firms (e.g. Dellaportas et al. 2005, pp. 48–49).

Ethics and professional practice

There is little doubt that the general public concern about ethical issues has impacted on business practice. Most professional bodies have some form of ethical statement in respect of the operation of their organisations. Professional accounting bodies usually have codes of ethics with which they expect their members to comply. These have changed over the years from statements governing how members should interact with other members to codes placing greater emphasis on ensuring that members' behaviour complies with perceived public expectations. Members' involvement with large corporate collapses and fraud scandals obviously reflect badly on the profession, although the vast majority of members do not become embroiled in such matters.

The notion of codes of ethics of professional bodies is inextricably linked to the notion of professionalism. Parker (1987) has shown that as professional accounting bodies in Australia developed so too did ethical rules for accountants—they were a part of the professional bodies' requirements of members. Late in the 20th century the two major professional accounting bodies in Australia (CPA Australia and ICAA) developed a *Joint code of professional conduct*. This was a set of ethical requirements common to both professional bodies. However, with the growing internationalisation of accounting regulation, the *Joint code* was replaced by a Professional Standard, *APES 110 code of ethics for professional accountants*. This was a requirement of the International Federation of Accountants (IFAC). Members (national professional bodies) are not permitted to issue ethical requirements less stringent than those proposed by IFAC so, as with the accounting standards (IFRS), the Australian professional accounting bodies have adopted the IFAC statement (with some very minor differences being clearly indicated with the letters AUST).[3]

Although the details of this and other codes are interesting, the primary concern here is with theoretical considerations.[4] To this end, some elements of these codes are important: for example, what is meant by the term 'profession'? What is the 'public interest'? How does the imposition of codes of behaviour relate to the discussion of regulation in previous chapters? In addition, the APES Code claims to have set out a 'conceptual framework' (for determining ethical behaviour). What are its elements? It is also interesting to note that the Code requires members to comply not only with the terms of the Code but also with the spirit of the Code. So, how is this achieved?

The idea of a profession

One of the earliest statements in the Code is the claim that 'A distinguishing mark of the accountancy profession is the acceptance of the responsibility to act in the public interest'. However, the meaning of 'profession' is elusive and it has been the subject of considerable debate over the years. As Longstaff (1995) states, 'professions do not have a right to exist. They are not the product of a law of nature . . . Rather, the professions are a social artefact.'

In earlier (pre-modern) times there were only three recognised professions—law, medicine and divinity. Sometimes officers in the army or navy were also afforded the title. A typical dictionary definition is likely to suggest that a profession is an occupational group characterised by claims to a high level of technical competence or expertise, autonomy in recruitment and discipline, and a commitment to public service.[5] Many lists of characteristics of 'a profession' have been provided by different authors and six of the most commonly mentioned in these lists[6] are:

1 Possession of a skill based on theoretical knowledge
2 Provision of training and an education
3 Testing of competence of members
4 Organisation
5 Adherence to a code of conduct
6 Altruistic service.

It is interesting to note that in all of these discussions on a definition for 'profession' a commitment to public service and ethics is a dominant characteristic.[7] More recently, the discussion has moved away from defining 'profession' to an interest in the power that professions have in societies—that is, the power of professionals to delimit and control their work. Traditionally professionals have exercised a high degree of self-regulation free from external control. It has been suggested that:

> . . . professions are exclusive occupational groups which exercise jurisdiction over particular areas of work. This jurisdiction is held to rest on the control of a more-or-less abstract, esoteric and intellectual body of knowledge (Abbott, in Kuper and Kuper 2003, p. 677).

For some, the status of a profession is more a reflection of self-interest—that is, maintaining control over entry in order to command high material rewards—than public service. But Samuels argues that 'the destructive consequences of untrammelled economic exploitation are held at bay by professionalism . . . where service rather than profit becomes the professional label' (quoted by Longstaff 1995, p. 3). Thus, societies tolerate such occupational grouping in the belief that the interests of the community will be promoted; in fact, privileges are accorded professionals in return for social benefits. This has echoes of Hobbes's social contract and Rawls's rules.

It is clear from the earlier quotation from the accounting Code that service in the public interest is seen as a defining professional attribute. This certainly meets Longstaff's requirement that 'If accountants are to remain part of a true profession, then their response to the community should be an unambiguous declaration of allegiance to the overriding principle of public service' (p. 17). But does this hold in practice? What role did accountants play in recent corporate fraud scandals and collapses? Why was the profession silent in the debate on the AWB wheat sales to Iraq scandal?[8]

In the public interest

While there have been many pronouncements about 'public service' and 'public interest', determining any sensible meaning of these terms is fraught with ambiguity. Not only does this issue involve all the philosophical concerns discussed above but it also has strong political implications. 'Public interest' can be defined or described only in the context of political preconceptions. Plato indicated that 'any theory of man, implicit or explicit, will be reflected in a theory of the state', and Aristotle held that ethics was just a branch of politics. This is simply because we are all members of a community, a society, over which there will be some form of governance. What is important is to determine the appropriate role of the state and the level of such governance. This is not a simple matter. To some extent the argument is circular in that the state influences what the public interest is, yet it is the public interest that shapes the form of the state; it is a matter of balancing individual interest with community or group interests, and this has been a concern of philosophers for thousands of years. For development of the individual Hobbes and his followers argued for strong government, but in the modernist era (Western) societies have rejected absolutist governments. Thus, any use of terms such as 'in the public interest' necessitates some notion of balance between individual and community interests. In recent times these interests have been described as 'rights' and so the debate revolves around the question: what are individual rights as opposed to communal rights? This is the question for which Rawls provided a solution—his just society (discussed above).

The public interest will always be determined by the form a society takes. There are many different societal 'forms'. For example, some are dominated by a particular religion; some by a strict class or caste system; some by a single political party which has central economic planning; some by strong traditional family ties; some will be governed by military interests; and some are dominated by those able to wield strong economic power. In practice, most societies are influenced by a combination of many of these factors, with varying emphasis on each. Consequently, in an Islamic state, business and professional ethics are determined by Islamic precepts (Sharia law).[9] In a totalitarian—say, communist—state, they are determined by the state (government). In a military dictatorship, military law or might determines acceptable order. In a society with a caste system, relationships between certain classes are prohibited or clearly defined. And modern (or late) capitalist societies generally sanction the pursuit of economic gain and consumerism, but with varying degrees of restriction. This is the core of the issue at hand: the balancing of social or community benefits against the pursuit of individual economic gain.

At the core of capitalist societies is the ideology of individualism—the freedom to make (economic and other) choices. This individual freedom has to be balanced with some level of community or social responsibility. Many commentators (philosophers, sociologists, politicians and the like) argue that this balance is determined through reason—that is, rationally:

> Many ethical theorists believe that it is reason itself that makes these demands, to go beyond intuitionism into a more fully articulated ethical theory. They think that what I have called rationalism simply follows from being rational (Williams 1985, p. 101).[10]

This raises the equally complex matter of defining rationality. Rationality involves knowledge, and knowledge is power. Knowledge is presented by those in power positions as objective knowledge about human beings—rationality. Therefore, those with this 'knowledge' will present it as universal—it is rational so it must apply everywhere (universally). Anyone who disagrees with this 'knowledge' is adjudged irrational, even 'mad'. Thus, rationality is defined by the powerful and represents the dominant societal ideology. The 'powerful' represent those who wield political power or influence. Hence, what is in the public interest will be determined politically, which is consistent with what Plato is espousing in the quotation above—the significance of a 'theory of the state'. It is also a necessary prerequisite for Rawls's just society. For Rawls, the process of arriving at a definition of 'public interest' must be transparent because his just society is comprised of people committed to living closely together as a society. Therefore, they should arrive at publicly stateable, and thus *rational*, principles. Recall from the earlier discussion of his work that there is a 'contractible' obligation of members of a society to have some agreed beliefs and authoritative procedures—the publicly stateable principles—for resolving conflicts and avoiding violence.

To summarise the discussion so far, among the defining characteristics of a profession is having a code of ethical conduct which demonstrates that its members will offer their services to the public and work in the public interest. However, when examined more closely, it is revealed that while this may sound attractive it involves the confusing and complex task of determining just what the public interest is—a highly contestable and elusive concept. This in turn involves the equally complex processes of determining just what rationality is and of balancing the rights of individuals and groups. Many theoretical positions on these topics have been presented over the years, but the issues still remain clouded, open to conjecture and complicated, because every suggested position has strong political overtones.

Balancing individual and group rights

A dominant theme in this book is the role of regulation in contemporary capitalist societies such as Australia. The question again arises in determining which policies to pursue in balancing the rights of individuals against those of broader groups, or society generally. It is relevant to this discussion because it has been shown that questions of ethics always intimately involve political considerations—problems for public policy as well as for the lifestyles of individual members of society. However, the individual and the community represent the two extreme positions, and there are very many situations between these positions as contemporary societies are made up of many groups of citizens (and many instances of cross membership of these groups). For example, a profession is one group. Therefore, there may be a conflict of interests for an accountant who may have to balance his or her interests as a member of a professional accounting body with those of his or her religious (or family or other) community, leading to the question: which takes precedence? Ethical considerations are not always linear!

Modern Western societies claim to promote and protect individual freedoms. Such freedoms take various forms and Rist (2002) has called the two extremes, 'Tolerant Diversity' and 'Corporate Unity' (p. 229). Societies are tolerant of the desires of individuals in the interests of diversity in society; however, individual goals tend to be 'destructive of the goals of others' so regulation is necessary to allow opportunity for others. It is very difficult to decide the form and extent of such regulation in order to promote fairness for all: 'it will be *unfair* to some to tolerate the "excesses" of others, or that there is no *reason* to tolerate the claims of one at the expense of another' (p. 229, emphasis in the original).

A variation on individualism is the development of group individualism—pressure groups 'whose leaders view their organizations as extensions and organs of themselves' (p. 230). These include minority groups, as well as other similar organisations such as gay rights groups, the religious right, women's rights groups, and even seemingly less socially desirable groups such as the gun lobby. Toleration is the catchcry and Rawls would have the state as arbiter in determining the fairest distribution of freedoms. Just how it does this is quite perplexing. Although democracy is the political form in many countries, not only are governments voted in by a minority of the population—especially where voting is not compulsory—but they are subject to pressures from various interest groups and, increasingly, the lobbying by some groups that goes beyond traditional national boundaries. As Rist (p. 231) has so eloquently pointed out:

> Confronted with the gradual materialization of the global village, its ever expanding demands fuelled by advertising and consumerism at the economic level, and potentially even more destructive at the political level: threatened, that is, by an exteriorized unity of mankind without community; what sort of public policy should we advocate?

This is evident in accounting in the lobbying of the IASB and other bodies for the (successful) adoption of IFRS. Professional accounting bodies themselves have created further uncertainties in respect of defining public interest. They have done this through their peculiar growth strategy of aggressively extending their membership and spheres of influence across national boundaries. Thus we have professional bodies granted a charter (which usually states that the public interest is the foremost consideration) in the UK having branches through Asia, Africa and Australasia. Even Australian bodies have similar growth expansion strategies. Are they really representing their members' (professional) interests or, more importantly, advancing the public interest, or have they taken on a form of their own ('bigger is better') whereby the body representing professionals is not being very professional itself?

The issue of public interest continues to be a deeply contested notion, yet it remains the cornerstone of claims to professional status. Puxty et al. (1994) have demonstrated that in the UK professional accounting bodies have resisted responsibility for the detection of fraud being thrust upon auditors. In fact, the chairman of a committee set up by the ICAEW is quoted as saying in a report:

> . . . the normal business relationship between the auditor and the client company was founded on trust and confidence. We do not feel that the business could be sensibly conducted if the auditor was recognised as a mole or informant who could secretly inform a Government agency that he suspected wrongdoing in the conduct of a client's affairs . . .'
> (Lord Benson, quoted in Puxty et al. 1994).

Given the public reaction to scandals such as the Enron collapse in the US and HIH's demise in Australia, it would seem that Benson's sentiments do not convey a sense of the auditor's role in protecting the public interest.[11] Puxty et al. also show how, over the years, accountancy bodies in the UK have lobbied company reform committees to prevent companies being required to make full financial disclosures in published financial statements. Clearly this is action in the interests of the clients of their members and not in the public interest. These are the sort of pressures (the lobbying by apparently influential interested parties) facing regulators and would seem to be an argument against self-regulation by the profession—another claimed hallmark of professionalism. As stated earlier, knowledge is power, so if those with that knowledge claim a special status and that they are preserving the public interest, that knowledge must be used judiciously.

Righteousness in an age of uncertainty

It was relatively easy for those like Kant, the citadel of certainty, to know right from wrong. For him, morality had nothing to do with happiness, as the utilitarianists believed; rather, a moral action was done out of a sense of duty, such duty being determined through *reason*. The certainty he expressed became a hallmark of modernist thinking. However, as the discussion so far has demonstrated, an accountant today would be far from certain as to which of the many arguments on ethics would lead to the most appropriate course of action. Unfortunately, we do not have the certainties that the modernists claimed and have to choose from a wide range of alternative courses of action. There is no *rational* basis for morality; rather it is shaped by circumstance, politics and the ideology of 'the powerful'—those with the capacity to persuade, or to prescribe what is appropriate. For example, a young accountant may be directed to follow a course of action in a particular situation because a superior says it is best for the firm and the client even though she or he believes it to be unethical.

The lack of moral certainty has led to appalling situations such as genocide, repression, torture, terrorism, environmental destruction and other evils, many of which have been justified on the basis of some so-called principle—and even public interest! In the business environment this has been manifest in the untrammelled greed, nepotism and corporate corruption that have often ended in economic injury or the ruin of many innocent participants. Despite the enthusiasm of modernist thinkers, this lack of certainty has long been recognised and can be dated back several thousand years to Ancient Greek scholars such as Protagoras (and the Sophists) and Socrates's friend Antistheses (and the Cynics), but it is also associated with the late 19th-century philosopher, Friedrich Nietzsche. It was to overcome this uncertainty that Alasdair MacIntyre resorted to a notion of another Greek scholar—Aristotle— when developing his virtue theory, discussed earlier in the chapter.

Aristotle argued that a 'good man' was one who possessed what he called *eudaimonia*, a word which has been difficult to translate but which would include notions of blessedness, happiness and prosperity. 'The virtues are precisely those qualities, the possession of which will enable an individual to achieve *eudaimonia*' (MacIntyre 1984, p. 149). In using Aristotle's notion of virtues MacIntyre obviously had a problem in attempting to define them in today's society. However, he believed that they could be derived from traditions—the wisdom of the ages.

Francis (1990) has addressed this question insofar as it affects accountants. He suggests five possible virtues that may be unique to the practice of accounting:

Honesty,

concern for the economic status of others,

sensitivity to the values of co-operation and conflict,

communicative character of accounting, and

dissemination of economic information.

However, there exist obstacles to the realisation of the virtues and he suggests three of these as:

the dominance of external rewards,

the corrupting power of intuitions, and

the failure to distinguish between virtues and laws.

The 'worship of money', he argues, has, in recent times, infected accounting practice and he concludes that 'Accounting, if it is to be virtuous, must celebrate itself as the unique creation of human labour and moral agency that it is' (Francis 1990, p. 15).

As accountants have long believed that they act value-neutrally, presumably they would also consider that there could be no issues in respect of gender in accounting. However, there are many who believe that gender is an important consideration in many facets of our societies. This does *not* mean there is an essential difference in the *nature* of men and women. The issue of whether there is an essential female nature is not relevant and, besides, some would argue that that view is merely an ideological construct. As with MacIntyre's position, the issue here concerns virtues rather than rights. Attention was drawn to the significance of gender in respect of ethics when Carol Gilligan pointed out that Kohlberg had used only a male sample in developing his stages of moral development. And as Reiter (1997) indicated, 'Gilligan showed that in moral discourse male subjects exhibit an orientation toward maximum autonomy and objectivity and an adherence to universal principles, while female subjects produce contextual responses' (p. 300). This gives rise to different ethical perspectives—the former has been referred to as the **ethics of rights** and the latter, as the **ethics of care**. In Kohlberg's model (a rights theory approach) the individual moves to greater independence and self-sufficiency. Gilligan (and others), however, argue that the ideal of a concerned and caring adulthood is a more appropriate basis for a just society. In practice, traditional 'female virtues' have been seen to be those of greater cooperation and caring; hence the name 'the ethics of care', which is associated more with feminine characteristics.

Reiter has argued that an ethics of care approach could assist the accounting profession in respect of matters of auditor independence in at least three ways:

1 In responding to crises concerning auditor independence, the profession's rhetoric moves away from the ethics of rights or separative thinking. But, to what extent does the profession move towards a more caring approach?

2 The analytical framework of the ethics of care versus the ethics of rights enhances understanding of some of the root problems with auditor independence.

3 Application of the ethics of care ideal to accounting practice enables us to see the adequacies and inadequacies of the profession's response to current and future problems in financial reporting and assurance (p. 299).

It may well be that an ethics of care perspective would have enabled the profession to respond more effectively to the criticism it attracted over recent major corporate collapses!

Morality versus ethics: discourse ethics

For most people (and in much of the discussion here) ethics and morality are fairly synonymous. However, for some this is just not so. Bernard Williams, 'a leading influence in philosophical ethics in the latter half of the twentieth century . . . rejected the codification of ethics into moral theories that views such as Kantianism and (above all) utilitarianism see as essential to philosophical thinking about ethics, arguing that our ethical life is too untidy to be captured by any systematic moral theory'.[12] Thus, for Williams, the 'moral system' is too abstract and artificial to be used as the basis of ethical practice. For example, utilitarianism is 'too simple' a systemisation of our ethical thinking. While Kantianism is too impersonal, abstracting moral thought from the identity of persons, utilitarianism abstracts from any goodness of the actions of individuals to who produces good consequences. Thus Williams opposes any attempts to reduce ethical ideas to a morality system mainly because there are too many situations with ethical implications.

Another philosopher who believes that there is a distinction between morality and ethics is Jurgens Habermas. He has developed a complex theoretical framework for understanding ethical issues, which is referred to as **discourse ethics**. For Habermas (1991), discourse is not simply language or speech but is a reflective form of speech that aims to reach a rationally motivated consensus (p. 42). The notion of rationally motivated consensus is important because discourse is not an esoteric activity of philosophers but an everyday mechanism for regulating societal conflicts. In other words, it is an observable process which aims to repair failed consensus in order to establish a rational social order. Discourse attempts to make good a validity claim to rightness—it is the way a speaker convinces the hearer of a particular claim. It is not a simple process and Habermas has had to devote a considerable amount of his writing to establishing it as a serious discipline with particular rules. It has become an essential part of his social theory.

Habermas is very much a modernist with a belief in the importance of the Enlightenment principles. Thus the idea of *rationality* is an essential part of his work. So too is *communication*: those who communicate effectively are able to resolve conflicts through discourse. Consequently, he set out to establish the basis of rational communication. In doing this he distinguished between a **discourse of morality** and a **discourse of ethics**. The former is concerned with how we establish valid moral norms (which are used to resolve conflicts). The validity of a norm depends on the agreement of many people. Norms are behavioural rules which take the form of imperatives: for example, do not steal. For Habermas, mature moral agents are at Kohlberg's stage 6.

Whereas the discourse of morality seeks to establish valid norms, discourse ethics is concerned with *values*. Consequently, ethical discourse produces only advice which has conditional or relative validity, 'what is good for me or us', rather than a broader social behavioural rule. To that extent ethical discourse is purposive and much less general than moral discourse, which seeks universal principles. *APES 110 Code of ethics for professional accountants* is an example of discourse ethics in that it sets out the conditions of the values to be adopted by a group of individuals acting as the profession of accounting. If this is true, then it is important to know how the 'rules' (the values) are established and the language used to articulate them. They are certainly rules for how members should (must?) act in society and for reducing conflict between members.

As indicated, Habermas's work is complex but what this brief introduction to it demonstrates once again is the importance of language. For Habermas, language is critical to resolving conflict within groups or societies. Societies create language in order to facilitate the communication necessary for their proper functioning. Habermas has attempted to establish the rational basis for this communication in the belief that only then will communication work for the betterment of societies through avoiding and resolving conflict.

Threats to ethics

The question of ethics is a highly complex matter. It is a subject that has troubled thinkers and policy makers for thousands of years. Some, such as the utilitarians, have produced simplistic sets of principles. Some, such as Kant and his followers, have insisted on universal duties and obligations. Aristotelians, and neo-Aristotelians, believe that ethical behaviour is the result of the essential character of the individual. Whatever the approach taken to try and understand ethics, it remains a central concern of contemporary societies and the basis for their 'proper' functioning. It affects all aspects of society and is generally regarded as the hallmark of a profession. This has been recognised by accountants and the profession has issued a Code by which it expects its members to behave. However, members are expected to comply not only with the 'letter of the code' but also with the 'spirit'. Thus it is important that accountants have an appreciation of the subject well beyond the statement of the Code.

The philosopher, Simon Blackburn (2001), has suggested seven threats to ethics. First, there is the increasing secularisation of societies and the failure of religions to accommodate the problems of contemporary societies. Second, there is the issue of a lack of belief in universal principles of ethics. His third is egoism or selfishness. This, of course, is institutionalised in neo-liberal ideology and neo-classical economic theory. His fourth is closely related to his third, and he refers to it as 'evolutionary theory'. This can be interpreted to mean a belief in Social Darwinism—the mistaken belief that there is a fundamental scientific reason for acting in our own interest because it is necessary that only the fittest survive. Fifth, he lists determinism. This is the belief that there is not much point in acting altruistically because 'life' is predetermined. His sixth threat is unreasonable demands—we expect and demand too much. Finally, he lists false consciousness, by which he means we are often 'fooled' into actions for the wrong reasons so we need to carefully reflect on why we undertake these actions.

These are the threats that Blackburn sees as the most obvious. There may well be others. Anyone entering a professional vocation needs to be aware of the implications on others and society generally of one's actions and bear in mind that a professional is one who works to serve the public interest.

NOTES

1 Hence this is referred to as rule deontology.

2 Emotivism 'is the doctrine that all evaluative judgments are nothing but expressions of preference, expressions of attitude or feeling, insofar as they are moral or evaluative in character' (MacIntyre 1984, p. 12).

3 Implementation has been the responsibility of The Accounting Professional & Ethical Standards Board Limited (APESB), a body initially set up jointly by CPA Australia and the ICAA, but later joined by the National Institute of Accountants (NIA). Its webpage can be found at: <http://www.apesb.org.au>.

4 A more 'practical' orientation is taken by the American Accounting Association (AAA) (1990) which presents a so-called 'model of decision-making'; this is discussed by Dellaportas et al. (2005, Chapter 4).

5 In Wikipedia < http://en.wikipedia.org/wiki/Profession>, for example, the definition provided is: 'A profession is an occupation that requires extensive training and the study and mastery of specialized knowledge, and usually has a professional association, ethical code and process of certification or licensing'.

6 Summarised in Kuper, A & Kuper, J, *The social science encyclopedia*, 2nd edn, Routledge, London, 2003.

7 It is also interesting to note that the issue of defining a profession has been largely an Anglo-American concern, with Continental Europeans not appearing to be so troubled by the matter.

8 The AWB situation was a matter of national significance, yet the accounting professional bodies (appeared to) remained silent, even though accountants were involved as auditors and financial advisers.

9 'The case of Israel is unique in that secular Zionists ground the secular state on a religious tradition which they reject' (Rist 2002, p. 230).

10 Early in the 20th century there were ethical theorists who believed that there were basic truths known by intuition—sort of *a priori*. However, this position came under such critical scrutiny that it became no longer acceptable. Later the notion was revived in the work of linguistic theorists (e.g. Chomsky): for example, we know by intuition that certain uses of language are unacceptable.

11 See CCH Australia Ltd 2001, *Collapse Incorporated*, especially Chapter 2, Andrew White, 'Flow on effects of recent collapses'.

12 The Stanford encyclopedia of philosophy, <http://plato.stanford.edu/entries/williams-bernard/>.

REFERENCES AND FURTHER READING

American Accounting Association (AAA) 1990, *Ethics in the accounting curriculum: cases and readings*, AAA, Sarasota, Florida, US.

Blackburn, Simon 2001, *Ethics: a very short introduction*, Oxford University Press, Oxford, UK.

CCH Australia Limited 2001, *Collapse Incorporated*, CCH Australia Ltd, Sydney.

Cheffers, M & Pakaluk, M 2005, *A new approach to understanding accounting ethics*, Allen David Press, Massachusetts, US.

Dellaportas, S, Gibson, K, Alagiah, R, Hutchinson, M, Leung, P & Van Homrigh, D 2005, *Ethics, governance and accountability: a professional perspective*, John Wiley & Sons Australia Ltd, Milton, Qld.

Francis, Jere R 1990, 'After virtue? Accounting as a moral discursive practice', *Accounting, Auditing and Accountability Journal*, vol. 3, pp. 5–17.

Gaffikin, MJR & Lindawati 2005, 'The moral reasoning of public accountants in the development of a code of ethics: the case of Indonesia', unpublished paper.

Habermas, J 1991, *The theory of communicative action: Volume 1—Reason and the rationalization of society*, Polity Press, Cambridge, UK.

Harpham, GG 1999, *Shadows of ethics*, Duke University Press, Durham, North Carolina, US.

Kohlberg, Lawrence 1969, 'Stage and sequence: the cognitive development approach to socialization', in Goslin, DA, ed., *Handbook of socialization theory and research*, Rand McNally, New York, pp. 347–480.

Kuper, A & Kuper, J 2003, eds, *The social science encyclopedia*, 2nd edn, Routledge, London.

Longstaff, S 1995, 'Was Socrates an accountant?', paper delivered to AAANZ Conference, La Trobe University, Melbourne, 11 July 1995.

MacIntyre, Alasdair 1984, *After virtue*, 2nd edn, University of Notre Dame Press, Indiana, US.

Nozick, R 1974, *Anarchy, state and utopia*, Basic Books, New York.

Parker, L 1987, 'A historical analysis of ethical pronouncements and debate in the Australian accounting profession', *Abacus*, vol. 23, pp. 122–140.

Puxty, A, Sikka, P & Willmott, H 1994, '(Re)forming the circle: education, ethics and accountancy practices', *Accounting Education*, vol. 3. pp. 77–92.

Puxty, A, Sikka, P & Willmott, H 1997, 'Mediating interests: the accountancy bodies' responses to the McFarlane Report', *Accounting and Business Research*, vol. 27, pp. 323–340.

Rawls, John 1971, *A theory of justice*, Harvard University Press, Harvard, US.

Reiter, Sara 1997, 'The ethics of care and new paradigms for accounting practice', *Accounting, Auditing and Accountability Journal*, vol. 10, pp. 299–324.

Rist, John M 2002, *Real ethics: reconsidering the foundations of morality*, Cambridge University Press, Cambridge, UK.

Williams, Bernard 1985, *Ethics and the limits of philosophy*, Fontana Press, Glasgow, Scotland.

CHAPTER 9

Corporate Social Responsibility and Environmental Accounting

S imilarly to the previous two chapters, this chapter examines the extent to which businesses should be concerned with social goals beyond those critical to maximisation of their material resources. Two major themes emerge: first, the impact of the growth in economic and political power of the corporation and, second, how business interests can respond to the urgent need for increased sensitivity to the physical environment. These issues have moved well beyond being of peripheral interest to a few concerned individuals to being central issues at international meetings of political and community leaders. An important example is: how will climate change impact our societies? Corporations, as the major exploiters of the world's scarce resources, have an obligation to be proactive in developing a sustainable future for the world. ■

The nature of corporations has changed significantly over the last 200 years, and corporations now play a critical role in the economic functioning of most economies. As their significance has grown there have been calls from many quarters for them to demonstrate greater awareness of the broader needs of society. It has been argued that, as legally created entities, corporations should demonstrate some of the societal responsibilities required of other 'citizens'. A traditional view is that corporations have been given privileges of legal protection, legal and economic rights, and access to societies' scarce resources, and therefore they have attendant responsibilities.

It is important to appreciate that the growth in economic significance of corporations has in turn resulted in the growth in political significance of the corporation. As one commentator has suggested:

> The twentieth century has been characterised by three developments of great political importance: the growth of democracy, the growth of corporate power, and the growth of corporate propaganda as a means of protecting corporate power against democracy (Carey 1995, p. ix).

Theories of the corporation

Over the history of the corporation different perspectives have emerged. Many of these have been presented as 'theories' of the corporation. Originally, the company or corporation was a mechanism for combining the capital resources of several people in order to pursue a business venture. With industrialisation in the 19th century the need for capital to undertake such ventures sharply increased, so the company was seen as an essential facilitator of economic and business activity. To encourage investment in companies, legislation was passed to afford some protection to the investors, notably the notion of limited liability. (Prior to this there had been many instances of unscrupulous company promoters using the company form of business organisation to defraud those wishing to invest in those companies.) At the same time it was recognised that legislation to protect those dealing with the company—creditors, lenders, employees and other interested parties, those whom we now refer to as stakeholders—was also necessary.

While this is probably well known it is important to recall, because it provides the background for many of the theories of corporations, which in turn determine the responsibilities we believe, or can argue, a corporation has. When considering why corporations exist, several questions come to mind: Does the corporation exist as a concession granted it by the state? Does it exist as an important instrument promoting economic activity within a state? Is there some 'natural law' that holds that people within a society have the right to associate (for some common pursuit)?

A legal case before the House of Lords in the UK near the end of the 19th century established the corporation's legal existence[1], although there had been debate over the matter for many years prior to this. It is generally held that the corporation is an artificial entity created by the state; that is, the corporation exists as a concession or privilege of the state, hence the name given to this perspective, **concession theory**. The important point here is that the state 'concedes' the right of the corporation to exist and, in doing this, the state acknowledges, by implication, the interests of the public over the private interest of the individual.

The concession theory perspective was important prior to the passing of general company legislation because the earliest companies had to be created by specific legislation. For example, the first joint stock company, The East India Company, was established by the granting of a Royal Charter on 31 December 1600.[2] With the passage in the UK of the Joint Stock Companies Act of 1844, the formation of companies was greatly facilitated and was much more generalised. Consequently, the view emerged that it was an individual's right to be involved with the formation of a company. This was the basis of the **aggregate theory** perspective. From this perspective the individual property owner has the right to contract with his or her property and forming a company is one form this contracting could take. This perspective can be viewed as the opposite of concession theory.

There are also various **economic theories**, or perspectives, of corporations. Here the concern is with the economic significance of the corporation rather than its legal status, as indicated in Chapter 3. Thus, according to **agency theory**, a firm (an economic concept) is seen merely as a nexus of contracts—arrangements entered into by the various interested parties. The firm (invariably a corporation) is not seen to exist as a separate entity. As such theories of corporations are based on economic theory, the idea of economic rationality is predominant and thus the maximisation of investor returns is the only aim of the corporation.

In **communitarian theory**, as its name implies, the corporation is viewed as much more than a set of private arrangements (contracts), as in the economic and aggregate theories, and more than a public creation, as in concession theory. It is both private (providing returns for the risk-taking investors) and public (in serving the interests of the communities in which it exists). The **natural entity theory** also differs from the previous theories in that the corporation is more than a set of arrangements (contracts), yet it is not an artificial entity but a 'natural entity', not so much created by the state but its existence is recognised by the state.

There are probably many more theories of the corporation but the important (and obvious) point to note is that the theoretical perspective adopted will determine what responsibilities the corporation is held to have.

There are at least two other dimensions that need to be addressed when considering the broader responsibilities of corporations. First, is the changing nature of the corporation over time, and second is the matter of what is referred to as corporate governance—the procedures, practices, policies and problems which affect the way in which corporations are directed, administered and controlled. This issue emerges as potentially problematic with the separation of ownership from control.

The changing nature of corporations

The initial purpose of the corporation was the accumulation of capital to enable high-cost business ventures to be undertaken. Although this was a primary aim of this form of business organisation at its inception, the issue became more significant with growing industrialisation and the birth and growth of the railways in the 19th century. Legislation was enacted to facilitate the growth of corporations, with slightly different emphases in different countries. For example, in the UK, where at this time industrialisation was occurring most rapidly, there was an urgent need for funds to build factories and to take advantage of industrial and technological innovations in machinery and the like, to further develop manufacturing. Corporations were seen as important institutions for the accumulation of such capital. This was a major reason for the enactment of limited liability for investors in company shares—protection of shareholders was a major focus of the legislation. In the United States, there was a similar need for the accumulation of capital, in this case to finance the expansion of the railways,[3] but the emphasis in the corporate legislation of the various states was the protection of those dealing with the corporations. In both situations the corporation was seen as necessary for capital accumulation, but the point being made here is that there were different perspectives of the nature of the corporation. These differences have grown to become very important considerations today, as is evident in the differing theories described above.

The corporation is now a very different type of organisation from earlier conceptions of it, and how it is treated, including its accounting, is also very different. What was once fairly straightforward accounting for stewardship—whether primarily for shareholders or for creditors—is no longer sufficient as corporations have grown to have 'lives of their own'; witness, for example, the growth of consolidation accounting where economic 'reality' takes precedence over legal 'reality'. In fact, that corporations quickly became (major) shareholders in other corporations became a concern to policy makers in the first decades of the 20th century. Earlier, in the US, the government had passed legislation to break up the concentration of economic power that had emerged from what were called trusts—combinations of large firms formed into huge corporations, such as US Steel. It was believed that the huge economic power wielded by controllers of these corporations (e.g. JP Morgan and Rockefeller) would inevitably lead to political power.

By the 1930s attitudes had shifted, and in a book first published in 1932 Berle and Means (1968) raised the problem of the corporate governance that had been created, they argued, from the separation of ownership from control. To Berle and Means the nature of the corporation had changed dramatically as a result of the transfer of control from owners to managers, which could result in unchecked corporate power with serious consequences for society. This process was referred to as managerialism. However, later (post World War II), American sociologists began to disagree with Berle and Means' thesis, arguing that the separation of control from ownership actually made the process more democratic. Economic corporate theorists recognised the problem with managerialism; however, agency theorists believed that the problem could be overcome by alignment of incentives and monitoring (see Chapter 3). By making managers shareholders (granting of stock options) managers would have interests aligned with those of other shareholders. In addition, monitoring systems could be implemented. Finally, they argued, managers would have concerns about the 'market for reputations'—they would not want to get a 'bad name'—and so they would work in the interests of the corporation, in other words the shareholders.

The issue of corporate governance is interesting and complex and there is a vast literature devoted to the subject. This is not the place to enter into that debate, but it is important to appreciate how the corporation is perceived and how it is managed as it has a direct bearing on the extent to which a corporation acts in a socially responsible manner. The issues raised by Berle and Means have been debated endlessly, with many initially agreeing with them (leading to regulation in the 1930s), then swinging away, and later swinging back to their view. Developments well after Berle and Means were writing have again directed attention to their thesis. These include the rise of transnational corporations, the seemingly excessive remuneration of directors and managers, and the continuing spectacular corporate collapses. Berle and Means conclude their book with sentiments which still seem very topical:

> The rise of the modern corporation has brought a concentration of economic power which can compete on equal terms with the modern state . . . Where its own interests are concerned, it even attempts to dominate the state. The future may see the economic

organism, now typified by the corporation, not only on an equal plane with the state, but possibly even superseding it as the dominant form of social organization (p. 313).

Corporations as psychopaths?

If Berle and Means are correct—and there is a lot of evidence to suggest they may well be—then, as 'the dominant form of social organization', corporations have a responsibility to act in a socially responsible manner. They are now 'obliged to serve the interests of society as a whole, much as governments were' (Bakan 2004, p. 19).

In the late 1980s, with the rise of the Thatcher–Reagan leadership, there was a marked change in the dominant political ideology of the Anglo-American world. The age of the market economy ideology was born. This was evident, for example, in the change in emphasis in the policies of the international economic organisations— the IMF, the World Bank and the WTO—as described in Chapter 6. The ideas of the economist, Milton Friedman, had a strong influence on the 'new' ideology. An oft-quoted (earlier) statement by Friedman said in effect that the only social responsibility a corporation had was to its shareholders. For him, while corporations were good for society—they generated economic activity which benefited all of society—they should never try to do good for society unless it was in the shareholders' interests. Friedman went as far as indicating that it was a moral imperative that corporations maximise returns to shareholders. Thus, this would prohibit any activities in the interests of societal or environmental goals that would diminish shareholder returns. With government policies reinforcing this ideology, enormous power was vested in corporations. Given that corporations have greater access to resources than individuals, they have disproportionate power to defend themselves against any wrongdoings. There are many who believe that corporations, and those who run them, have used this power often to the detriment of others in the societies in which they operate. Traditionally, corporate governance in other countries has been different from the Anglo-American approach, but with the growth in global financial and other markets this approach has spread to other parts of the world. And the 'exploitation' has been exacerbated in countries with weak, sometimes corrupt, governments!

In his book, *The Corporation*, Joel Bakan (2004) has made a stinging attack on the modern corporation.[4] His basic premise is based on a type of natural entity theoretical approach in that he argues that, under current corporate legislation, the corporation is a person. Nineteenth-century law in both the US and the UK had 'transformed the corporation into a person with its own identity, separate from the flesh-and-blood people who were its owners and managers and empowered, like real persons, to conduct business in its own name, acquire assets, employ workers, pay taxes, and go to court to assert its rights and defend its action' (p. 16). But this person is devoid of the morality and conscience commonly part of other persons. His analysis demonstrates that, on the basis of its personality and characteristics, this person—the corporation—fully meets the clinical definition of a psychopath! This sounds very melodramatic, yet Bakan is not the first to employ such an analogy. In 1933 a US Supreme Court judge, Justice Louis Brandeis, likened corporations to 'Frankenstein monsters'—once they exist they threaten to overpower their creators[5] (quoted in Bakan 2004, p. 149). To Brandeis, corporations were created by government regulation which later proved inadequate to prevent the harm they caused to society.

Psychopaths are irresponsible, manipulative, grandiose, reckless, remorseless and superficial. To Bakan (a law professor), corporations display all these characteristics. They are irresponsible in that in pursuing their goals they put others at risk, for example, by often ignoring employee safety or employment tenure. They are manipulative, evidenced in misleading and false marketing or false financial statements. They are grandiose in that they insist they are the biggest and/or the best (manifest in the financial media or stock market rankings). They are remorseless, as is evident in their strict pursuit of cost benefits at the expense of product safety or environmental degradation. They are superficial in the manner in which they relate to people (and other institutions, including other corporations). In his book (and the film) Bakan presents considerable empirical evidence in the form of many cases to illustrate his argument. It is very important to note that Bakan does *not* claim that *all* corporations are psychopathic. It is the organisational structure of the corporation that he targets. Consequently, the 'corporate theory' he adopts is important: his view is that the corporation is a created entity, a 'person'. Obviously, if he assumed an economic theory perspective, as did Friedman, his conclusions would be very different! However, on the evidence he produces, it is very hard not to agree with many of his conclusions; even conservative business commentators agree.[6]

Corporate social responsibility

Paradoxically, Bakan and corporate economic theorists concur that the corporation is legally bound to increase shareholders' wealth through the pursuit of profits. Thus, the sole responsibility of the officers of the corporation is to work to that end. They are not permitted to pursue altruistic or social goals (other than to maximise profits). To illustrate this Bakan uses the case of The Body Shop. Founder Anita Roddick developed a company that had definite and serious socially and environmentally responsible goals. These lasted as long as the company remained a company under her control. When a public offering was floated on the London Stock Exchange, as the company needed to raise funds to grow the business, outside managers were brought in to head the company and make it 'more efficient'. Roddick continued to work hard to maintain the company's progressive values and programs but her efforts were subsequently overpowered by those of other directors: a direct result of her having to make (in her words) 'a pact with the devil' (that is, the initial public offering).

Many companies claim to be acting socially responsibly and many researchers have investigated such corporate social responsibility (CSR), developing theories, such as stakeholder theory, or legitimacy theory, or some other theory, as explanations as to why corporations so act. To some radical commentators CSR is little more than a confidence trick. For example, Claire Fauset claims that CSR is:

> an effective strategy for: bolstering a company's public image; avoiding regulation; gaining legitimacy and access to markets and decision makers; and shifting the ground towards privatisation of public functions. CSR enables business to propose ineffective, voluntary, market-based solutions to social and environmental crises under the guise of being responsible. This deflects blame for problems caused by corporate operations away from the company, and protects companies' interests while hampering efforts to tackle the root causes of social and environmental injustice (Corporate Watch 2006, p. 2).

The above discussion has concentrated on corporations, and to many it may seem unduly negative or even cynical. The world does face serious social and environmental problems and it would be churlish to overlook the work of many well-intentioned, hard-working, sincere and committed researchers, commentators and organisations dedicated to finding solutions to these problems. However, talking and writing about CSR and associated problems has become a 'large industry' and it is difficult to determine which suggestions would be the most effective in solving the world's problems of social injustice and environmental degradation. There are many organisations claiming to be socially and environmentally 'sensitive' while turning a blind eye or even supporting the promotion of corporate or individual greed, fraud and exploitation. At the forefront are many corporations and some business organisations, together with individual business and accounting commentators.

Bakan (2004) does not advocate the abandonment of the corporate form of business organisation. However, he does argue that there is a need to improve the regulatory system:

> ■ to bring corporations back to democratic control to ensure they respect the interests of citizens, communities and the environment

- by making staffing of enforcement agencies more realistic ('more teeth')
- by prohibiting actions that may cause harm to people's health, safety and the environment
- to improve genuine accountability
- to protect the role of workers' and other associations that can monitor corporate behaviour in respect of the environment, consumer and human rights (pp. 161–162).

In addition, he believes it is important to strengthen political democracy, to create a robust public sphere, to challenge and change away from the market fundamentalism of the neo-liberalism ideology that has captured international institutions such as the IMF, the World Bank and the WTO. For example, lobbying of governments on behalf of corporate interests has become an accepted practice (often because of promises to further the interests and resources of politicians). This is a practice that greatly diminishes democratic processes and one that is heavily criticised when it occurs in developing countries,[7] yet is quite 'respectable', as lobbying, in so-called developed democracies!

The problems associated with corporate power have been exacerbated by the processes of globalisation. Traditionally, large corporations from Japan and Continental Europe have had governance traditions different from those of the Anglo-American world. They have had closer associations with governments, unions and banks and have been more disposed to having built-in mechanisms for social responsibility. However, with the growth of financial and market globalisation, these corporations have had to adopt a more Anglo-American approach, while their governments have retreated to a more laissez-faire position. This is not to suggest that only Anglo-American corporations have abused their corporate status, even though some in the armaments, pharmaceutical and energy industries have been rumoured to have been involved in antisocial behaviour. There are abuses by corporations from all countries. What is apparent is that CSR concerns are no longer purely national matters, they are global.

Defining CSR reporting

For many years accountants eschewed involvement in any activities that were not purely economic, with the excuse that they were ill equipped to define measurable social and environmental activities that corporations could engage in. That involved value judgements, and accounting was value neutral they claimed! Previts and Merino (1998, p. 240) have suggested that the 1920s marked the beginnings of the debate on businesses' social responsibility but there was no legal basis on which concerned individuals could act. In the 1960s, there was (renewed) considerable interest in the broader social responsibilities of business. Several economists became involved and several suggestions were put forward, but accountants were slow to become involved. However, by the late 1960s and early 1970s several accountants expressed an interest in accountants participating in developing social goals. The expertise they hoped to bring to the matter was the ability to provide reportable measures of social activities engaged in by corporations and other institutions—that is, social accounting. Whereas the term 'social accounting' had been used to refer to national income accounting (macroeconomic income measurement) in the 1970s, Seidler and Seidler (1975) suggested that:

> . . . social accounting is the modification and application, by accountants, of the skills, techniques and discipline of conventional (managerial and financial) accounting, to the analysis and solution of problems of a social nature (p. ix).

However, because of the possible terminological confusion, Linowes (1968), a partner in a major accounting firm who became a leading advocate of accountants' involvement in social activities, preferred the term 'socioeconomic accounting'.[8] For him it indicated 'the application of accounting in the field of the social sciences' (p. 37), which included sociology, political science and economics. Nevertheless, as its name implies, it was primarily directed to economic considerations.

The books by Seidler and Seidler (1975) and Estes (1973) are anthologies—collections of articles and papers by many different contributors. Seidler and Seidler suggest that whereas Estes' book provides an excellent introduction to the concepts and philosophies of social accounting, their book is an attempt 'to move accountants a bit further into social accounting' (p. viii). Consequently, the book presents many cases and examples of the issues and problems involved in social accounting. It is interesting to note that contributors include many notable economists such as JM Clark, West Churchman, Baumol, Hirshleifer and Shapiro. It is interesting because it indicates that the subject was being taken very seriously. It is also interesting to note that subjects addressed included problems of air pollution and water quality management, two of many issues that have now become extremely significant. Paramount amongst the concerns was the ability to report on social programs and it was felt that this was an area in which accountants could make major contributions. Various models were proposed and debated. One firm, Abt Associates Inc., took the issue very seriously and developed a comprehensive social audit model which resulted in its 1972 annual report being one of the few actual attempts to implement social accounting.

Prior to the involvement of accountants, those interested in corporate social performance had employed many terms normally associated with accounting. Hence the expression 'social audit' was often used but it bore little resemblance to what is commonly understood as a financial audit.[9] Abt Associates used the term, and in its 1972 annual report stated that it:

> . . . pioneered its social audit in the 1971 annual report. A social balance sheet and a social income statement was [sic] prepared which tabulated the effects the Company had on 'society', defined as staff, the local community, clients and the general public.

The company's efforts were way ahead of their time and it undertook to make representations which many corporations today have yet to match. Because of their innovative nature, some commentators have suggested that many of the measurements were arbitrary and too subjective. These claims have persistently been made by those opposed to any form of corporate social performance reporting and are obviously based on preconceptions of the measures accountants 'should be concerned with'— namely, so-called objective economic measures! This has been the major hurdle that advocates of social performance reporting have had to overcome. Even though the AICPA issued, in 1972, a monograph entitled *Corporate social measurement*, many accountants resisted social reporting. Unfortunately the oil crisis of the 1970s seemed to have turned attention to traditional economic measurement, and interest in social accounting in the US waned in the late 1970s.

Nevertheless, many scholars persisted with the attempt to add a social responsibility dimension to accounting. Estes produced another book with a strong emphasis on the implementation of social reporting models (1976). Others attempted to address the question using a managerial accounting emphasis, for example, Livingstone and Gunn (1974). Yet others provided a definition for the corporate social audit (Bauer and Fenn 1972). In the UK, Trevor Gambling (1974) adopted a more theoretical and philosophical orientation, attempting to relate 'social accounting' to broader issues of culture and national income reporting.

Reporting CSR

The idea of socially responsible business is not at all new. In Classical Greek times those engaged in business were expected to practise a high standard of morality in trade. In the Middle Ages, in Europe, the Church ensured that those engaged in 'industry and commerce' behaved according to the Church's code of moral conduct. Pursuit of profit for personal gain only achieved ascendancy with the intensification of the industrial revolution and a reformed religion. The growth of the corporation then reinforced the notion of investment for financial return.

There were always those who believed that people involved in business had a responsibility to society in pursuing their trade, culminating in an outpouring of such sentiment in the US in the 1960s. This occurred for a variety of reasons, including the growing general social consciousness expressed in the actions of a range of groups such as the peace movement. This was the height of the Cold War and there were some who felt that socially responsible business would serve as a good showcase for the advantages of Western-style democracy. There were probably countless other reasons, not the least of which was the relative economic buoyancy of that decade.

According to Estes (1976, p. 19) corporate social performance fell under four broad headings:

1   Community involvement—socially oriented activities that tend to primarily benefit the general public, including general philanthropy, education, health, housing and the like
2   Human resources—those internal activities directed to the well-being of employees including remuneration, training, and safe and healthy working conditions
3   Physical resources and environmental contributions—for example, responsible environmental protection policies
4   Product or service contribution—product quality, responsible labelling, and marketing and consumer education.

Nearly thirty years later there are much the same concerns and the Global Reporting Initiative (GRI 2000) lists performance indicators under three main headings:

1   Economic
2   Environmental
3   Social.

Under the social heading there are sub-headings for:

a   Labour practices and decent work
b   Human rights
c   Society (community)
d   Product responsibility.

However, a major change is that the GRI refers to its reporting framework as **Sustainability Reporting Guidelines**. The important change is the use of the term 'sustainability', a word which has much broader implications than social and environmental reporting. Recent research in accounting has embraced the term and the implications of its broader concerns.

With the worsening economic conditions of the 1970s, largely as a result of the oil embargo, interest in corporate social reporting waned. While there were still many advocating the need for social accounting, interest did not pick up again until the late 1980s when a large number of articles reporting the results of research were published. Unfortunately, much of this research was more concerned with form than with substance; that is, it was more interested in describing reporting trends—the extent of reporting of 'social activities' in corporate financial statements. Although this may have been a useful starting point, there were few attempts to grapple with the underlying structural issues. Much of the research was merely 'reinventing the wheel', reproducing the discussion of the 1960s and 1970s.

During the 1990s, however, there was a huge increase in research interest in social issues, some researchers turning their attention to the question of *why* corporations reported social activities. For example, in a paper presented at a conference in 1994, Lindblom argued that an explanation could be found in their seeking legitimacy.[10] The argument rested on a *concession theory* of the corporation. A corporation is dependent on social and political support (that is, corporate legislation) and therefore its survival and growth is in turn dependent on its delivery of socially responsible activities. This explanation of corporate social reporting came to be known as **legitimacy theory**. Lindblom's paper inspired many researchers to extend the explanation and to attempt to provide empirical evidence to support it (for example, Deegan and Rankin 1996; Deegan, Rankin and Tobin 2002; O'Donovan 1999, 2002; Wilmshurst and Frost 2000). The appearance of legitimacy theory predates the Lindblom (1994) paper, but it is that paper that seems to have sparked the interest of many of the researchers. Five years earlier, Guthrie and Parker (1989) had argued against the use of legitimacy theory to explain CSR, yet later accounting researchers rarely referred to their work.

The basis of legitimacy theory is the notion of a social contract similar to that of Hobbes, as detailed in Chapter 8, but it is still consistent with the concession theory of the corporation. Thus, although supporters of legitimacy theory suggest that firms will be penalised if they do not operate consistently in accordance with community expectations (consistent with their social contract), it is difficult to see how any penalty could be imposed if no law has been infringed. As Bakan (2004) has shown, corporations seem to be able to work antisocially with impunity. Unfortunately, pressure from community groups tends to be aggressively counteracted by modern large corporations, and community group success is rare. Nevertheless, supporters of legitimacy theory have been working to provide empirical support and there are several corporations that do act socially responsibly and report such activities, especially in respect of environmental issues.

Closely related to legitimacy theory is another explanation for voluntary corporate social reporting, which is referred to as **stakeholder theory**. Although the expression is widely used, it is not a single theoretical explanation and is better viewed as an overall term which addresses the relationship between the various stakeholders in an organisation. In respect of a corporation, it encompasses far more than just the interests of the shareholders. It is an expression of the *communitarian perspective* of corporations. Even though it usually refers to those with a financial interest in the corporation (those with a financial 'stake') it can be interpreted more broadly to include also governmental bodies, political groups, trade associations, trade unions, communities, associated corporations, prospective employees, prospective customers, the public at large and, often, even competitors. There are at least two implications of this interpretation. First, explanations based on this framework will be open to criticism of lack of specificity. And second, this interpretation has strong ethical associations. Use of the term is not restricted to the accounting literature: it is used by some organisational theorists in the discipline of management.

The ethical interpretation of stakeholder theory clearly illustrates a communitarian perspective of the corporation. Managers are expected to treat all stakeholders' interests equally. At times this will involve managing in the interests of the shareholders (the private interests) and at times it will mean sacrificing the shareholders' interests in favour of the broader interests of all (other) stakeholders (the public interest). Several researchers, adopting a neo-empirical research perspective, have undertaken studies to discover empirical determinants of stakeholder theory. In so doing they have broadened the scope of stakeholder theory to include such aspects as the power relationships between the various stakeholders and managers and even regulators. It is questionable whether this has produced any meaningful results as it is not only open to the criticisms levelled at all neo-empirical-type research but also the contestability of the subject matter itself, which will diminish any claim to objectivity.

Accounting and the environment

Hardly a day passes without some reference in the media to the problems the world is facing in respect of the environment. Concern over the environment has become one of the biggest issues facing the world community. It is a subject with enormous implications. Being such an important subject, the environment and its related issues can be discussed and debated at very many levels. It affects communities at local, national and global levels. It is of interest to very many intellectual communities including scientists, engineers, social scientists, politicians, lawyers, educationalists and philosophers. It is no wonder, therefore, that there has been a growing interest in environmental issues in the accounting community. So can accountants play a role in issues concerning the environment and, if so, what is the role? Purists would argue that accounting serves only business and commercial interests and therefore accountants should avoid involvement in this issue. However, this is fast becoming an outdated and irrelevant perspective as businesses, as well as governments, are well aware of the environmental implications of their activities and the communities' sensitivities to them. It is only in some unfortunate developing economies that policy makers are allowing business and commercial interests to override those of the environment.[11]

The resurgence of interest in CSR in the late 1980s and 1990s was largely due to the growing interest in environmental concerns. The early discussion on social reporting included environmental factors as part of the social report. For example, the Abt Associates Inc. Social Operations and Income Statement includes a sub-heading for Environment (for, for example, reduced pollution, air pollution, paper recycling and water pollution—see Bauer and Fenn 1972, p. 24). However, as interest in social reporting waned interest in environmental (ecological) factors increased (as the green political movement grew so did 'green accounting') and much of the research examined ways in which corporations could report on environmental elements. In fact, in 1992, a book of environmental papers entitled *Green reporting*, edited by David Owen, was published. What was previously referred to as 'corporate social reporting' or 'social audit' or 'socioeconomic accounting' increasingly came to be referred to as social and environmental reporting (SER) or, more generally, as social and environmental accounting.

Traditional economic analysis has regarded goods or services generated by an economic activity where the costs and benefits do not fall upon the decision-taking agent (e.g. the producer) as (economic) externalities (as first noted in Chapter 4). They are the difference between 'social' and 'private' costs and benefits. The best known example relates to pollution created by production processes. Accountants simply followed this naive economic belief and did not include externalities in conventional financial reports. As societal environmental consciousness grew, some accounting researchers turned their attention to determining ways in which externalities such as environmental costs (e.g. pollution) could be reported in financial statements. However, their efforts were doomed to failure. If traditional economic analysis ignores externalities and if conventional accounting derives from traditional economic theory, then how could externalities be reported? Problems of definition, measurement and valuation would (and did) arise. And in addition to problems of measurement there were philosophical issues. If the environment were reduced to economic measures, how would this affect the way the environment was treated by accountants? There are examples of cynical developers costing in to their projects fines they would get from violating environmental regulations—an example of economic considerations taking priority over social considerations. Reduced to this the environment is brought down to simple cost–benefit economic analysis and there is little support for the notion of the so-called social contract!

To effect meaningful reporting of environmental factors new perspectives on 'business' activity were necessary. Consequently, there was a shift in the approach in the 1990s.

Accounting and sustainable development

In 1987, under the auspices of the United Nations, the World Commission on Environment and Development, under the chairmanship of GH Brundtland, published a report entitled *Our common future*. The report came to be known as the Brundtland Report and was 'a pivotal document' in the sustainable development debate (Bebbington 2001, p. 131). It was widely quoted at the 1992 Earth Summit in Rio de Janeiro and subsequent similar meetings. The report defined sustainable development as:

> . . . development that meets the needs of the present world without compromising the ability of future generations to meet their own needs.

Although intended to relate to the need for environmental protection, the word 'sustainability' has, as Deegan (2000) suggests, 'become a central part of the language of government and business worldwide' (p. 301). However, it is important to note that the term extends well beyond SER or CSR. As early as 1996, two researchers (Fowke and Prasad 1996) had determined over 80 definitions of sustainable development (SD) and it is not uncommon to come across expressions such as institutional sustainability, economic and financial sustainability, ecological sustainability and energetic sustainability, to name but a few.

Researchers Bebbington and Gray have worked extensively on relating SD to accounting and they have suggested that it has been applied both to legitimate (that is, sustainable) business activity and to challenging such activity. They argue that there are four 'camps' in the literature:

> 1 those who argue that accounting should steer well clear from issues involving nature, ecology and sustainability because it can only lead to damaging beliefs in humanity

2   those who reduce nature, ecology and sustainability to contingent liabilities and impaired assets—that is doing exactly what the first camp argues

3   those who offer non-analytical professionally oriented managerial solutions which tend to be rather trite

4   those who 'suggest that accountants and accounting may be able to support the pursuit of SD but that how this could be done is problematic' (Bebbington and Gray 2001, p. 561).

Thus, while there is concern about environmental issues and willingness by some accountants to become involved in providing suggestions as to how to overcome these problems, there are difficulties in producing fruitful solutions. Lamberton (2005) has traced the history of sustainability accounting and attributes to Gray much of its conceptual development (p. 8). He states that Gray has identified three different methods of sustainability accounting:

1   Sustainable cost
2   Natural capital inventory accounting
3   Input–output analysis.

In developing the first, Lamberton argues that Gray has drawn on the notion of capital maintenance and applied it to the biosphere (p. 8). That is, a sustainable firm would maintain natural capital intact for future generations. However, there would be problems in determining the external costs—the predictable problems of definition and valuation. Nevertheless, he suggests that some researchers have made headway in arriving at acceptable measures of costs. Whether this is so remains to be seen!

In the second approach the stocks of natural capital over time are recorded, with diminutions in the stock representing the environmental cost. This is conceptually sound but again there would be problems with definition and valuation. In respect of definition, Gray has suggested four categories—critical (e.g. ozone layer); non-renewable/non-substitutable (e.g. oil); non-renewable/substitutable (e.g. energy use); and renewable (e.g. timber). Well intentioned though this is, it breaks down the problem into smaller units rather than overcoming it, so long as conventional measures and valuations are expected.

The third method avoids the immediate problem of measurement and valuation by examining 'the physical flow of materials and energy inputs and product and waste outputs in physical units' (Lamberton 2005, p. 10).

Regulating environmental reporting

Most of the work on developing meaningful social and environmental reporting has been in the context of voluntary disclosure by firms. However, this has been problematic and has led Lehman (2004) to suggest that 'if concern about the environment is important then environmental disclosure under the auspices of voluntary regime is clearly inadequate' (p. 3). Once again, regulation surfaces as an important consideration.

To date there have been no extensive regulations relating to social and environmental reporting. Much of what has emerged from various interested bodies has been advisory guidelines, relying on voluntary responses by corporations. Nevertheless, there have been some minor regulatory attempts. For example, in Australia, early extractive industry accounting standards required reporting entities to account for environmental restoration costs. Section 299(1)(f) of the *Australian Corporations Act 2001* requires companies to report on environmental performance in their annual report. This provision was originally enacted in 1998 and subsequently reissued as part of the 2001 Act. While this is the first Australian mandatory requirement, Frost (2007) says that similar requirements exist in several other countries, including Sweden, Norway, The Netherlands, Denmark, and even the US and the European Union. Frost concludes that the enactment of this provision has led to a significant increase in environmental disclosures by Australian companies (p. 210).

Many other pronouncements have also been 'persuasive' in encouraging greater disclosure. For example, in 2000 the Mineral Council of Australia (MCA) issued a *Code for environmental management*, with which members (signatories) are required to comply by, amongst other things, issuing audited financial reports. In fact, the MCA has gone well beyond just environmental considerations and issued *The Australian minerals industry framework for sustainable development*, which is designed to encourage leading companies to commit to upholding fundamental human rights and respecting cultures, customs and values in their dealings with employees and others affected by their activities.[12]

Also in 2000 Environment Australia published *A framework for public environmental reporting: an Australian approach*.[13] Subsequently, in 2003, this same body published *Triple bottom line reporting in Australia: a guide to reporting against environmental indicators*. In the foreword, the then Minister for the Environment and Heritage, Dr David Kemp, states that this guide is necessary because:

> There is growing recognition that business has a crucial role to play in helping Australia to become more sustainable. As a result many Australian organisations are responding by reducing their environmental impacts and risks, for example, by decreasing water use and minimising greenhouse emissions. In addition, a wide range of stakeholders, including the

finance sector, are beginning to consider corporate environmental performance in their purchasing and investment decisions, and thus seek robust information on an organisation's environmental performance.

Although not designed for mandatory regulation of corporate reporting, the guide is intended to support voluntary reporting on environmental performance by organisations in Australia because triple bottom line (TBL) reporting is becoming an accepted approach by which organisations can demonstrate that they have strategies for sustainable growth.

The guide also states that:

The number of organisations worldwide producing reports containing environmental performance information continues to grow, particularly amongst larger organisations. The recent KPMG survey found that 45 percent of the world's top 250 companies now publish a separate corporate report with details of environmental and/or social performance, up from 35 percent in 1999 (p. 16).

Interestingly, it states that a recent study revealed that 72% of Japanese companies produce environmental reports, making it the top ranked country in the world; Australia ranked 12th with 14%. Environment Australia was influenced by many other developments and reports, but a major influence in establishing the need for such a guide was the report by the Global Reporting Initiative (GRI), an official collaborating centre of the United Nations Environment Programme, entitled *GRI sustainability reporting guidelines*.

A triple bottom line report is designed to show the performance of a company in respect of traditional economic measures, social activity and environmental protection measures—hence the name. A TBL report employs conventional measures and descriptions so whether it is likely to produce the desired results is a matter open to interpretation. In light of the earlier discussion on the role of corporations in contemporary society, it could merely be what Fauset claimed, namely 'an effective strategy for: bolstering a company's public image' (Corporate Watch 2006, p. 2).

Is there wood in the trees or a tree in the woods?

There is little doubt that there is and should be considerable concern about the management of the world's environment. Many issues such as global warming and climate change are daily news items. All of us have an obligation to be aware of our effect on the environment—our 'footprint'. However, can we effect any solutions?

Is accounting a discipline whose practitioners can assist in resolving the world's problems?

Early attempts by accounting researchers to provide meaningful statements of the environmental impact of business activity were, however well intentioned, understandably superficial and unsophisticated. Researchers tried for many years to determine the form and manner in which organisations could report the environmental impact of their activities. It was only towards the end of the 20th century that attention was turned to deeper analyses of the issues. In doing so, longer term and broader issues were raised—such as the actions needed for a sustainable future. This subject involves many more issues than direct environmental impact; it involves economic, environmental and social planning and performance. It also involves notions which have been referred to as **eco-efficiency** and **eco-justice**. Efficiency is a conventional management concept. Justice is a far more complex concept and to be meaningfully addressed involves questions of social justice, ethics, and the impact of global economic activity. For example, how do the activities of large corporations in developing countries affect the lives of the poor and less economically advantaged? How do they affect traditional tribal and cultural means of existence? Eco-justice measures are needed to establish acceptable solutions to these and other big questions.

It is difficult to make sense of the myriad proposed solutions offered by researchers. Figure 9.1 presents a schema to assist with understanding the broad picture. The vertical axis represents deeply held fundamental beliefs—ontological and ideological positions. At the top of the vertical axis are economic theories of the corporation expressed by people such as Milton Friedman (corporations exist purely for the economic advancement of the shareholders and have no other external social obligations). At the bottom of this axis are those who are committed to a philosophical position embedded in social theory. Researchers here would subscribe to a communitarian theory of corporations (for example, SER sceptics such as Puxty (1986) and Cooper (1992), and Bebbington and Gray's (2001) first 'camp'). Neither position would support corporations attempting to measure and report corporate social and environmental activities, but for very different reasons. On the horizontal axis are those who believe it is possible and desirable that corporations report their social and environmental activities. At one end are researchers who have encouraged CSR (for example, Deegan and Rankin 1996) and others who investigate the extent of CSR from time to time. Those in this group would subscribe to the concession theory of the corporation. At the other end are those committed to sustainable development, those who hold that corporate activity should include much more than just reporting on social and environmental performance and extend to a commitment to social and environmental programs to ensure the future of the world. For this group

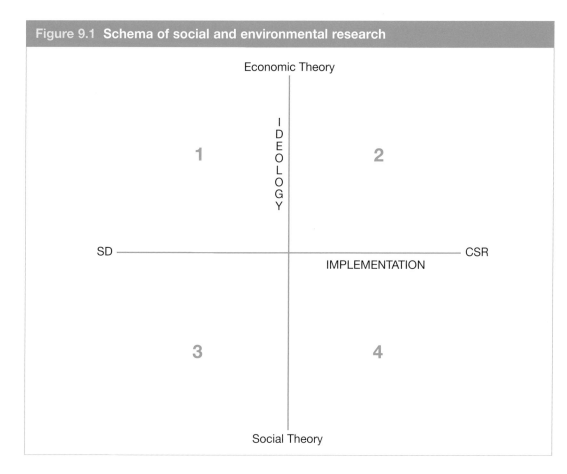

Figure 9.1 Schema of social and environmental research

Economic Theory

IDEOLOGY

1

2

SD ———————————— CSR
IMPLEMENTATION

3

4

Social Theory

corporations are inevitable. Their work (for example, Bebbington 2001) would be based on a natural entity perspective of corporations. The work of Bakan (2004) would best fit at the intersection of the two axes as he believes corporations are primarily economic organisations whose activities have broader social goals, but he is totally cynical of attempts to define 'corporate' and report social goals.

The two axes create four quadrants and, for convenience, most work would fall into one of these and would be positioned in proximity to one of the axes depending on the position taken. Examples are:

Quadrant 1 This group would subscribe to SD but view the fundamental basis of business activity as economic. In order for accountants and accounting to be involved it would be necessary for interdisciplinary work involving also scientists and ecologists. Examples include the GRI (2000), Saravanamuthu (2004), and even Gambling (1974).

Quadrant 2 Work addressing TBL (for example, Bebbington and Gray's (2001) second 'camp') would fit well here.

Quadrant 3 Work debating issues of eco-justice would fall into this quadrant. It would also include that which examines deeper accountability issues such as ecology and environmental ethics, as does Andrew (2000), and epistemological issues, as do Everett and Neu (2000).

Quadrant 4 Social audit works would fit appropriately into this quadrant.

Any diagram that classifies research, such as Figure 9.1, is inevitably simplistic but is useful for pedagogical purposes. It is two-dimensional, yet the work ranges from the simple to the highly complex dealing with a great many issues. Another dimension, a diagonal line crossing from quadrant 3 to quadrant 2, could be added to represent the type of research. Research towards the upper end (quadrant 2) would tend to be quantitative, and that towards the opposite end would tend to be qualitative.

What is the purpose of the contemporary corporation?

This chapter opened with an examination of the nature and development of the corporation. It is without doubt the single most important economic organisation in contemporary society. Despite its origins as a device for facilitating economic and commercial activity, it has grown to have the capacity to wield power greater than that of the state (government). Berle and Means' prediction from many years ago has proved correct: corporations now wield tremendous political power derived from their economic strength. Corporations, then, must assume some of the roles previously regarded as belonging to government—those designed for the betterment and protection of society. Much of the argument Bakan (2004) presents is indisputable. One of his arguments, however, is for greater *effective* regulation to control corporations. But in some countries this is not practicable as corporations have long controlled their governments. While sometimes this control is exercised by national corporations, most often it is in the hands of transnationals, which by their very nature are difficult to regulate or control. Many exploit resources in developing and poorer countries, disrupting traditional cultural systems.

On the other hand, there are many corporations whose executives seem genuinely concerned with the state of the world. Enlightened executives see the long-term survival of their corporations tied to the long-term survival of the world—the environment and societies. Here, interests of the corporation and society coalesce. It is very difficult to generalise about managerial behaviour in order to understand why some corporations seem to act more in the interests of society while some cynically pursue 'self-interest' irrespective of the cost. Assessing corporate behaviour involves research into globalisation, ethics, regulation, politics and sociology, as well as economics. In the past, accountants have not concerned themselves with anything other than the technicalities involved in providing users with information. However, determining who the users are has become more complex, as is recognised in so-called stakeholder theory. Consequently, the issue of what information to report has become more complex and there has been considerable effort expended on broadening the range of information from the economic to that which reflects broader societal interests. Questions remain, however, as to whether this has been useful and whether it is appropriate for accountants to be involved.

Research to date has not provided answers to those who argue that the involvement of accountants and accounting in these environmental and social issues is philosophically and morally inappropriate. For example, what value should be placed on certain environmental, cultural and heritage items—should trees in public parks and gardens be valued? We (in Western societies at least) now live in an age of consumerism—or 'late capitalism', as it is sometimes referred to—where everything seems to be measured in economic terms. Common sense suggests that this is inappropriate, and there is evidence to demonstrate that this is so—for example, massive environmental degradation, global warming, widespread poverty, social disruption, terrorism. It is important to tackle these and many other issues to ensure the survival of the world. In so doing it is perhaps necessary to realise what the great economist Keynes was reputed to have said:

> The difficulty lies not so much in developing new ideas as in escaping from old ones.

NOTES

1 *Salomon v. Salomon & Co Ltd* (1897) AC 22.

2 This is a simplified version. The Charter was followed by several specific pieces of legislation directed to The East India Company, such as securing the Company monopoly rights over trading interests. The point being made here is that specific legal actions were needed to set up the Company. There are several examples of similar companies being created in a similar manner in different countries many years prior to the setting up of this Company!

3 Of course, the growth of railways was also important in other countries, including the UK, as was the need for industrial growth. The discussion here is just for illustration.

4 The book has also been produced as a documentary film and has been shown in cinemas and broadcast on television (see <http://www.thecorporation.tv>).

5 *Frankenstein* is a novel by Mary Shelley (first published in 1819) in which a scientist, Victor Frankenstein, creates a man who, when endowed with life, could not be controlled by the scientist and ran amok until he finally destroyed himself by committing suicide after the death of his creator. Although the creature was never given a name, popularly it is usually referred to by the name of the scientist creator—Frankenstein.

6 For example, in 'The lunatic you work for', a review in *The Economist*, 8 May 2004.

7 Often referred to as corruption, bribery, graft and nepotism, and in other similar colourful terms!

8 This was the same term used by Belkaoui (1984) in a major book on the subject.

9 The term now seems to reflect the non-financial behaviour of a firm. Thus, a social auditor 'is a "critical friend" (ideally an outsider) who periodically checks "the books" and asks probing questions to help the organisation reflect systematically on the effectiveness of its internal operations as well as on its broad external impact', <http://www.caledonia.org.uk/social2.htm>, accessed 18 August 2007.

10 The expression had been used earlier in other related disciplines and Linblom had presented a paper employing the notion of legitimacy at the American Accounting Association meeting in 1983 but neither this nor the later paper were published in journals. One of the earliest supporters of legitimacy theory in relation to accounting reporting was Patten (1991) but he was by no means the first.

11 Of course, Bakan (2004) argues that this occurs more generally.

12 See the MCA's *Human rights factsheet*, issued in June 2005, <http://www.minerals.org.au/>.

13 See <http://www.environment.gov.au/>.

REFERENCES AND FURTHER READING

Andrew, Jane 2000, 'The accounting craft and the environmental crisis: reconsidering environmental ethics', *Accounting Forum*, vol. 24, pp. 199–221.

Bakan, Joel 2004, *The Corporation—the pathological pursuit of profit and power*, Constable and Robinson Ltd, London.

Bauer, RA & Fenn Jr, DH 1972, *The corporate social audit*, Volume 5 in *Social science frontiers*, Russell Sage Foundation, New York.

Bebbington, Jan 2001, 'Sustainable development: a review of the international development, business and accounting literature', *Accounting Forum*, vol. 25, pp. 128–157.

Bebbington, J & Gray, R 2001, 'An account of "sustainability": failure, success and a reconceptualization', *Critical Perspectives on Accounting*, vol. 12, pp. 557–587.

Belkaoui, Ahmed 1984, *Socio-economic accounting*, Quorum Books, Westport, Connecticut, US.

Berle, AA & Means, GC 1968, *The modern corporation and private property*, Harcourt, Brace and World, New York.

Carey, Alex 1995, *Taking the risk out of democracy: propaganda in the US and Australia*, University of Illinois Press, Urbana, Illinois, US.

Cooper, C 1992, 'The non and nom of accounting for (m)other nature', *Accounting, Auditing and Accountability Journal*, vol. 5, pp. 16–39.

Corporate Watch 2006, *What's wrong with corporate social responsibility?*, <http://www.corporatewatch.org/?lid=2670>.

Deegan, C 2000, *Financial accounting theory*, McGraw-Hill Book Company Australia Pty Ltd, Roseville, NSW.

Deegan, C & Rankin, M 1996, 'Do Australian companies report environmental news objectively? An analysis of environmental disclosures by firms prosecuted successfully by the Environmental Protection Authority', *Accounting, Auditing and Accountability Journal*, vol. 9, pp. 52–69.

Deegan, C, Rankin, M & Tobin, J 2002, 'An examination of the corporate social and environmental disclosures of BHP from 1983–1997: a test of legitimacy theory', *Accounting, Auditing and Accountability Journal*, vol. 15, pp. 312–343.

Environment Australia 2000, *A framework for public environmental reporting: an Australian approach*, Department of Environment and Heritage, Canberra.

Environment Australia 2003, *Triple bottom line reporting in Australia: a guide to reporting against environmental indicators*, Department of Environment and Heritage, Canberra.

Estes, Ralph 1973, *Accounting and society*, Melville Publishing Company, Los Angeles, US.

Estes, Ralph 1976, *Corporate social accounting*, John Wiley and Sons Inc, New York.

Everett, J & Neu, D 2000, 'Ecological modernization and the limits of environmental accounting', *Accounting Forum*, vol. 24, pp. 5–29.

Fowke, R & Prasad, D 1996, 'Sustainable development, cities and local government', *Australian Planner*, vol. 33, pp. 61–66.

Frost, Geoffrey R 2007, 'The introduction of mandatory environmental reporting guidelines: Australian evidence', *Abacus*, vol. 43, pp. 190–212.

Gambling, T 1974, *Societal accounting*, George Allen and Unwin, London.

Global Reporting Initiative 2000, *Sustainability reporting guidelines on economic, environmental and social performance*, Global Reporting Initiative, Boston, US.

Guthrie, James & Parker, Lee 1989, 'Corporate social reporting: rebuttal of legitimacy theory', *Accounting and Business Research*, vol. 19, pp. 343–352.

Lamberton, G 2005, 'Sustainability accounting: a brief history and conceptual framework', *Accounting Forum*, vol. 29, pp. 7–26.

Lehman, G 2004, 'Social and environmental accounting: trends and thoughts for the future', *Accounting Forum*, vol. 28, pp. 1–5.

Lindblom, CK 1994, 'The implications of organizational legitimacy for corporate social performance and disclosure', paper presented at Critical Perspectives in Accounting Conference, New York.

Linowes, DF 1968, 'Socio-economic accounting', *Journal of Accountancy*, November, pp. 37–42; reprinted in Estes 1973, op. cit., pp. 4–14.

Livingstone, JL & Gunn, SC 1974, *Accounting for social goals*, Harper & Row, New York.

O'Donovan, G 1999, 'Managing legitimacy through increased social reporting: an exploratory study', *Interdisciplinary Environmental Review*, vol. 1, pp. 63–99.

O'Donovan, G 2002, 'Environmental disclosures in the annual report: extending the applicability and predictive power of legitimacy theory, *Accounting, Auditing and Accountability Journal*, vol. 15, pp. 344–371.

Owen, Dave 1992, *Green reporting*, Chapman and Hall, London.

Patten, DM 1991, 'Exposure, legitimacy and social disclosure', *Journal of Accounting and Public Policy*, vol. 10, pp. 297–308.

Previts, Gary John & Merino, Barbara Dubis 1998, *A history of accountancy in the United States*, Ohio State University Press, Columbus, US.

Puxty, Anthony G 1986, 'Social accounting as imminent legitimation: a critique of a technicist ideology', *Advances in Public Interest Accounting*, vol. 1, pp. 95–111.

Saravanamuthu, Kala 2004, 'What is measured counts: harmonized corporate reporting and sustainable economic development', *Critical Perspectives on Accounting*, vol. 15, pp. 295–302.

Seidler, Lee J & Seidler, Lynn L 1975, *Social accounting: theory, issues, and cases*, Melville Publishing Company, Los Angeles, US.

Unerman, J, ed. 2007, *Sustainability accounting and accountability*, Routledge, London.

United Nations World Commission on Environment and Development 1987, *Our common future (the Brundtland Report)*, Oxford University Press, Oxford, UK.

Wilmshurst, T D and G R Frost (2000), 'Corporate Environmental Reporting: A Test of Legitimacy Theory', *Accounting, Auditing and Accountability Journal*, vol. 3, pp. 10–26.

P A R T

Theory and the Future of Accounting

CHAPTER 10

A Theory for Accounting?

There are many issues facing the profession of accounting today. These involve the problems raised by globalisation, the imposition of increased regulation and the diminished role of self-regulation, and the difficulty in defining professionalism, as well as concerns about the appropriate response to demands for greater ethical behaviour of practitioners, building a sustainable future in the light of seemingly impending environmental disasters and the increasing complexity of some business practices. In the past many have felt that a soundly developed accounting theory would resolve many of these issues but there has been a distinct failure to develop an acceptable theory. This has implications for the intellectual status of accounting as an independent discipline. Does it mean that accounting is merely a craft at the whim and fancy of its practitioners or can it still be a professional practice that will truly serve the interests of the societies in which it operates? These are the matters raised in this chapter. ■

It was indicated at the outset of this book that the intention was to examine the family history—the genealogy—of accounting theory in order to arrive at a better understanding of what accounting theory is and how it has shaped accounting practice. In so doing it was necessary to determine the elements of theories and how they were developed. In terms of current notions of theories and theorising, most of the developments in accounting theoretical thought have occurred since the beginning of the 20th century. It was also necessary to restrict developments in accounting thought to those that were expressed in the English language. Even so, the meaning attached to the theory has varied widely. Most views have been shaped by influences from other disciplines, the most dominant of those influences being economic theory, and very often ideas developed in the economics discipline have been imported unquestioningly into accounting. There is no doubt that traditionally accounting has largely been concerned with economic matters and that there are other facets of accounting that, until recently, have been overlooked. This belated recognition has resulted in a widening of perceptions of the place of theory and how it is formed, and there are now many competing visions of what constitutes theory—some, unfortunately, more short-sighted than others.

It was also stated in Chapter 1 that the basis of a theory is a conception of knowledge—what it is, and how reliable and dependable knowledge is created. After reviewing the extant accounting theory and research it is somewhat disappointing to discover that even well-established scholars confuse some of the notions central to the knowledge creation process. This is manifest in epistemological and methodological positions inconsistent with stated ontological stances. Even more disrupting are political interventions in the knowledge creation process, with many scholars being seemingly unaware that this is occurring. Accountants have long argued that the practice of accounting is a value-neutral process of generating information useful to users. However, a closer examination of the practice of accounting leads to the inevitable conclusion that all claims to truth, certainty and permanent foundations of knowledge have to be approached with some scepticism. For example, the theorists of the 1960s produced theoretical expositions claiming to have determined what represented the true income of the firm. Yet they all vehemently disagreed with each other! The next generation of theorists argued that they could produce an objective understanding of accounting by observing accounting practice, apparently oblivious to the fact that what they chose to observe was subjectively determined!

Accounting as a discipline

On 29 December 1923, an early accounting professor, Henry Rand Hatfield (1866–1945), presented a talk to fellow academics entitled 'An historical defense of bookkeeping' in which, as the title implies, he employed historical evidence to demonstrate the noble ancestry of the discipline of accounting (bookkeeping). He was doing this to counter the charges levelled at him by non-accounting academics over his chosen discipline: was accounting really an independent discipline worthy of its place in universities? Although not as commonly encountered today, there are still some who question the intellectual credentials of accounting. There are probably countless reasons for this, but one thing is certain: there have to be good arguments with which to defend this charge, particularly in light of accounting having been implicated in the spectacular corporate collapses of the early part of this century. For example, as presented in this book, there has been a failure to establish an acceptable theoretical basis for the practice of accounting despite most of the 20th century being devoted to a search for one. Individual theorists, communities of researchers, professional bodies and other groups have developed many theories, none of which has been able to fully satisfy those in the discipline.

One characteristic of accounting is the failure of those practising it to fully embrace the research produced by those engaged in accounting research. This is especially so in financial accounting. In fact it would be fair to say that in many sections of the practising community there seems even to be a suspicion of accounting research. Although in some instances this is understandable—where, for example, some earlier researchers have 'talked past' practice—similar division does not appear in other professional disciplines such as medicine and engineering. Business and commercial practices are highly complex, involving large numbers of quite disparate sections of society, so it is not possible to make complete behavioural generalisations. Mainstream accounting researchers have been slow to recognise this and have persisted in pursuing and undertaking research that many practitioners believe to be too esoteric and remote and not easily translatable into the practice of accounting, which remains not much more than that set out over five hundred years ago.[1] The effect has been to drive an even bigger wedge between the groups. To be fair, in recent times there has been a reorientation by many researchers in an attempt to address problems of practice such as issues in determining accounting standards. Nevertheless, there seems to be a lack of awareness by many mainstream researchers of the broader context in which accounting exists.

Accounting serves the interest of, and impacts on, very many groups in society, yet mainstream researchers persist in investigating only small sectional interests. This, together with suspicion of accounting research by many practitioners, suggests that accounting is an unintellectual craft—that is, it avoids involvement in activities normally regarded as contributing to the intellectual capital of a society, despite claims to the contrary by some professional accounting bodies! Moreover, some groups within accounting are proud to be non-intellectual in the belief that they objectively serve the practical interests of business and should not be involved in contributing to broader social goals and policies. If this is true, then it flies in the face of claims to professionalism. Recall from Chapter 8 that being a profession requires servicing the public interest on the basis of specialist knowledge and skills.

Aristotle believed there were many intellectual virtues or characteristics that complemented moral (and ethical) virtues. These are:

episteme ('scientific' knowledge)

nous (capacity for intuitive reasoning)

phronesis (the ability to deliberate well on matters of human welfare)

teche (skill or art)

sophia (wisdom and theoretical excellence).

Generally, intellectuals may be described as persons, typically well educated, who engage their intellect in work which they believe to be of cultural importance.[2] Specifically, intellectuals are those associated with the propagation and advancement of knowledge as well as the articulation of the values of society. In the Middle Ages, in Europe, the intellectuals were the clerical scholastics. Recall from Chapter 1 that they were the literate group whose primary function was to define human existence in relation to Classical knowledge and the Bible. The Enlightenment was an age of the celebration of the intellectual and many issues of philosophy and science were defined then—for example, the rules of scientific method, which still exist today. In the 19th-century Anglo-American world, the term 'intellectual' developed pejorative connotations and was used to refer to those who existed in ivory towers, remaining unconscious of everyday problems. It is perhaps this attitude that persists in the minds of some accounting practitioners and their attitudes to accounting research. In many totalitarian societies in the 20th century intellectuals were physically eliminated, as in Nazi Germany and in the 'killing fields' of the Pol Pot regime in Cambodia.

The French philosopher, Pierre Bourdieu (1930–2002), wrote about intellectuals and was wary of them—he believed, in his country at least, that they had considerable cultural capital and authority. However, he did argue that they played an important role in society—they had the ability to intervene in social issues because they were independent of political and economic influences and considerations (Webb et al. 2002, p. 18). For Bourdieu, intellectuals had an obligation to be involved in social and professional issues—to intervene in the interests of social justice through the processes of reasoning and analysis. However, such intervention is not unproblematic and Neu et al. (2001) provide some disturbing evidence that abuse of political power can override the benefits of intellectual intervention. One instance was when the (then)

British government had determined to close coal mines in the UK. Some researchers (intellectuals) intervened to show that the government's case was based on dubious accounting numbers. However, not only did the government use its political power to quash their arguments but it was also supported in this by the accounting professional body. The research undertaken by the intellectuals was overridden by political expediency. It seems that the professional accounting body was quite prepared to sacrifice intellectual independence in order to win political favour. This invites the question as to whether the accounting profession is at all interested in preserving its intellectual capital. Or does the potential for political power and privilege override intellectual integrity? This is not to argue that the professional body in this case should not have disagreed with the analysis of the researchers—to do so and to debate the issues would have been sound intellectual practice—but it was the manner in which the opposition was played out that raised this important question.

This, of course, returns us to the importance of political considerations in decision making and the power of dominant parties. Consequently, how committed is the discipline/profession to the intellectual development and analysis of knowledge?

Intellectual capital

Edvinsson and Malone suggest that:

> Intellectual capital is a combination of human capital—the brains, skills, insights, and potential of those in an organization—and structural capital—things like the capital wrapped up in customers, processes, databases, brands, and IT systems. It is the ability to transform knowledge and intangible assets into wealth creating resources, by multiplying human capital with structural capital (quoted in Holman 2005, p. 1).

Intellectual capital has become a topical subject in the management and accounting literatures. There have been many books published on it, as well as at least one journal—*The Journal of Intellectual Capital*—devoted to it. Developing and preserving the intellectual capital of an organisation is seen as sound management. But does this apply to the accounting profession? While most professional accounting bodies are committed to the 'education' of their current and future members, does this mean a commitment to the values normally regarded as intellectualism? Within organisational analysis, the expression 'intellectual capital' is confined to measurable attributes and much of the discussion in the literature is directed towards defining measurable characteristics. For example, there is considerable debate on the issue of measuring the 'worth' of intellectual property, and often traditional asset measurement techniques are employed. But what about the 'brains, skills, insights' suggested in the Edvinsson and Malone definition, let alone Aristotle's 'wisdom and theoretical excellence'?

The above are all highly debatable topics and there is unlikely to be any acceptable solution. What is of far greater importance is the *attitude* towards 'intellectualism' that can be inferred from the actions of those engaged in accounting practice, education and research. The instances detailed by Neu et al. (2001) are disturbing in that they could be representative of attitudes towards all intellectual interventions that run counter to the preferred political position. If so, there are serious political and power implications in any so-called disinterested pursuit of sound accounting knowledge. In fact, many would say that it is naive even to suggest that political considerations are not involved in all everyday decisions. The point is, however, that the development of knowledge has to take into account the political dimension. This is evident from the accounting research permitted to be undertaken in many US (and other) business schools—some respectable research styles (often involving qualitative research) are not only discouraged, they are banned—hardly what would be expected from an intellectual forum. Moreover, editors of journals refuse to accept research employing research methodologies that do not conform to their often narrow predilections. As Beaver (1996, p. 114) states, editorial policies of journals 'have a dramatic influence on the directions of accounting research'. Tinker and Puxty (1995) and Macintosh (2004) provide excellent detailed illustrations of this. Such editors, and the business schools, wield enormous coercive power. This is a situation in which 'what (knowledge) is accepted, what rejected, and how change takes place is political and sociological more than epistemological' (Gouldner, cited by Arrington 1986, p. 20).

It is significant that in discussing accounting research Beaver (1996) is totally oblivious to research that does not conform to his narrow vision. For him, accounting research comprises either that which examines accounting data as measurement or that which examines accounting data as information. His emphasis is 'on research design rather than findings' and all his research conforms to what is referred to as capital markets research. Yet he claims that the single most important factor in future research (FAR) will be the results of 'the creative process of talented individuals' (p. 114), but the form and content of capital markets research is so narrowly prescribed that it is difficult to reconcile such research with what is generally regarded as the creative process. There is no doubt that there are very intelligent individuals engaged in this type of research but because it is so narrowly prescribed it is unintellectual: it conforms neither to Edvinsson and Malone's 'practical' notion of what is intellectual nor to all of Aristotle's more general intellectual virtues. Being intellectual does not mean agreeing with all research perspectives but it does imply tolerance of alternative views on the basis that some *might* produce fruitful or meaningful research that adds to the knowledge of the discipline.

The previous chapters have presented some of the many theoretical issues in accounting. First and foremost there are the ontological and epistemological issues that shape the methodologies through which knowledge of accounting is constructed. Unfortunately, in accounting, these issues are not always well understood and myths circulate throughout the discipline. For example, the pervasive positive–normative distinction emerged from economics with disastrous consequences, as many accounting academics teach their students that a line can be drawn between what can be called a positive theory and what can be called a normative one. The term 'positive' arose from Comte's assertion that the basis of his positivism lay in knowledge resulting from facts derived from direct experience—which he called 'positive'. The term 'normative' is derived from norms or systems of values. Late in the 19th century the economist, John Neville Keynes, the father of the better-known John Maynard Keynes, called for the discipline of economics to rely more on positive knowledge (in the Comptean sense) than normative knowledge, by which he presumably meant that economists should seek more empirical evidence. When Watts and Zimmerman (1978) wrote of positive accounting theory (PAT) a myth was created that has persisted in accounting—that there can be positive theories and normative theories. Many adherents of PAT fail to appreciate the intricacies of positivism (see Christenson 1983), yet the term 'normative' has become a pejorative term in accounting. All knowledge emerges from a consensus of beliefs rather than a correspondence with the natural world. Any attempt to produce knowledge of the world entails subjective choices. What we choose to investigate and how and what we observe are the result of choices (they are theory laden); the language in which we express this knowledge is derived from social consensus. The PAT adherents mistakenly cling to the outmoded and misguided notion that knowledge can be determined objectively—that there can be knowledge which corresponds to nature.

As the issues facing accounting are encountered it becomes obvious that any claims to objectivity are misguided. According to Arrington (1986), 'we [accounting researchers] are naive with respect to the political and ideological commitments which inform our research since we have erroneously presumed that we can function as "value-free", "objective" scholars' (p. 2). In fact, accounting knowledge is subject to political, legal (regulation), global, ethical and social, as well as economic, pressures.

Valuation

Most of mainstream accounting research concentrated on purely conventional economic considerations. Despite this, the responses of the early modernist theorists (pre-1970) and those of the later modernists (post-1970) were very different. However, on closer examination it is apparent that the differences stem from differing methodological emphases. For the early modernist theorists, such as Chambers, it was critical to state assumptions and carefully define terms. Thus, these became the foundations of his later theorising—it is entirely consistent with his stated assumptions and definitions. In the work of the later modernists it was necessary to infer their assumptions and definitions from their data. For Chambers (1966), the internal consistency of his 'argument' was crucial. For the later theorists it was the validity of their inferences and the testing of their hypotheses that became critical. Both types of theories are positivist and, as such, are based on empiricism, but the early modernists did not have access to the large databases and information processing technologies used by the later modernists. The fact that the later modernists selected data primarily from securities markets narrowed the scope of their theoretical interests, and it is possible to infer from this their theoretical intentions.

Although there were very different methodological emphases, both the early and the later modernists were essentially concerned with valuation, probably the most single important issue for (economics-oriented) accounting researchers for the best part of the last one hundred years. The early modernists were concerned with determining appropriate general asset valuations from which a 'true income' (they are sometimes referred to as the true income theorists) could be determined and reported in financial statements. The later modernists turned their attention to overall 'firm valuations' that would be reflected in securities prices. Despite this, however, never far away was the notion of intrinsic value.

Surprisingly, both approaches depend on a belief in the efficiency of markets. The early modernist theorists were working at a time of rising price levels—inflationary conditions. Historical cost accounting had given rise to many significant problems. In a static price level situation a balance sheet, logically, is a list of unallocated cost resources and commitments where cost approximates some notion of 'value'. However, when price levels change, a list of balances is virtually meaningless. The adding of the individual components further contributes to the lack of any meaningful information as each item measures different attributes (different dates give rise to different measuring units). With the emphasis of accounting on providing information useful for decision making—the decision usefulness emphasis—a balance sheet does not provide decision makers with any useful information. It was felt that the balance sheet should provide information on the firm's financial position. For Chambers, management needed to know what financial resources the firm had in order to make decisions about future actions and directions the firm would take. Consequently, he argued that this information would best be reflected in the market selling prices of its assets—the financial resources available to management was the sum of the market *selling* price of its resources (if they were to be sold at this point in time) net of the firm's immediate financial commitments. Other theorists argued that it was the maintenance of physical capacity that would ensure the survival of the firm. Therefore, the relevant measures of resources would be the *replacement* market prices of its assets—that is, how much it would cost the firm to replace its assets in order to maintain the same level of productivity. In both systems, income was the excess of the 'value' of the net assets of the firm over a period after an adjustment for the immediate effect of rises in the general price levels. Chambers's system was referred to as continuously contemporary accounting (CoCoA), or exit price accounting; the other was known as replacement value accounting (RVA), replacement cost accounting (RCA) or current cost accounting (CCA) (there were minor differences in the three variants but this is not the place to detail them—essentially they all involved the use of current replacement prices). Both systems were discussed in Chapter 2. The objective of the two main approaches was to provide decision makers (users of financial statements) with a meaningful statement of the firm's financial position, which was not reflected in historical cost accounting statements due (mainly) to the effects of fluctuating (in reality, rising) price levels. The survival of the firm was obviously important and under the former system the emphasis was on the financial resources needed to maintain survival; in the latter it was on the level of resources needed to maintain physical survival. This is essentially what is referred to in the IASB's *Framework* as 'capital maintenance'.

A third, more abstract measurement notion also emerged at this time. This was known as deprival value. The **deprival value** of an asset is the lower of its replacement cost and the higher of its net present value (NPV) and its net realisable value (NRV), or current selling price. The asset is valued at reporting date at an amount that represents the loss that might be expected to be incurred by the firm if it were deprived of the use of the asset or the expected future economic benefits derived from it. The concept achieved added significance in Australia in the 1990s because it was the method prescribed by the Steering Committee on National Performance Monitoring of Government Trading Enterprises (1994) for government trading entities. It included reference to the replacement cost (RC) and the current exit price—the net realisable value—of an asset as well as to its net present value, a fourth asset measurement notion.

Economic value

The later modernist theorists rejected the valuation work of the earlier theorists and turned to economic theory. In 1929 Canning, an economics professor, published a book *The economics of accountancy*. In his book Canning argued that the accountants' notion of value was retrospective and had no theoretical basis. He believed that they should adopt an economic theory of value: the value of an asset should reflect the expected future benefits to be derived from it (as discussed in Chapter 2). Because the neo-empirical researchers drew their ideas from economic theory it is not difficult to see that they readily adopted Canning's notion and economic value became a central tenet of their accounting research. Basically, the economic value of an asset is the present value of the future cash flows it generates. This is represented by:

$$PV_t = \sum_{j=1+r}^{T} CF_j(1 + r)^{t-1}$$

where PV_t is the present value at time t, CF represents the cash flow and r is the interest rate. **Economic income** is essentially the increment in the PV over a period $(PV_{t+1} - PV_t)$. Note that the prescribed measurement of assets recommended in the various conceptual frameworks is closely related to this notion (but there are exceptions!).

It is important to appreciate that the above concepts are so defined in conditions of certainty and (near) perfect market conditions. These are unrealistic assumptions and much of the research undertaken by later modernists was designed to explain how empirically determined measures vary from those expected in such perfect market conditions. However, economic value is envisaged as a *market value*. In the language of economics, economic value is a *stock concept* and economic income is a *flow concept*. Most of the neo-empirical research, discussed in Chapter 3, is premised on notions of economic value and economic income.

Market value

Another matter on which both the early and late theorists were agreed was the need in accounting for a more rigorous appreciation of what market value entailed. A major difference was that the early modernists were interested in valuing individual assets held by the firm, the summation of which, less commitments, representing a 'value' of the firm. The later modernists 'valued' the firm in terms of its total market capitalisation (its shares). Thus, both approaches were very different and both had their own sets of inherent problems. Whereas the former was subject to several markets (assets), the latter assumed securities markets (only) were best placed to determine a firm's value. However, there was a tendency to reify 'the market' as some all-knowing, omniscient arbiter of all worldly problems! A market is simply a meeting point of those wishing to make exchanges and, like all social institutions, is subject to human foibles. Markets are subject to manipulation and rely on political and social power to maintain their viability. Arguments that they are neutral arbiters rest on circular reasoning. Consequently, in most instances there is unlikely to be a single market 'value' so decision makers have to choose from a *range* of 'values' and they need some basis for making such choices. For example, if I wish to sell my car, I will receive different offers depending on how I proceed—private open sale, private sale to friends or family, trade-in, etc. Are they different markets? What then is the 'value' of my car? Inevitably it comes down to my objectives. In many instances there will be no 'problem'—for example, where there are many similar transactions—but it cannot be argued that certainty exists. To be fair, most researchers realise this and their research is designed to explain anomalous effects of market imperfections.

In accounting, many problems arise as a result of the way in which accounting has been (and often must be) practised. For example, there will be issues of recognition (of assets, liabilities, revenues and expenses, etc.), those arising from the necessity for accruals (as a result of the need for regular periodic reporting) and those resulting from the conservative practices of accountants (a traditional behavioural tendency to caution).

Accounting is employed in a great many instances other than in public companies, so calculating the value of a firm on the basis of its market capitalisation is a limited notion of value. There are many public sector institutions which satisfy accountability responsibilities through the provision of financial reports. These institutions include government trading enterprises (GTEs) which are, in effect, like other corporations but without the share ownership structure (for example, an electricity utility, selling electricity to consumers). Consequently, value cannot be determined through market capitalisation. However, valuation of a GTE and its resources is important for at least two reasons: first, the survival of the entity and, second (and related to the first), establishing the pricing of its goods or services. For example, with the electricity utility, what price should it charge its customers for supplying electricity? As mentioned above, a body charged with regulating and monitoring GTEs, the Steering Committee on National Performance Monitoring of Government Trading Enterprises (1994), required entities to use deprival value for the measurement of their assets.

Other public sector organisations also have to provide accrual-based financial statements but do not have any market from which they can determine a 'value' to use as the base for measuring assets. Similarly, there are many not-for-profit organisations that need to produce financial statements.

Thus, notions of value are important in many organisations other than private corporations. Consequently, valuation has been a major problem for the accounting profession for some time. It is interesting to note that prior to the adoption of accrual accounting by the public sector a cash-based accounting system was used. The reporting entity accounted in terms of receipts and disbursements of cash. The purchase of a piece of equipment (a non-current asset) was recorded as a cash disbursement. A register of equipment therefore had to be maintained, but in non-financial terms, so valuation was not necessary. The move to accrual accounting by the public sector raised the question of asset valuation. Accrual accounting gives rise to the need for valuation and this is why it has become a subject of research interest.

Other values

The world of commerce has become quite complex. This is certainly true of financial instruments, especially the question of how they are reported in financial statements as they assume a greater significance in a firm's financial structure. Although a much older practice, in the 1980s it became popular to record such assets as **mark to market**. Essentially, this involves assigning such 'assets' the current market price for that or a similar financial instrument. In the US, as of 1997, some businesses (such as securities traders) have been permitted to employ mark to market accounting for taxation purposes. Any security or commodity held at balance date (usually 31 December) is permitted to be valued at the then current market price. This can be construed as a partial acceptance of exit price accounting advocated by Chambers and others. Note that at this time it applies only to financial securities (held by traders). However, there has been considerable discussion of another valuation notion very similar to the exit price, namely **fair value**.

In the US, the Financial Accounting Standards Board (FASB) has issued an accounting standard, *SFAS 157 Fair value measurements*. The International Accounting Standards Board (IASB) intends issuing a similar standard in 2008. It had previously provided a definition in IFRS1, Appendix A: 'fair value is the amount for which an asset could be exchanged, or a liability settled, between knowledgeable, willing parties in an arm's length transaction'. A very similar definition exists in *SFAS 157*. However, two views of this have emerged. First, as would be expected, adherents of the efficient market hypothesis (EMH) believe that (rationally) fair value is essentially the market price. Others have less faith in rational market behaviour and so argue that fair value is not the market price (recall the discussion on noisy trading in Chapter 3). Therefore, while it would be reasonable to assume that fair value is the market price because of market irregularities (that is, markets are not perfect), it is not as simple as that. Nevertheless, the term 'fair value' would seem to imply a close relation to market price. It is similar, too, to what Chambers was advocating.[3] All this implies dissatisfaction with the use of traditional historical cost measures only. To be consistent with the idea of decision usefulness of financial reports, it is clear that it is necessary to take account of many more considerations than envisaged in traditional (historical cost) accounting. This is also true of accounting generally—there are necessary considerations beyond mere economic arguments.

Images of accounting

Over a quarter of a century ago Davis et al. (1982) wrote of the images that had shaped accounting theory:

> Working within a framework of defining a numerical view of reality, accountants draw on different images of the accounting process to elaborate different theories of accounting (p. 307).

They suggested four images in financial accounting, namely:

- Accounting as a historical record
- Accounting as current economic reality
- Accounting as an information system, and
- Accounting as a commodity.

The argument is interesting in that it calls into question the belief that accounting exists as part of a fixed reality, which has led to the mistaken belief that accountants are merely neutral recorders of the objective facts of this economic reality. This sort of belief is central to modernist thought. Ironically, Davis et al. were not arguing for a move away from modernist thinking but they did *observe* that accounting theory had been shaped by very different perspectives of what accounting is, thus destroying the notion of a fixed foundation to accounting knowledge. There have been many developments since the time of their writing, and their ideas have been extensively expanded upon. For example, Arrington and Francis (1989) argued that the social sciences were moving out of an era of modernism—'it is an untenable philosophical position' (p. 1)—and it was long past the time for accounting researchers to have abandoned 'any desire to somehow "ground" knowledge in an external and transcendental metaphysics like the positivist's faith in observation or the Marxist's faith in historical determinism' (p. 1).

Referring to an earlier paper by Burchell et al., Graham and Neu (2005) acknowledge that accounting serves complex purposes both within organisations and within the wider social practice in which the organisations exist:

> accounting systems serve to reduce uncertainty about organizational decisions, sometimes providing calculable answers, sometimes enabling learning, sometimes providing ammunition for political conflicts, and sometimes merely helping to rationalize past decisions (p. 451).

It is important that those concerned with accounting recognise this and develop new systems of thought for understanding this broader vision of accounting. This would requires an *intellectual* appreciation of the place, significance and establishment of accounting knowledge, which returns us to the earlier discussion.

Also recognising the increasing power of accounting to shape organisational, political and social contexts, Sikka et al. (1995) argue that 'accountants have colonized "regulatory spaces" to shape notions of truth, fairness and proper business conduct' (p. 113). Thus, they see more sinister motives. They suggest that accountants *are* aware of the broader significance of accounting in society and have used this knowledge as an instrument of power—to take advantage of this knowledge to manipulate society for their own aims. They suggest that there have been one or two academic accountants who have worked hard to increase public awareness of the uses and abuses of accounting knowledge. Like Neu et al. (2001), they feel that 'professional interests' have worked to silence the voices of these intellectuals. However, they go further to ask whether 'As intellectuals, are accounting academics concerned to act in ways that engage more directly with the values of fairness, justice, greater democratic participation, openness and accountability?' (p. 114). They concur with Edward Said who argued that an intellectual was someone 'whose place it is "to confront orthodoxy and dogma" and to "represent all those people and issues that are routinely forgotten or swept under the rug" but without claiming that such challenges are themselves value-free' (p. 115).

'Retaining an independent voice and being adept at survival is a challenge to all intellectuals' (p. 118). Unfortunately, the past has shown us that few in the accounting academe have been prepared to take on such challenges and the overall preference has been to feel comfortable and secure with the status quo. Consequently, accounting knowledge has been slow to develop and has remained the property of powerful business interests and the dominant economic theory. This has been manifest in the research that many business schools have been 'permitted' to undertake, reinforced by the editorial policies of many journals, as mentioned previously. In accounting, conservatism persists in more than just valuation practices!

That accounting serves the interests of powerful management and owners is nowhere more apparent than in management accounting. Management accountants have been instrumental in designing and implementing systems of control and performance measurement designed only to benefit those interests. They have reinforced the notions of scientific management popular early in the 20th century but subsequently denigrated by employee interests and industrial and other sociologists aware of their dehumanising effects. A good example is the case of Telstra Australia reported on an ABC TV *Four Corners* program (reporter Quentin McDermott, 8 June 2007) where it was observed that:

> . . . increasingly Telstra's 40 000-plus workers say they are feeling the pain. Some angrily accuse the company of forcing cultural change too far, too fast and with scant regard to their welfare and dignity.

The program went on to report on the fate of one long-serving line technician who, it was argued, had an exemplary past record as one of the top technicians—if not the top. After new control measures were introduced by the company, he became so disillusioned and depressed that he committed suicide. Obviously there is no absolute proof that the suicide resulted from the new control measures, but another Telstra worker, also with an excellent past employment record, Sally Sandic, also committed suicide after such measures were introduced by the company.

This is a good example of what has been termed 'the increasing influence of accounting calculus', or 'the numerical view of reality' to which Davis et al. (1982) were referring. Classical economists referred to the factors of production as land, labour and capital. Therefore, management accountants have seen workers simply as a factor of production that can be reduced to numerical measures. Previously these numbers were money numbers but reference to recent management accounting textbooks shows that non-monetary measures are now being recommended as part of performance indicators to be used as part of the control mechanisms of management. Many of these developments apply equally to public sector organisations and the private sector.

Extending the boundaries of concern

Bourdieu believed that 'researchers should constantly take into account their own presuppositions about their field of research, and understand the extent to which their way of seeing informs what they are likely to see' (Webb et al. 2002, p. 65). One of these 'presuppositions' relates to language. For a long time most people took language for granted, but during the 20th century awareness began to grow of how essential language was to knowledge, and investigations into the structures, uses and importance of language began to assume momentous importance. There have been, and still are, a number of 'disciplines' devoted to the study of language, although going by different names. While this is not the place to enter a discussion of these various 'paradigms', a list of *some* of them and an example of a person associated with each, as presented in Table 10.1 (overleaf), illustrates the extent of language (or linguistic) analysis in the 20th century.

Table 10.1 Some examples of language, or linguistic, paradigms

Description of language paradigm	Example of associated theorist
Structuralism	Saussure
Semiotics	Peirce
Theory of signs	Morris
Analytical linguistics	Wittgenstein
Ordinary language philosophy	Austin
Semiology	Barthes
Hermeneutics	Gadamer
Generative grammar	Chomsky
Discourse analysis	Stubbs
Rhetoric 'theory'	McCloskey
Critical discourse analysis	Foucault
Deconstruction	Derrida

In addition to these paradigms, there are several associated fields of study such as communications theory, information theory, contextual analysis and conversational analysis.

An appreciation of language is vital to understanding the practice and theory of accounting. Recall from Chapter 1 that the essential criterion of knowledge is communication—knowledge exists only when it is communicated (who knows what the sound of a tree falling in an uninhabited forest is?). Recall from Chapter 3 that a criticism of positive accounting theory related to how its exponents used language to *persuade* others they were right (the use they make of rhetoric). Recall from Chapter 6 how international accounting regulations (e.g. IFRS) assume a translation (from English) of universal concepts is unproblematic. And recall from Chapters 8 and 9 that notions such as 'in the public interest' and 'sustainable development' are contentious and highly contested. Moreover, let us not forget that the metaphor, 'accounting is the language of business', has been used regularly over the years!

Positivists (which would include Morris, Wittgenstein and Austin from the list in Table 10.1) argued that there could be a neutral language whereby signs (words) could *correspond* to empirical objects. Semiotics is generally the science of signs. Proponents of positivist semiotics, such as Morris, classified signs as being **syntactic** (the relation of sign to sign, with therefore no relation to everyday objects), **semantic** (the relation of sign to everyday objects) or **pragmatic** (the human behavioural response to signs). Whereas syntactical signs (e.g. mathematical notation) conveyed no meaning, complex theories of semantics and logic were used to argue that there could be a unique meaning conveyed by signs such that truths could be established.[4] The positivists' intention was to create a philosophy of language consistent with the philosophy of science. This led to sterility and also to a disenchantment with attempts to determine 'a philosophy of meaning' through linguistic analysis, some suggesting that the 'philosophy of language suffered too long from the metaphysical presuppositions of positivism' (Rorty 1992, p. 361, referring to the work of Fodor and Katz).

One unfortunate lasting legacy of the positivists' work is the analytic–synthetic dichotomy.[5] This suggests that there is a distinction between everyday language and a meta (theoretical) language. **Synthetic statements** (note 'statements', not 'signs'—i.e. words) have everyday world referents and are logically contingent, while **analytic statements** are purely internal and true by virtue of their meaning (they are tautologous). Positive accounting theorists believe that there can be statements which are purely analytic and, generally (but not solely), these would be those that are expressed mathematically. These are then combined with synthetic statements— empirically determined statements—to form theory, which is then claimed to be objective. This line of thinking follows a line of modernist thought from Descartes (1596–1650) that there could be clear, unambiguous words which could be moulded into a calculus-like language so that knowledge could be created with the precision, clarity and power of mathematics.

Unfortunately, positive accounting theorists (and other accounting positivists) 'missed the boat'. Philosophers and social scientists had taken what Boland (1989) and others had referred to as a 'hermeneutic turn', and had come to

> . . . the realization of our own deep, personal involvement in interpreting our inherently symbolic and multi-vocal everyday language in constructing all we know (p. 216).

That is, an acceptance that knowledge of an event or experiment can only be determined through interpretation; meaning (and therefore knowledge) is derived from the *interpretations* of the researcher. Recall from Chapter 1 that the scholastics— the religious scholars of the Dark Ages—were engaged in hermeneutical study in interpreting the Bible. Interpretation and accounting was discussed in Chapter 7. The term 'hermeneutics' now extends to theories and methods for understanding human action and artefacts. Terms (relevant to the present discussion) associated with it include **text**, **discourse** and **rhetoric** (and, of course, **interpretation**). Text has commonly been used to refer to the written word. However, in the 20th century it became much more widely used to refer to those things that convey meaning. In fact some philosophers (such as Foucault and Derrida) argue that all meaning (and, therefore, knowledge) is derived from the interpretation of texts, and interpretation in turn is always contextual—that is, meaning is always context dependent. If this is so, then it is not possible to stand 'outside' and attain an objective basis for knowledge. Our world is, then, intentional—we create it and communicate it through language. Meaning is produced by language. Therefore, a corporation is 'produced' by its financial statements—we conceive of the corporation through the system of signs (words and numbers) that comprise its financial statements. We say things like 'it is a good company' or a 'weak company' and so on. We arrive at this 'reality' through a sort of **deconstruction** process. That is, we interpret the corporation in terms of the analysis of its financial statements we engage in, using the categories we create and privilege (or, in other words, the hierarchical order we impose) and, once created, these categories take on meaning (e.g. liquidity). This illustration is a little 'forced' and simplistic but it does suggest the importance of 'language' to the way we determine the world. To people like Derrida knowledge emerges from our deconstructing language. Arrington and Francis (1989) provide a much more sophisticated appreciation of the significance of deconstruction to accounting. Amongst other things they believe:

> . . . that accounting has the capacity to construct realities in a manner that dictates the conditions of human life and the current theories of accounting are infused with unexamined commitments to particular moral and social orders (p. 4).

Neo-empirical accounting researchers subscribe to the positivist possibility of objective and universal truths—the notion that truth, by its very nature, exists outside any perspectival bias. Their research is designed to move closer to uncovering these truths and is therefore, in their eyes, scientific. This overlooks the major contention in the work of Thomas Kuhn that science progresses through a community of scholars working around an accepted paradigm, as explained in Chapter 1. A paradigm, as a set of presuppositions which constitute a body of evidence, dominates until superseded by another with greater explanatory power. Post-Kuhnian scholarship demonstrates that part of the dominance of a particular paradigm results from the social and political power created though the capacity of its adherents to *persuade* others—the use of rhetoric. Therefore, a large part of the success of a paradigm is due to use of language. Consequently, some philosophers and researchers have argued that meaning is created through the transformation of experiences through dialogical relations—the discourse between participants. A result has been the growth of what is referred to as **discourse analysis**.

For some, the term 'discourse' is defined simply as 'a formal discussion of a topic' (e.g. Descartes's *Discourse on method*, 1637). Foucault (1972) used it to refer to 'the general domain of all statements, sometimes as an individualizable group of statements, and sometimes as regulated practice that accounts for a number of statements' (p. 80). The former refers to linguistic qualities, and much discourse analysis is technical analysis of language. The latter is much more general and is concerned with power as a central condition of society and how language is used to incorporate this power. It is more usually known as critical discourse analysis (CDA), which Wodak (2004) defines as:

> . . . fundamentally interested in analysing opaque as well as transparent structural relationships of dominance, discrimination, power and control as manifested in language (p. 199).

A good example of how CDA could be employed in accounting research would be in an analysis of the continuing debate between advocates of rules-based accounting standards and supporters of principles-based standards (discussed in Chapter 6). Although purportedly about the best approach to formulating accounting standards, the debate has strong undertones of the power relationships (and issues of control) between the FASB and the IASB. This is the essence of Foucault's CDA in which discourse reveals the power of knowledge in determining not only *what* can be said but *who* can say it.

This brief discussion of the importance of language to knowledge suggests that if we are serious about understanding knowledge in (and of) accounting then it is vital that we examine how language establishes this knowledge. Language, however, does not remain static and therefore it would be wrong to suggest that we could move to a fixed point in accounting. That is, we could not produce a single objective concept of knowledge of accounting that could be expressed in a universally valid vocabulary. It might be more appropriate (to paraphrase Wodak 2004) to seek fundamental categories, concepts and relationships organising accounting and other knowledge across time. But we should remember that:

> Every claim to knowledge is a discourse, a text, and is both a product of human manufacture and inseparable from the language which gives it expression (Arrington and Francis 1989, p. 4).

The broader context of accounting practice

This chapter has canvassed a wide range of topics that affect knowledge of accounting. Until recently, most accounting research was framed around dominant economic thinking. Consequently, the major issue in accounting has concerned valuation, and valuation entails measurement. However, to rely solely on economic thinking is to adopt a far too narrow perspective as there are many other factors that contribute to knowledge. Unfortunately, many accounting education programs ignore the essential interdisciplinary nature of (accounting) knowledge—they are too specialised. The effect is similar to what Lowe (1994) argued was the problem of programs in economics:

> Allowing students to graduate in economics without understanding its political implications, or in the technologies without appreciating their wide-ranging social implications, is like instructing army artillery officers in the mathematical principles of ballistics without telling them that the shells explode and kill people. It is almost culpably irresponsible (p. 20).

Thus, valuation is a much broader issue involving much more than purely economic considerations. What this chapter has shown is that it involves language and political power. To close our minds to this is to adopt an unintellectual position.

That accounting is subject to political implications is not a new insight; it has been discussed by well-known accounting writers. Watts (1995) fully acknowledges and provides an explanation of this. However, elsewhere, he also acknowledges that the methodology of PAT has relied on the 'methodology of economics, finance and science generally' (Watts and Zimmerman 1990, p. 153). In making this statement the authors are restating the narrow perspective adopted by PAT (and capital markets) researchers, that finance is heavily dependent on economics, and by 'science generally' they are probably espousing the outdated positivist perception of methodology. However, as indicated in Chapter 3, their appeal to the authority of science is an example of the use of rhetoric similar to that of a Minister of the Environment claiming that a potentially environmentally disastrous pulp mill has been scientifically proven to be safe despite the majority of the population being opposed to it!

In Chapter 1 it was stated that this book was an attempt to present a genealogy of accounting (thought). The notion of a genealogical description of a discipline was first conceived by the philosopher Nietzsche (1844–1900) and was taken up by later philosophers such as Foucault and Bourdieu. The important feature of genealogical explanation is recognition of the past—the importance of history:

> . . . [we] cannot grasp the dynamics of a field . . . without a historical, that is a genetic, analysis of its constitution and of the tensions that exist between positions of it, as well as between this field and other fields, and especially the field of power (Bourdieu and Wacquant, quoted in Webb et al., p. 53).

Foucault is perhaps better known than Bourdieu for his championing of genealogical methodology and he too was concerned with the power created through disciplinary discursive practices. His concern was with the material conditions of discourse which he defined as institutions, political events, and economic practices and processes (Foucault 1972). That is, he was concerned to show how those with power within a discipline define what knowledge is within that discipline. A genealogical history of a discipline shows that knowledge does not proceed linearly but discontinuously through a series of disparate events and accidents. Maybe capital markets research in accounting developed simply because researchers had access to financial securities databases and the technology for their analysis (the computer). This then gave a different definition of accounting from that which previously existed.

Therefore, a genealogical history is not a continuous, linear, cumulative progression of knowledge. As with a family history there are many threads which lead nowhere and many fortuitous events. The search for GAAP did not emerge from accountants wanting to develop a theoretical base for their discipline but from the disasters of the Great Depression. Nevertheless, such a search did contribute to what was accepted as the 'knowledge' of accounting.

Is there a theory for accounting?

It is not a new insight to claim that there can be no one theory of accounting. Other disciplines do not have a single theory—there is no theory of medicine, no theory of law, and no theory of engineering. However, the practice of each of these disciplines depends on theoretical understanding. As Aristotle said, practice proceeds from theory. There are many very significant societal problems in which accounting needs to play a role. Of particular urgency are those concerning environmental issues, ethical issues, globalisation issues—and there are many more.

The environment in which accounting is practised has recently changed dramatically, partly as a result of the above issues and partly because of increasing regulation. Those engaged in the practice of accounting have to adopt approaches that are well beyond those of the past, and thus an appreciation of the interdisciplinary nature of accounting theory and research is essential. Accounting is shaped by the demands placed on it, but it also shapes the environments with which it interacts. Consequently, accountants need to be aware of social, political, legal and linguistic considerations, and not just serve the economic interests of a few members of society. It may be necessary, as some have argued, for there to be new accountings.

NOTES

1 Of course, there have been many modifications as business practices and the economic environment have become more complex.

2 Jary, D & Jary, J 1991, *Collins dictionary of sociology*, HarperCollins, Glasgow, Scotland.

3 However, the Standards specify the situations in which the use of fair value measurements are appropriate.

4 This brief and simple explanation obviously does not do justice to the depth of the philosophical inquiry and debate, but this is not the place to extend the discussion. The important point to note relating to the positivists' view is their belief in a correspondence theory of truth.

5 The distinction was made by Kant but later adopted as a main tenet of positivism.

REFERENCES AND FURTHER READING

Arrington, CE 1986, 'The rhetoric of inquiry and accounting research', Working Paper 86-02, The University of Iowa, US.

Arrington, CE & JR Francis 1989, Letting the chat out of the bag: deconstruction, privilege and accounting research', *Accounting, Organizations and Society*, vol. 14, pp. 1–28.

Beaver, William 1996, 'Directions of accounting research: NEAR and FAR', *Accounting Horizons*, pp. 112–121.

Boland, RJ 1989, 'The coming hermeneutic turn in accounting research', in O Johnson, ed., *Methodology and accounting research: does the past have a future?*, pp. 215–233, University of Illinois, Champaign, Illinois, US.

Canning, John B 1929, *The economics of accountancy*, Ronald Press, New York.

Chambers, RJ 1966, *Accounting, evaluation and economic behavior*, Prentice Hall, Englewood Cliffs, New Jersey, US.

Christenson, C 1983, 'The methodology of positive accounting', *The Accounting Review*, vol. 58, pp. 1–22.

Davis, S, Menon, K & Morgan, G 1982, 'The images that have shaped accounting theory', *Accounting, Organizations and Society*, vol. 7, pp. 307–318.

Foucault, M 1972, *The archaeology of knowledge*, Tavistock Publications, Bristol, UK.

Graham, C & Neu, D 2005, 'Accounting for globalization', *Accounting Forum*, vol. 27, pp. 449–471.

Holmen, Jay 2005, 'Intellectual capital reporting', *Management Accounting Quarterly*, vol. 6, no. 4, pp. 1–7.

Lavoie, Don 1987, 'The accounting of interpretations and the interpretation of accounts: the communicative function of "the language of business"', *Accounting, Organizations and Society*, vol. 12, pp. 579–604.

Lowe, Ian 1994, *Our universities are turning us into the ignorant country*, University of New South Wales Press, Sydney.

Macintosh, NB 2004, 'A ghostly CAR ride', *Critical Perspectives on Accounting*, vol. 15, pp. 675–695.

Neu, D, Cooper, D & Everett, J 2001, 'Critical accounting interventions', *Critical Perspectives on Accounting*, vol. 12, pp. 735–752.

Rorty, R 1992, *The linguistic turn—essays in philosophical method*, University of Chicago Press, Chicago, US.

Sikka, P, Wilmott, H & Puxty, T 1995, 'The mountains are still there: accounting academics and the bearings of intellectuals', *Accounting, Auditing and Accountability Journal*, vol. 3, pp. 113–140.

Steering Committee on National Performance Monitoring of Government Trading Enterprises 1994, *Guidelines on accounting policy for valuation of assets of government trading enterprises using current valuation methods*, Melbourne.

Tinker, Tony & Puxty, Tony 1995, *Policing accounting knowledge: the market for excuses affair*, Markus Weiner Publishers, Princeton, New Jersey, US.

Watts, RL 1995, 'Accounting choice theory and market-based research in accounting', in S Jones, C Romano & J Ratnatunga, eds, *Accounting theory: a contemporary review*, pp. 430–455, Harcourt Brace, Sydney.

Watts, RL & Zimmerman, JL 1978, 'Towards a positive theory of the determinants of accounting standards', *The Accounting Review*, vol. 53, pp. 112–134.

Watts, RL & Zimmerman, JL 1990, 'Positive accounting theory: a ten year review', *The Accounting Review*, vol. 65, pp. 131–156.

Webb, Jen, Schirato, Tony & Danaher, Geoff 2002, *Understanding Bourdieu*, Allen and Unwin, Crows Nest, NSW.

Wodak, Ruth 2004, 'Critical discourse analysis', in Clive Searle et al., eds, *Qualitative research practices*, pp. 197–213, Sage, London.

Glossary

a posteriori Knowledge which is dependent on experience. Philosophical empiricism holds that all knowledge is *a posteriori*. There is now a tendency for philosophers to argue that the distinction between *a priori* and *a posteriori* is false and serves no useful purpose.

a priori Knowledge independent of experience. Importantly, *a priori* knowledge is distinguished by its method of proof *not* by how we came to acquire it. It is a highly contested notion which is dependent on the particular epistemology adopted and the context in which it is used. For example, mathematical truths are said to be known *a priori* (2 + 2 = 4), and in ethics we know *a priori* that promises ought to be kept. Its opposite is *a posteriori*.

agency theory A theory developed to explain the ways in which agents, linked by contractual arrangements with a firm, influence its behaviour such as its organisational and capital structure, remuneration policies, accounting techniques and attitudes towards risk-taking. Costs incurred in administering principal-agent relationships are referred to as agency costs.

agent (in accounting, finance and law) A person who, or entity which, acts on behalf of another person or entity (the principal).

aggregate theory (of corporations) The perspective that an individual property owner has the right to contract with her or his property and forming a company is one form this contracting can take.

analytic statements Statements which are purely internal and true by virtue of their meaning (tautologous).

association studies Capital market research studies which test for a positive correlation between an accounting performance measure (e.g. earnings of cash flow from operations) and share returns.

bonding cost Costs incurred by agents to indicate to principals that they are acting appropriately on their behalf.

capital assets pricing model (CAPM) A model that describes the relationship between risk and expected return of securities. The expected return of a security or a portfolio equals the rate on a risk-free security plus a risk premium.

categorical imperative Kant's term for any universal moral obligation (duty).

causality The principle that every change or event has a cause.

CoCoA Continuously contemporary accounting—a theory developed by Raymond Chambers.

commodification Where economic value is assigned to something not previously considered in economic terms (e.g. an idea, identity, gender); the treatment of things as if they were a tradeable commodity.

communitarian theory (of corporations) The view that the corporation is much more than a set of private arrangements (contracts) as in the economic and aggregate theories, and more than a public creation as in concession theory.

comparative accounting The study of factors deemed to be the cause of national differences in accounting.

compliance Maintaining adherence to rules and regulations.

concession theory (or corporations) The view that the corporation exists as a concession or privilege of the state which 'concedes' the right of the corporation to exist, thereby acknowledging the interests of the public over the private interest of individuals.

conditionalities Conditions imposed on borrowing countries by the International Monetary Fund and the World Bank.

context of discovery The view held by positivist philosophers of science and others such as Karl Popper that the origination of new theories is a psychological process incapable of scientific explanation.

context of justification The view held by positivist philosophers of science and others such as Karl Popper that the success or failure of theory lies in the capacity of its advocates to justify it through rigorous testing and compliance with the accepted methods of scientific theorising.

contracting costs A term applied in agency theory to refer to the costs of maintaining the relationship between principals and agents such as monitoring costs, boding costs and residual losses.

corporate governance The set of processes, customs, policies, laws and institutions affecting the way in which a corporation is administered or controlled.

critical theory The name applied to the philosophy of the Frankfurt School of Philosophy of the early 20th century and extended in the work of Jurgens Habermas; also used to refer to non-positivist philosophies.

deconstruction A project to reveal the ambivalence in all texts which can only be understood in relation to other texts and not in relation to any kind of literal meaning.

deontology An approach to ethics that centres on an individual's duty or obligation and which highlights the 'rightness' or 'wrongness' of actions.

glossary

deprival value The loss expected to be incurred by an entity if it were deprived of the service potential or future economic benefits of an asset (measured or assessed at a particular date).

derived measures Measures that are dependent on other measures. For example, in accounting, profit is dependent on measures of revenue and expenses.

deterrence In respect of regulation, an approach that provides penalties for non-compliance with the regulations.

discourse Originally the process of (linguistic) communication between two or more persons but now broadened to refer to systems of thoughts composed of ideas, attitudes, courses of action, beliefs and practices that systematically construct the subjects and the worlds of which they speak.

discourse analysis Analysis of texts in any form but specifically regarding regularities which can be made in respect of any text on signs of social organisation.

discourse ethics Discovering ethical positions through discursive practice (e.g. discussion, debate and argumentation) associated with philosophers Habermas and Foucault (each with their distinctive position).

discourse of ethics Systems of thought, ideas and beliefs in regard to what is ethical.

discourse of morality Systems of thought, ideas and beliefs in regard to what is regarded as moral behaviour.

eco-efficiency A concept describing a vision for the production of economically valuable goods and services while reducing the ecological impacts of production; in other words, producing more with less.

eco-justice Working for the well-being of all people in a sustainable manner. It is usually used to refer to justice which is concerned with the ability of the most vulnerable people—communities of colour and/or low income, and all children—to live in clean, healthy environments.

economic income Strictly defined as cash flow plus change in present value, but used to refer to the notion of income as a flow of future benefits as opposed to accounting income which is a retrospective calculation (the result of past transactions).

economic theories (of corporations) Perspectives of the corporation based on the assumptions of economic theories.

economic value In accounting this refers to the subjective measure which relates to the maximum amount of things that a person is willing to give up to have a particular thing.

efficient market hypothesis (EMH) The notion developed by economists that financial markets reflect all available information. There are three versions—the weak, the semi-strong and the strong—defined in terms of how quickly security prices reflect information.

emotivism The term used by the analytical philosopher, AJ Ayer, to argue that all ethical statements were based on emotional responses rather than facts.

empiricism A belief that all meaningful knowledge can only be derived through sensory experience. In a weaker form it refers to methods of knowledge acquisition in which experiential knowledge is privileged over other sources of knowledge.

empiricist epistemology A theory of knowledge that relies solely on empirical knowledge—that is, knowledge that is acquired from sensory experience.

entity theory A view that arose in the early years of the 20th century largely as a result of the separation of ownership from control brought about by the development of the modern corporation in which the entity (corporation) is the centre of accounting interest.

ethics of care A view of ethics that emphasises what some see as the feminine qualities of nurturing, rather than concentrating on individual rights.

ethics of rights The view that questions of ethics should rest on what we are entitled to as a matter of principle.

event study An analysis of whether there was a statistically significant reaction in the financial markets to a past occurrence of a given type of event that is hypothesised to affect a firm's market value. The event that affects a firm's market value may be within the firm's control, such as the event of the announcement of a stock split.

externalities Costs incurred by an organisation but not borne by that organisation. Technically it can be defined as third party (or spillover) effects arising from the production and/or consumption of goods and services for which no appropriate compensation is paid (e.g. pollution costs arising from a firm's production activity where these costs are borne by society generally rather than the firm).

fair value Generally refers to the current market price; therefore the fair value of an asset is the amount for which the asset could be bought or sold in a current transaction between willing parties (other than in liquidation). Similarly, the fair

glossary

value of a liability is the amount at which a liability can be settled between willing parties (other than in liquidation).

falsified Demonstrated to be untrue (false).

fiat (measurement by fiat) Measurement where we have only a pre-scientific or commonsense concept rather than the capacity to directly measure a property or attribute; in accounting, where regulations state the basis of measurement.

free-rider effect The situation where some consumers benefit from a service without paying for it at the expense of others who do pay for that service.

fundamental measures Measures that directly relate to the property or attribute being evaluated, such as weight or height.

GAAP Generally accepted accounting principles.

genealogy In theory, a mode of historical inquiry in which it is argued that the actual causes of a thing's origins and its eventual uses are not continuously connected. It differs from traditional views of history as a continuous development and holds that knowledge is always rooted in power.

harmonisation In accounting, the process of developing a set of universally applicable set of accounting standards.

hegemony Originally it meant leader, prominent power or dominant state or person but is now used in the context of the ideological domination of one class by another.

hermeneutics The process of acquiring knowledge through interpretation.

hypothetico-deductivism A dominant view of scientific method in which the process of theorising starts with a hypothesis from which the theorist then deduces what one would expect to find in the empirical world as a result of that hypothesis.

ideographic (idiographic) Focussing on cultural and historical aspects, as in the human sciences (usually contrasted with *nomothetic*).

incommensurable In relation to scientific theory, a concept that all observations are theory relative and consequently that one theory cannot be measured or compared against another.

induction A method of reasoning from the general to the specific; the process of making generalisations on the basis of observed instances.

information asymmetry A situation in which at least some relevant information is known to some but not all parties involved. It causes markets to become inefficient, since not all the market participants have access to the information they need for their decision-making processes.

instrumentalism A philosophy of science directed towards establishing technical control over the environment because it is end results which matter.

intellectual capital A term with various definitions in different theories of management and economics. One popular definition is knowledge that can be exploited for some money-making or other useful purpose.

intellectual virtues Those characteristics that Aristotle believed were necessary for a person to be a good citizen and which complemented his or her moral virtues.

interpretation Understanding derived from the text.

interval scale A measurement scale in which the numbers are assigned on the basis of an order but also where there are equal differences between measurements representing equivalent intervals.

legitimacy theory An explanation for why entities voluntarily disclose information on their social performance based on the idea that as society grants the entity privileges (such as access to resources) it has an obligation to be accountable to society.

logical positivism The (positivist) philosophical doctrine of a group of philosophers associated with Vienna in the 1920s adopted (and modified) by later philosophers; also referred to as logical empiricism. Verification and testing are important tenets.

mainstream accounting research Positivist accounting research the results of which are usually published in widely circulated accounting journals.

mark to market The assignment of a value to a position held in a financial instrument based on the current market price for that instrument or similar instruments.

measurement The application of numbers to properties or attributes of an object or event.

measurement scales Different criteria or levels of measurement: where numbers replace names (*nominal scale*, e.g. player numbers in a sporting team); when attributes are placed in quantity order (*ordinal scale*, e.g. the ranking order of those sitting an examination); where there is a rational zero with equal spaces or intervals between each measurement (*interval scale*, e.g. temperatures); where the measures are compared one to another (*ratio scale*, e.g. as used in financial statement analysis); and even higher levels of mathematical

glossary

properties. The scale adopted will determine the permissible operations with the numbers.

methodology The philosophical evaluation of investigative techniques within a discipline; sometimes incorrectly referred to as 'the methods of inquiry'.

methods The investigative techniques applied in research.

modernity The period in which modern forms of social and economic organisation have existed (replacing the previous feudal order), marked by a belief that knowledge could only be derived through the use of scientific reasoning.

monitoring cost Costs incurred to ensure an agent acts on behalf of the principal.

moral absolutism A belief that there are universal principles of moral behaviour— there are absolute standards by which all moral questions can be judged.

moral hazard A situation which occurs when consumers not paying for a service or product over-consume without regard to the costs being borne by others.

moral relativism The view that what is right is purely a local matter, to be judged within the local community within a given time. Consequently what is considered appropriate behaviour within one community cannot be judged by someone from another community.

moral virtue According to Aristotle and some later philosophers, a human characteristic essential to rationally choose the best course of action. For Aristotle it was an essential prerequisite to practical wisdom; in his *Nicomachean Ethics* Aristotle lists several examples of moral virtues.

natural entity theory (of corporations) The view that the corporation has a natural right to exist.

noise trading An expression used in behavioural finance to refer to situations where uniformed investors buy and sell financial securities at so-called irrational prices, thus creating noise (strange movements) in the price of securities.

nominal scale A measurement scale in which names are assigned as labels.

nomothetic Focussing on establishing general laws as in a natural science model of knowledge (in contrast to *ideographic*).

non-realist ontology An ontological position that does not subscribe to a realist ontology—for example, a social constructionist ontology.

objectively determined A notion that holds that knowledge can be obtained without any individual's personal beliefs or preferences.

ontological commitment The assumptions in a theory as to what kinds of entities exist.

ontology The theory of being, philosophically concerned with establishing the fundamental things which exist in the world.

opportunistic behaviour Behaviour that seeks to maximise benefits and advantages (such economic, political or social).

ordinal scale A measurement scale in which the numbers assigned to objects represent the rank order (1st, 2nd, 3rd, etc.) of the entities measured.

paradigm An example or representative instance of a concept or theoretical approach; in the growth of science context it is the theoretical centre of a school of thought.

Pareto efficiency The allocation of resources such that someone can be made better off while no one else is made worse off.

positivism A doctrine conceived by the philosopher Auguste Comte which claims that the only true knowledge is scientific knowledge and that this should be the basis for the study of society (sociology); the term now refers to an approach to the acquisition of knowledge which seeks to ape the methodology of the physical sciences.

positivist science The scientific method espoused by positivists.

poststructuralism A term loosely used to describe theorists influenced by a number of French philosophers of the later 20th century, some of whom had previously been structuralists but later rejected many of its assumptions. It is not a single movement but comprises many philosophers critical of many of the fundamental assumptions of Western philosophy.

pragmatics (in the theory of signs) The relationship of signs to (human) behaviour.

pragmatism A school of philosophy that originated in the US in the late 19th century with CS Peirce, extended in the early 20th-century philosophies of James and Dewey and revived in the second half of the century in the works of Richard Rorty. Pragmatists consider the practical consequences or real effects to be vital components of both meaning and truth.

principal (in accounting, finance and law) The person for whom, or entity for which, another entity (agent) acts, being duly authorised to do so.

principles-based standards Accounting standards which defer to underlying principles, as opposed to lists of rules to be complied with.

profit skimming This occurs when a supplier will supply only those customers that lead to the greatest profit returns and ignores supply to others.

proprietary theory The dominant view of accounting for most of the first half of the *glossary*

20th century, it is the view that the proprietor is the centre of accounting interest and, therefore, financial statements are prepared from his or her viewpoint. Proprietary theory is often reflected in the accounting equation presented as $P = A - L$ (where P is proprietorship, A represents assets and L represents liabilities).

psychological egoism The view that humans are always motivated by (rational) self-interest (even when they appear to be acting in a community interest).

public choice theory A branch of economics, developed in the 1950s, which uses the same principles that economists use to analyse people's actions in the marketplace and applies them to people's actions in collective decision making, assuming that people are motivated by self-interest.

random walk hypothesis A view held in finance theory stating that stock market prices evolve according to a random walk and thus the prices of the stock market cannot be predicted.

ratio scale A measurement scale in which each measure stands in a relationship to a natural zero.

rational choice theory A view held by some sociologists, economists and political scientists that all action is fundamentally 'rational' in character and that people calculate the likely costs and benefits of any action before deciding what to do. It denies the existence of any kinds of action other than the purely rational and calculative and has been used in constructing formal, and often so-called predictive, models of human behaviour.

rational self-interest The belief that when faced with several courses of action people will choose that which gives the best overall outcome for them. It is the basis of economic rationality in which it is assumed it is rational to pursue a course of action that is designed to maximise economic rewards.

realist ontology The belief that there is a world which exists independent of us—objects exist independently of our conception or perception of them.

reduction The notion that empirical data about associations found in small-scale units can be generalised to relationships and characteristics of larger units.

relativism Knowledge is created and justified in terms of the social practices of the time and place in which it arises; beliefs can be understood only in their cultural, linguistic and historical context. Not a single concept but a family of views—for example, it can apply to ethics or moral principles.

residual loss The costs incurred over and above bonding and monitoring costs in a principal–agent relationship (e.g. where management uses a company's resources for its own use).

return The economic rewards from an economic decision to invest.

rhetoric Originally developed in Classical Greek time as a discipline to teach people to speak effectively, it is now applied to the art of persuasive communication—the use of language to persuade.

risk (Generally speaking) the likelihood that an investment decision leads to a loss; the probability of an event occurring that will have an impact on the achievement of objectives (which has led to measures of risk employing probability measures).

rules-based standards Accounting standards which emphasise compliance and deterrence, as opposed to *principles-based standards*.

scientific reasoning The process of reasoning on the basis of the same methods purportedly employed by scientists.

semantics (in the theory of signs) The relationship of signs to everyday objects.

sign An entity which signifies another entity; something that stands for something else.

simplicity The property, condition or quality of being simple or uncombined; in theory, the belief that the simplistic explanation is the best.

social audit The reporting by an entity on its performance in meeting broad social goals.

social constructionism The ontological position that the beliefs and meanings of a society create knowledge of the world—that the social context of inquiry constructs knowledge. Any reality is only that which exists in the context where it is relevant to us (society)—knowledge is always relative to its social setting.

social contract (theory) The view that a person's moral and/or political obligations are dependent upon a contract or agreement between them and society. Although it is considered that human beings are naturally free they forgo some of their natural liberty for the interests of a civil society.

sociology Originally a term devised by the philosopher Auguste Comte to indicate the science of society, it now refers to the systematic study of the functioning, organisation, developments and types of human societies without implying any particular attachment to a method of science.

stakeholder theory An explanation for why entities voluntarily disclose information on their social performance based on the idea that the entity has a large number of interested parties to which it should be accountable.

glossary

statistical inference Inference about a population from a random sample drawn from it, or, more generally (in popular usage), drawing conclusions from statistics derived from accepted and commonly applied techniques and processes.

structuralism Theories which assume there are structural relationships between concepts and social institutions. Originally associated with linguistics, it was later used extensively by researchers and theorists in the social sciences, humanities and history of science.

syllogism A form of argument where a conclusion follows from two or more premises; a deductive argument.

syntactics (in the theory of signs) The relationship of sign to sign.

synthetic statements Statements which have everyday world referents (refer to the everyday world) and are logically contingent (make 'sense' logically).

testability In theory specifically a notion central to positivist philosophy that a hypothesis or theoretical statement must be capable of undergoing certain tests to establish its purported verity; more generally, in research parlance, a proposition capable of being tested against the evidence.

testing Subjecting a hypothesis or proposed theory to a series of tests in order to determine its robustness—that is, its capacity to stand up to claimed real world situations.

text Originally this referred to the written word, but in 20th-century philosophy it was extended to include anything that conveyed meaning.

transfer pricing The pricing of goods and services within a multi-divisional organisation, but more usually refers to the costs charged by multinational and transnational corporations to divisions operating in countries other than those in which the main division exists.

triple bottom-line An entity's performance in relation to financial, social and environmental matters.

truth The opposite of falsity or fakery; there are several theories of truth, the oldest being the *correspondence theory of truth* in which it means 'that which corresponds to the facts', but today this is only believed by naive empiricists. An alternative is the *coherence theory of truth* in which the truth of a proposition is where it is part of a comprehensive system in which it entails other propositions or is consistent with every other proposition. There is also a *consensus theory of truth* in which it is a matter of social or scientific agreements on reality; and it is also a notion in logic where it is said that for a conclusion to be true the premises must be true. It was for a long time an important consideration in accounting and auditing where financial statements were to present a *true and fair view* of the financial affairs of the reporting entity.

universability test Kant's principle by which we can determine whether an action is appropriate by considering it to be something everyone would do. For example, we should not steal because if everyone did so chaos would exist.

utilitarianism A school of thought that holds that utility is the greatest happiness of the greatest number in a society.

value relevance research Research that investigates the empirical relation between security market prices (values) and particular accounting numbers with a view to providing a basis for accounting standards.

verifiable Capable of verification—that is, the process of ascertaining that a proposition (or a theory or an opinion) is true.

verification A principle of the logical positivists as a criterion of science that to be accepted as a meaningful (scientific) statement a proposition must be verifiable.

virtue theory The view, expressed in its modern form by the philosopher Alasdair MacIntyre, that when considering ethics we should concentrate on who people are—or should be—rather than what they do; a reference back to Aristotle's view that we should be 'virtuous' citizens.

Washington Consensus An agreement between the International Monetary Fund, the World Bank and the US Treasury which state the necessary criteria for countries applying for a loan.

windfall profits Profits that ensue from an unexpected (or unanticipated) event.

Index

index

index

index

index

index